Advance Praise for *GodViews*

"Jack Haberer has participated in and explored the various dynamics of the major struggles of the Presbyterian denomination. Like a prism breaking down a beam of light, he has discerned five different perspectives, GodViews, at work in our debate and struggle. By helping us see more than two points of view in our current struggles, he has helped us take a fresh look at what is happening and given us some tools to work together with more respect and insight."

—Laird Stuart,
co-moderator of Covenant Network of Presbyterians
and pastor of Calvary Presbyterian Church,
San Francisco

"Our divided churches should welcome sincere efforts to interpret the 'good faith' of some Christians to various other Christians of 'good faith' who have somewhat different emphases. This book is interpretive, insightful, and nonjudgmental. *GodViews* is constructive and *Christian!*"

—Peggy Shriver,
coauthor of *The Divided Church:
Moving Liberals & Conservatives from Diatribe to Dialogue*

"*GodViews* is a book 'for just such a time as this'! I can't imagine a more timely or important book for Presbyterians, indeed for all Christians who seek to deal with the diversity in their churches while seeking the unity that Christ intends.

"Pastor Haberer provides wonderful insight with his concept of 'God-Views,' five different 'missional visions'—all rooted in the gospel—by which Christians approach their faith and life. He helps us understand that we truly need each other to be the body of Christ and invites the church to move from debate to dialogue so that our respective GodViews may enrich and correct one another and mold us into the vital Christian-community that God intends the Church to be.

"This is truly a great book, and it couldn't be more timely! I hope every Presbyterian (and especially every minister and elder) will read it and, more importantly, take its message to heart!"

—Clifton Kirkpatrick,
Stated Clerk, PC(USA)

"In *GodViews: The Convictions That Drive Us and Divide Us,* Jack Haberer writes the way he talks—with energy and clarity. While reading this book, I found myself identifying with a couple of GodViews. All of them will certainly help me better understand the complicated dynamics of the issues facing our church today.

"I highly recommend this book. It heads us in a helpful direction. *GodViews* points us toward a new framework within which we can listen to and understand each other with greater clarity. It points us toward each other *as members of the Body of Christ.*"

—John Detterick,
Executive Director, PC(USA)

GodViews

GodViews

The Convictions That
Drive Us and Divide Us

Jack Haberer

G
GENEVA

Geneva Press
Louisville, Kentucky

Book design by Sharon Adams
Cover design by designpointinc.com

First edition
Published by Geneva Press
Louisville, Kentucky

This book is printed on acid-free paper that meets the
American National Standards Institute Z39.48 standard.☉

PRINTED IN THE UNITED STATES OF AMERICA
01 02 03 04 05 06 07 08 09 10—10 9 8 7 6 5 4 3 2 1

Library of Congress Cataloging-in-Publication
Data is on file at the Library of Congress,
Washington, D.C.

ISBN 0-664-50190-7

*To **B**etty **M**oore:*
church statesperson,
renewal leader,
mentor, and
friend.

❖

Contents

Foreword

by M. Craig Barnes

*T*his is a wonderfully helpful book, written by a thoughtful pastor who clearly loves and understands the Presbyterian Church. Periodically the debates of this church, our church, threaten to tear apart its unity, and it is this concern that Pastor Haberer addresses.

But beware. There are several things this book does not do. It doesn't offer a solution to the sexuality debates that have preoccupied the mainline churches for the last twenty years. It doesn't even do a very good job of telling the reader who is right and who is wrong in these debates. The book doesn't offer a simple analysis of the muddy middle or the extremist fringes of the church's membership. And it certainly doesn't add one more sentimental appeal for unity by asking, "Why can't we all just get along?"

There is nothing simple or sentimental about the book. In fact, it is the author's intent to add a little complexity to our understanding of the church. Thank you, Jesus.

While clarity may be found in the extreme positions of a debate, truth seldom is. Jack Haberer has the courage to write a book that will not be popular among those who want to read that they are right, and that the problem with the church is "them." Nor will the book be popular among those who are tired of the theological divisions and are dying to find a quick way out of the debates. This book is a book for those who are committed to the church for the long haul, who believe that there is more truth than any of us possess, and who still have faith that the Holy Spirit is not done with us. In short, it's a book for grown-ups.

Pastor Haberer takes the time to introduce us to ourselves. He carefully interprets five different missional visions, which he calls *GodViews*, that are represented in the church: Confessionalist, Devotionalist, Ecclesiast, Altruist, and Activist. He not only analyzes each's theological and psychological disposition, but also introduces us to each one's biblical warrant. Each GodView is presented evenly, and the dangers of each view are explained at some length.

Whenever a creative author develops groupings, there is always a danger of oversimplification. Most of us are guided by at least two of these GodViews and should acknowledge that we ought to embrace all of them. Haberer is careful not only to acknowledge this objection but makes it his primary thesis. No perspective can understand itself apart from the other perspectives on God that always exist in every denomination.

Every time a church has split apart over a particular issue, it is not long before the debates resume in both splinters because all of the GodViews will exist within each of them. The issues may change, but that doesn't drive the debate as much as the varied views of God.

Many in the Presbyterian church are trying to maintain our unity by getting people who disagree over important issues to listen to each other's stories. The assumption is that if you recognize the presence of God in other people's lives then you will have to recognize their lifestyles as well. This is essentially a horizontal way of doing theology. That is not what this book is doing.

Instead, the author is getting us all to lift our faces upward to the one God. His understanding of truth is that it is revealed vertically, from God to us in the Word. The genius of the book is that it helps you understand what God's word looks like from the perspective of an uplifted face other than your own.

At times, while reading the manuscript, I felt like I was in family counseling. The author-therapist tenderly, but relentlessly, presses the point that the other members of my family aren't trying to drive me crazy. They're just wired differently. And here's the important point: their wiring was given to them by God. Accepting that is critical to my ability to accept them and my place among them.

When you finish reading the book and turn your face back to your brothers and sisters in the family of God, you'll find that you still disagree about very, very important issues. The difference the book makes is that you will be clearer that these are indeed your brothers and sisters. Our great theological debates are never more than a family squabble. That doesn't demean the importance of the debate, but it does set a dramatically different tone for how we speak to each other, and the options we consider for resolving the debates. You may not always like your brothers and sisters and at times are even hurt by them, but you can never get rid of them because, well, they're family.

Foreword

by John M. Buchanan

*D*uring the years since I was ordained to the ministry of Word and sacrament, I have listened to, witnessed, and participated in strenuous Presbyterian struggles over civil rights, poverty, the Vietnam War, the feminist movement and a host of other difficult issues. Through all those conflicts, never did I hear Presbyterians suggest that the only way to resolve our conflicts was to divide the church.

Some of those debates were pretty hot, I recall. The first time I attended a meeting of the General Assembly, the floor was temporarily "occupied" by the "Submarine Church," a revolutionary youth movement that had decided there was not much hope for the creaky structures of the church; that it was time to tear it down and start all over again. Some commissioners thought the Submarine Church had a point and deserved a hearing. Other commissioners were furious and thought the demonstrators should be arrested for disturbing the peace. Both sides had considerable difficulty being in the same room together, not to mention having a civil conversation. Still I do not recall anyone suggesting that the other side should leave the Presbyterian Church.

Not until recently have I heard "schism" proposed as a viable alternative for my church. In the midst of pre-assembly preparing and organizing several years ago, a newspaper reporter observed that we had already become two churches and asked why didn't we Presbyterians honestly acknowledge what had happened, divide the assets, and go our separate ways.

Does it matter? Does it matter to the Christian mission enterprise whether or not the Presbyterians stay together? Jack Haberer, a pastor-theologian who serves in and loves the Presbyterian Church as much as I do, thinks it matters a great deal. I agree with him. Every time I read how Paul gently chides the early church for its divisions in First Corinthians 1, I wonder what he might say to us. Every time I read Ephesians, as he admonishes the believers to "make every effort to maintain the unity of the Spirit in the bond of peace," I find myself wondering if we twenty-first-century Presbyterians are doing nearly enough to "maintain the unity of the Spirit" (4:3). And every time I read the words of Jesus' prayer for the disciples, "that they may all be one . . . so that the world may believe" (John 17:21), I grieve that so much of our institutional and individual energy, passion, hope, and love are being absorbed in fighting one another. So I am delighted with a book from the heart and mind of one who refuses to accept division as the only way to resolve the conflicts that beset us.

Jack Haberer and I do not agree on everything. In fact, we disagree about one of the basic issues currently before the church. The truth is that Jack Haberer and I became good and trusted friends not *in spite of* our disagreements, but *because* our contrary positions, resting on our respective understandings of scripture and mutual love for our church, forced us to take each other seriously.

In a recent essay, "Church Fears, Committed Conversations," Presbyterian theologian Joseph Small refers to C. P. Snow's observation that, "The number two is a very dangerous number, and that which attempts to divide anything into two should be regarded with suspicion." Jack Haberer observes that we are lured into "binary" or "two-party" thinking, that "relieves us of the responsibility to deal with uncomfortable issues, undesirable ideas, unattractive options and unappealing persons." I wish every Presbyterian decision-maker would ponder that helpful analysis and Haberer's sobering warning that binary, two-party thinking is a great way to win a war but a terrible way to run a church.

Not everyone is going to like this book. The author proposes no simple solutions to our conflicts, and he certainly doesn't recommend that we paper over our current difficulties. Rather, he challenges us, all of us, to remember that in Christ we already belong to one another and because of that, walking away from one another is unthinkable.

Please don't turn immediately to the conclusion of this lively book, but know that when you get there, you will find that the author has subtly moved from the question of saving the church from schism to the much more important matter of "How can the church be a faithful church through such times as these?" Simple and eloquent suggestions plot a plan for such faithfulness.

This is an important book by a thoughtful, faithful Presbyterian, written for all of us who, in Haberer's powerful words, are "resolutely determined to stay together, to struggle together, to study together, to serve together and worship together—thereby being the church Jesus has built upon the rock, against which the gates of hell shall not prevail."

Acknowledgments

*I*t's really hard to hold a lot of prejudices against people when they surround you with their inquiring minds, their generous spirits, and their determined commitment to serve the same God you love. So many high-caliber, Christian thinkers and leaders have contributed directly to this volume that it honestly must be considered a group effort.

At the beginning it was Mark Achtemeier and Andrew Purves who, having heard me thinking out loud about the complexities of the church, commissioned me to write "An Evangelical Perspective on Unity in Diversity" for their book, *A Passion for the Gospel* (Geneva Press, 2000). In the process, that project took on a life of its own, especially when Tom Long at Geneva Press encouraged me to dig further. My congregation, Clear Lake Presbyterian Church, provided time off and a stipend for a sabbatical, and the Louisville Institute, under the leadership of David Wood and Jim Lewis, provided a generous grant from the Lilly Foundation to pursue further research.

The sabbatical took me to several seminaries where I engaged in eye-opening dialogue with world-class scholars: Joe Coalter, Andy Dearman, Ellen Babinsky, Robert Shelton, Quinn Fox, Jack Rogers, Richard Mouw, Marianne Meye Thompson, John Thompson, Marguerite Schuster, Paul Pierson, Don Hagner, Ron Kernaghan, Chap Clark, Barbara Wheeler, Don Shriver, Peggy Shriver, Max Stackhouse, Stacy Johnson, Tom Gillespie, Sam and Eileen Moffatt, Bruce McCormick, George Hunsinger, and Freda Gardner. In the midst of such dialogues, I also engaged in other dialogues with such influential thinkers as Jerry Andrews, Richard Lovelace, Joe Rightmyer, Arnold Lovell, Doug Jacobsen, Robert Bullock, Tom Tewell, Joe Small, Cliff Kirkpatrick, Ralph Winter, Art Greer, Brent Edman, Mary Lynn Tobin, Sandra Lomasson, Carol Pagelson, Scott Anderson, and Cliff Frazier. Most significant among those dialogues were ones shared with Laird Stuart, with whom our private conversations were transformed into public forums, "Unity-in-Diversity" conferences, as sponsored by the Presbyteries of Sacramento, Kendall, and Idaho. The Presbytery of New Covenant also hosted two different events at which I spoke—special thanks going to Stewart Coffman for providing the opportunities for such engagement with colleagues.

The sabbatical also provided time to travel through Israel-Palestine, and while there, so many insights were gained through dialogues with Abuna Elias Chacour, Salim Munayer, Naim Ateek, Ronnie Cohen, Daniel and Becky Frank, Hattem Shehaddeh, and Bishop Awad.

As the project took shape, Jim Singleton, Peggy Shriver, Stacy Johnson, and David Dobson red-lined the manuscript, saving me from many missteps. My old friend and psychology scholar, Joe Pirone, helped refine my forays into his field of expertise.

Through the whole process I received enormous help and support from my church staff and elders, most especially associate pastors Jim Elder, Craig Goodwin and Nancy Goodwin, and church administrator, Janice Feather, who carried extra heavy loads through these past months. My assistant, Barb Robertson not only carried extra work, she also provided the first round of top-drawer editing help. Seven years of sharing staff leadership with Connie Nyquist, Barbara Carmichael and Reg Brown have probably done more than anything to teach me how to serve Christ as partners with those whose sense of call reflect contrary, albeit complementary, GodViews. Throughout the development of these ideas, I have been sustained by several prayer partners: Jimmy and Marilu McGregor, George and Joyce Coyer, Lynn and Julie Calhoun, Will and Allison Groten, Mike and Susie Ray, Byder Wilde, Sharon Jenkins, Maryanne Stickney, Judy Franklin, Barbara Henkel, and Carl Bookout.

Throughout this project I have drawn heavily from the well of love and wisdom so available from the love of my life, Barbie, and our children, David and Kelly. I've also reached back to my ecumenical family: Mom, the Roman Catholic director of religious education; sister Tobi, the non-denominational worship leader; sister Beth, the Episcopal missionary in Nepal; and brother Geoff, the vocalist with the Harlem Gospel Tabernacle Choir. They and their families continue to broaden my appreciation for the variety of faithful expressions of faith within Christ's church.

This project could never have happened were it not for the discipling I have received over the past decade from the Red Fox of evangelical Presbyterianism, Harry Hassall, and from other key leaders in the Presbyterian Coalition, such as Clayton Bell, John Huffman, Barry VanDeventer, David Dobler, David Snellgrove, and Mort McMillan.

Above all, it has been the mother superior of the evangelical renewal, Betty Moore—retired director of Presbyterians for Renewal and retired coordinator of the Presbyterian Coalition—who has shown me the ropes. In fact, over the past several years, Betty has downright mothered me: instructing me, encouraging me, laughing with me, crying with me, scolding me, pushing me. In the process, she has taught me how to love the church while contending with the church, and she has shown me how truly to believe that this discombobulated cluster of contentious folks are—as she has become to me—my family. I am so grateful for all she has taught me, and for that reason, it is to her that I dedicate this book.

Chapter 1

Carmel or Caesarea?

I expected my first trip to Israel to be an eye-opening experience, one that would illumine the ancient God-stories. I did not expect it to open my eyes to today's God-story.

Every nerve screamed with excitement on that first morning of discovery. After years of searching the depths of scripture, the bus ride winding up Mount Carmel proved almost more than my imagination could grasp. *Here.* Right here Elijah dueled with the prophets of Baal. Here the God of Abraham and Sarah, Isaac and Leah, Jacob and Rachel shut out the gods of the Canaan pantheon. Here divinity proved itself. Here and now, on an April 1998 morning, I was encountering the very "here" of God's visitation.

Our trans-Atlantic flight had delivered us to Israel the night before. Now, just eighteen hours later, we were ascending to a place whose history had captivated me for years. A major research paper in seminary ("exegesis" paper, to use seminary lingo) had led me through the study of the ancient Baal epic, discovered in 1928. I had parsed every Hebrew word and retranslated every phrase. I had learned that the drought brought on by Elijah's prophecy had targeted Baal for personal humiliation, since he was not only the prime minister of Canaanite mythology but also the god allegedly possessing the power over the elements of sun, lightning, and rain. I had learned that Queen Jezebel, who had imported such paganism, was driven by an ambition for unchallenged control in Israel that demanded putting Elijah's "troublemaking" out of the way forever. I had learned that Elijah's final success in calling fire down from heaven would prove the undoing of the queen's paganism and her power. Indeed, Elijah's faith was validated, God was shown to be almighty, and the prophets of Baal were brought to their fateful end. Truth had won.

Here we now were reengaging that truth-conquest. The bus driver parked just outside the gate of the monastery atop the mountain.

Walking through the gate, we entered the courtyard. To our right rose the small monastery, and to our left stood a tall statue of the sword-bearing prophet slaying a defeated pagan priest (a rather violent-looking image by today's standards). We walked across the courtyard, ascended steps around the left side of the monastery, and arrived at an open terrace. A wide panorama opened before us: to the west, the blue Mediterranean Sea; to the east, the Valley of Armageddon; and to the south, a row of mountains heading toward Jerusalem.

Ronnie, our tour guide, pointed southwest toward the coastline. "Look over there," he said. "Can you see those smokestacks?"

We squinted to see. As our eyes refocused we responded in turn, "Yes," "I see them," "There they are."

He continued, "That's Caesarea."

My thoughts catapulted about eight hundred years from the days of Elijah to the time of Peter. My thoughts ran particularly to the story of the conversion of Cornelius, the Roman soldier. Being a God-fearer—that is, a Roman who followed Jewish practices—his desire for God prompted him to send messengers down the coast to Joppa and urge the Apostle Peter to come and tell him the news of Jesus. Just before those messengers reached Joppa, Peter was shown a vision of a sheet filled with unkosher foods descending from heaven; he was told to eat what was there, and upon protesting its unlawfulness, heard a voice command, "What God has made clean, you must not call profane" (Acts 10:15). Released from those Levitical standards, Peter traced the coast northward a day's journey to Caesarea and led Cornelius to faith. In the process, the wall of exclusion between "God's chosen people" and the outsiders was destroyed, and the division between Jew and Gentile abolished.

Standing now upon the terrace, I suddenly found myself thinking about the church entering the twenty-first century. "This is where we live now," I pondered, my reverie ruffled by the potential implications. "This is where the church is—living in the tension between Carmel, the citadel of truth, and Caesarea, the port city of inclusiveness."

The timing could not have been more uncanny. Just a couple of weeks before, I had celebrated a Presbyterian triumph of truth. As moderator of the Presbyterian Coalition, I had helped encourage efforts to block ratification of Amendment A, known as the "Fidelity-Integrity" amendment, which would have weakened the denomination's prohibition against the ordination of avowed, unrepentant, sexually active homosexuals. For the three previous years I had spent an enormous amount of energy helping establish the policy of prohibition; then, most recently, I had expended more effort to defeat my opponents' watered-down alternative.

In the process I had cast my hopes, dreams, and convictions on the altar before Elijah. I had gone out on a limb, casting my lot with the prophet's determination to stand for the truth—no matter what the cost— so that God's will would be represented faithfully and proclaimed purely in the church. Mount Carmel felt like home. This citadel of truth was where I belonged.

Yet Caesarea, with its port opened wide to the sea, looked warm and welcoming, too—albeit in a different way. Here was the place from which God's good news had burst out of Israel's tribal monopoly. Here was the embarkation point for a gospel that ultimately welcomed into God's household my Irish and German ancestors. Caesarea is the Ellis Island of European Christians, Asian Christians, African Christians, et al. With its story of Gentile inclusion, Caesarea had welcomed my friends and me to faith, just as today it welcomed us to this holy land.

Entertaining these thoughts, I knew well that I was treading on dangerous ground. I certainly had been avoiding the Caesarea story for months. Throughout the amendment debates, my liberalizing opponents kept trying to make hay of this story in the hope of convincing us to loosen our standards and broaden the church.

Standing here on the terrace, I couldn't help myself. I had to ponder, "Perhaps God wants us to live in both Carmel *and* Caesarea at the same time."

These thoughts really were dangerous. I could not think them without immediately identifying with the disappointment felt by Scott Anderson, the gay man in Sacramento who, years before, had demitted his ministerial ordination when a church member threatened to out him. On the day we announced our amendment-vote victory, several days before leaving for Israel, I had interrupted my celebration long enough to call Scott to express my sympathy over yet another setback for him and his allies. Now, while taking in this Carmel-Caesarea vision, my thoughts were moving beyond detached sympathy to a more attached empathy. I did not doubt that we conservatives were following an understanding of God's truth regarding sexual ethics that had stood uninterrupted for three thousand years. I felt no remorse for standing in line with so many great figures of the Christian faith. I could not apologize for my efforts to proclaim Christ's liberating power from alternative sexual desires to live in heterosexual faithfulness. Yet I could not help but recognize that my opponents believed themselves to be following an understanding of God's love and grace that had wrestled against exclusivist trends ever since the days of the Apostles. I surely could feel compassion for the way they felt that the church's policy shut them out.

Looking out over such a vista and contemplating these thoughts forced one thing to become all too clear to deny: the word "inclusion" belongs in my Christian vocabulary. In the past, I would always shake my head in quiet derision when hearing that word uttered by denominational leaders, or when reading it in the *Christian Century* (yes, I do subscribe to the *Christian Century*, but like other evangelicals, I carry it around inside my latest copy of the more conservative *Christianity Today*). The religion of inclusiveness had seemed to be nothing more than another step down the stairway to the bottomless pit of modernist and postmodernist relativism. Having seen Caesarea, I could no longer dismiss inclusivism as the buzz-word of liberal foes. This port city burned an indelible mark in my mind's eye, penetrating my theological lead shield. It commissioned me—at a minimum—to take a whole new look at myself, asking, "If Jesus were here today, would I embrace him as did the Marys, Marthas, Matthews, and Marks . . . or would I be standing alongside the Pharisees, Sadducees, and scribes, opposing his inclusion of such people?"

Not an easy question to ponder while visiting the Holy Land.

A couple of weeks after returning home from Israel, Stated Clerk Cliff Kirkpatrick called with a proposition. "Jack, these amendment votes are tearing up the church. We've got to find a way to stop the bloodletting. Would you be willing to meet with a small group of leaders to talk about finding a different way?" I could hardly decline the senior constitutional officer of my denomination. He quickly arranged a meeting that included Roberta Hestenes, John Galloway, Barry VanDeventer, John Buchanan, Laird Stuart and me. Each person had well-established credentials. Roberta, one of the leading statespersons in American evangelicalism, had chaired the General Assembly committee that forged the "Fidelity-Chastity" amendment, supported by the Presbyterian Coalition and adopted successfully a year before. One year later, Laird had chaired the General Assembly committee that formed the alternative "Fidelity-Integrity" amendment, and John Buchanan, a former moderator of the General Assembly and present comoderator of the Covenant Network of Presbyterians, had helped spearhead the unsuccessful efforts at adopting this liberalized policy. John Galloway had worked quietly behind scenes from a neutral stance to bring such warring parties together, and Cliff's overall love for and service to the church pleaded for peace and unity. Barry, a presbytery executive, had worked with me in supporting the traditional position and would have brought keen constitutional expertise to our discussions. Unfortunately, other obligations forced him to cancel his attendance at the last minute.

Cliff asked me if I would prepare some thoughts to lead us in opening worship. We met at a beautiful estate home in suburban San Diego where a courtyard, supplied with backboard and basketballs, gave us an easy way to vent our competitive energies; a few airballs by us middle-aged pastors—all frustrated jocks at heart—served up enough humility to help break the ice. After a few embarrassed laughs we gathered in the living room and shared introductions. I opened my Bible to Acts 10, the story of the conversion of Cornelius. I recounted my recent visit to Caesarea and Carmel, underlining the geographical irony I had encountered there and highlighting the tension of faithfulness that challenges us here. After a song and a prayer, we began our discussions.

We shared our hopes and fears for the larger church. No one held any illusions about the near future, given the relatively close votes that had ratified the "Fidelity-Chastity" amendment and rejected the other. Cliff asked bluntly, "Is there another way to get through this?"

Roberta volunteered, "Well, I'm working on an article for the *Presbyterian Outlook* that calls for a time-out. What do you all think about that?" The conversation grew animated. Laird and John Buchanan acknowledged that the possibility of yet another defeat to their cause would be devastating. Roberta and I admitted that many evangelicals had made it clear that, if called to yet another denomination-wide amendment battle, they would refuse to participate. Many of them were talking seriously about leaving the denomination; we knew we could lose by default. We all acknowledged that the recent debates and votes had polarized the church, created many tensions within presbyteries, promoted the use of diatribes while quashing attempts at thoughtful dialogue, and drained a great deal of energy from our own ministries and those of the whole church. We all wanted to take a break. John Buchanan offered the suggestion that we use more biblical language, like "sabbath." I proposed that we issue a "Call to Sabbatical."

The call urged taking a season (no specified time, but at least a couple of years was implied) to back away from writing new legislative proposals. We urged our fellow Presbyterians to refrain from provoking judicial actions, i.e., neither shining flashlights in bedroom windows to catch sinners "in the act" nor engaging in "ecclesiastical disobedience" that would require others to enforce church law. Of course, such a call could carry no constitutional power. Neither could we presume to negotiate a commitment from our respective constituencies. If General Assembly commissioners wished to propose new legislation, they could. Judicial charges could always be filed. We just hoped that moral suasion would hold sway.

After lots of group editing, Cliff issued the Call to Sabbatical from his office.

Initial response to the Call was disconcerting. *The Presbyterian Layman,* a publication of the conservative Presbyterian Lay Committee, decried it as a sellout, snatching defeat from the proverbial jaws of victory. They also charged that it grew out of a clandestine negotiation session engaged by individuals unauthorized to do so (of course a "call" to sabbatical does not equate to a sabbatical "treaty," its only force being an appeal by the authors to the larger church to take a time-out). Presbyterians for Lesbian and Gay Concerns also decried it as a sellout, insisting that their liberal allies were too willing to accept defeat against the villainous legalism of the conservatives.

Nevertheless, the Call was embraced by a broad center of the church. When the General Assembly convened in Charlotte a few weeks later, the Call to Sabbatical echoed through the halls. Under the leadership of its newly elected moderator, Douglas Oldenberg, the Assembly chose to follow the lead. The only related action taken was that of calling for a national conference to contemplate "The Nature of the Unity We Seek in the Midst of Our Diversity."

The weeks following the Assembly felt pretty rocky for this leader. I had already announced my resignation from serving another term as moderator of the Presbyterian Coalition. Now it became clear that some were ready for me to step aside. Some board members felt betrayed by the Call. Others supported the idea, as expressed by Clayton Bell, then-pastor of Highland Park Presbyterian Church in Dallas, who said simply, "Folks, I questioned the Call at first, but I'm now convinced that God is in this."

Indeed, feedback over the next several months indicated that some evangelicals wanted to draw a hard line between "us" and "them." Others welcomed the prospect of finding a new way to deal with our conflicts in the church. While nobody seemed to know how to arrive there, many people expressed hope for a new model of relationships that would enable the church to stay together while reclaiming the central message of the gospel.

At the same time, many liberal opponents added their voices to the call to seek a new path. Some of them began by striking up conversation with evangelicals, startling us into discovering that the liberals were not as wild-eyed as we had earlier perceived. Some members of the liberal contingent acknowledged embarrassment over extremes taken by certain of their allies. Many liberals made clear that their support of gay rights only extends to homosexuals engaged in monogamous relationships, that multiple partnering is off-limits! Some from the liberal side articulated an understanding of the gospel that would have been scored an A+ by Billy Graham himself.

I had to admit my own embarrassment over having misinterpreted the intentions, the theology, and the ethics of these opponents. Face it: From where I sat, my thinking was that people who supported gay ordination must also have deleted the resurrection from the Apostles' Creed, must have embraced the worship of pagan gods, and certainly must have burned their Bibles. Now I realized that my caricatures of them were wildly inaccurate.

Many of us mutually recognized that we had stereotyped one another, caricatured one another, and demonized one another. Now we found ourselves becoming friends.

One early exchange of friendship came upon my arrival at the General Assembly following the Call. After finding a seat in the back row of the Pre-Assembly conference (the price for arriving late), the next persons to arrive and sit in the lone empty seats next to me were John and Sue Buchanan. John introduced me to Sue. He and I exchanged a polite hug. "How goes it, John?" I asked.

"About the same as for you, Jack," he responded. "Just keeping busy pulling the arrows out of my back." We both smiled sheepishly. A few minutes later, I served ice water to the two of them.

The next day he reported to me that after the event Sue asked him, "Who was that nice man who gave us the glasses of water?"

John grinned and told me, "I straightened up and told her, 'That's no nice man. That's the czar of the Coalition!'"

Strange friendships grew as we sought to live into the Call. More surprising friendships resulted from discussions regarding our unity-in-diversity. Given the recent developments, Moderator Oldenberg asked me to serve on the conference planning committee. Incorporating a wide spectrum of evangelicals, progressives, moderates, and racial-ethnic minorities, the committee set out to elevate the discussion from that of sexual ethics to larger theological issues. In the midst of the planning meetings, friendships continued to grow, among the most noteworthy being a friendship struck up between evangelical leader Joe Rightmyer, the director of Presbyterians for Renewal, and Scott Anderson.

In the midst of all these goings-on, at least a few of us began to realize that we must find a new way to be the church together. Some truths also emerged, most notably the revelation that our preconceptions were skewed. Most of the liberals weren't radicals. Most of the conservatives weren't fundamentalists. We demonstrated that we really do love the church and don't want to drive away those with whom we differ. We all caught each other by surprise.

The clearest conclusion that emerged for me was that the church is far too complex—and for most believers it is far too complicated—to continue to allow a simple, two-party theory to summarize the church's divisions. Us-and-them, good-guys-and-bad-guys, liberals-and-conservatives . . . such categorizations provide a great way to run a war, but they comprise a godawful way to run a church. While the term "diversity" may be misused, the church of Jesus Christ really does reflect a diversity of racial-ethnic origins, a diversity of visions for mission, a diversity of theological emphases—all existing together around a core theology that gives substance to the expression, "Variety is the spice of life." Put metaphorically, living in both Carmel, the citadel of truth, and Caesarea, the port city of inclusiveness, requires us to embrace ambiguities and complexities akin to those of the character of the godhead.

Is it realistic to talk about the church in categories more complex and ambiguous than simply liberal vs. conservative? To hear the arguments, to read the publications, and to meet together in fellowships all seem to push us into one party or the other. In fact, recent church history also seems to promote the two-party notion. Sadly, a common reading of history also suggests that the two parties must inevitably split apart, only to split again and again. Must that result emerge from the present arguments? Perhaps a better understanding of a few past conflicts can help us.

Chapter 2

So What's New?

We have been here before. Ever since the days of Martin Luther, the Western church has suffered innumerable splits between Christian sisters and brothers who determined that they could no longer stay together. Their service to God was too impeded by each others' presence to pretend to be "one body in Christ." Some church bodies are more prone to such splits, hence the common comment that Baptists are the only people who "multiply by dividing." But mainline church bodies have suffered many splits, too. Indeed, the great ecumenical century might actually be remembered as the decimated, sectarian century.

The War of the Century

What was the most significant event of twentieth-century Protestantism in the West? Many people would say the ordination of women or the integration of churches. Perhaps so. Other observers would insist on the massive missionary expansion around the world or the ecumenical efforts among church bodies. Again, perhaps. I would suggest that truly the most significant event of the whole century was the Scopes Monkey Trial. Immortalized in the movie *Inherit the Wind*, which has been refilmed and rereleased numerous times, this trial has cast its shadow through every decade since the trial took place. In fact, one could argue that every mainline split over the following seventy-five years was merely an aftershock of the still-unresolved conflict that came into focus in that 1925 Tennessee courtroom.

The indictment of John T. Scopes for teaching evolution drew two of the most celebrated lawyers in the land, William Jennings Bryan and Clarence Darrow, to face off against one another. Darrow, who was known as a legal champion for the unfortunate and oppressed, defended the school teacher. Bryan, a three-time unsuccessful

Democratic nominee for president and two-time unsuccessful candidate for moderator of the Presbyterian Church, prosecuted the case. Although known for his liberal political convictions, Bryan was a biblical literalist and religious fundamentalist. The American media covered this case as it had never done before, providing sensational details of each day's proceedings, often mocking Bryan's passion as driven by simplistic narrow-mindedness. Bryan ultimately won the case, but he died just a fortnight later. American-brand evangelical faith seemed to die with him.

That conservatism had been a defining mark of American Protestantism since the arrival of the first colonists from Europe. Although subsequent history has brought ebbs and flows (the Revolutionary era was more noted for its deism than evangelical faith), a cyclical pattern of renewal and awakening had kept alive a passion for the gospel and a broad adherence to biblical ethics and morals. That cycle burst into a flashpoint in the early decades of the twentieth century. The academic world was aflame with new ideas, stemming from the works of Darwin, Freud, and Marx. Schools of biblical criticism were not only questioning the authorship of the Pentateuch and the historical accuracy of gospel accounts of Jesus' life, but these ideas were breaking out of the academy and falling into the discourse of the general population. For example, Albert Schweitzer's first theological work, *The Quest for the Historical Jesus*, was read widely upon its release in 1906. A pervasive optimism in humanity's innate ability to improve its lot was surging as the new century burst forth. The Enlightenment was finally shining its light where average people could see it. For conservative Christians, worldliness was winning the war against biblical faith.

This battle between biblical faith and worldliness had endured many advances and setbacks through nineteen centuries. Standing fast on principle is not easy when new questions, new ideas, and new temptations keep changing the subject. How does a person hold to the faith-once-given while facing new and challenging questions and possibilities?

Consider the actions of one Jewish community. You probably recall that for thousands of years, Jews and Christians alike have condemned the use of horoscopes to predict the future. To look to an astrologer to predict the future implies that stars and planets exercise sovereign control over our lives—a claim that puts them in the place of God. Believing in the zodiac also makes people fatalistic, not only releasing individuals from obligation to give an accounting for their behavior but also creating self-fulfilling prophecies that hold them in bondage and deny the freedom God offers. Cries of "idolatry" and "paganism" have pounded out from pulpits in both synagogues and churches on this issue. But that reality presented a major problem to Jewish religious historians when in 1928 archaeologists unearthed the small, ancient synagogue Beth Alpha in central Israel, just west of the Jordan River. Built in the sixth century C.E., this small synagogue apparently served as the worship center for a little farming community at the foot of Mount Gilboa. For floor covering two mosaic artists produced a work that is beautiful in its simplicity. Fittingly, the nave shows the ark of the covenant flanked by two menorahs. The base of the mosaic depicts Abraham's presentation of Isaac as a sacrifice to God, accompanied by the Hebrew words for "Behold the ram." But in the center, dominating the whole mosaic, is a full twelve-house zodiac! Sacrilege!!! Why would such an aberration be there? How could a people so committed to serving the one God of the universe so compromise themselves as to build their worship of God on a base of astrology?

Because of the temple's presence in a national park, the government developed a video that considers the origin of such a curiosity. The video depicts the elders of this humble town seeking the lowest possible price from apprentice-level artists. When presented with plans for the work, the befuddled elders grasp for understanding. "We can't have a zodiac in our synagogue," says one after another. Finally one speaks up. "I don't see what the problem is," he responds. With a tinge of twentieth-century humor he adds, "Everybody's doing it."

Everybody has been doing it—or so it would seem—since the beginning of time. That is, every believer has been wrestling with the constantly changing opportunities and temptations with which the world's culture confronts the church's desire to be faithful to the revealed will of God.

When fundamentalists and modernists in the early part of the twentieth century came to rhetorical blows, they were wrestling with that same old problem, presenting itself in its newest terms. How can one still believe in the Bible's creation story when truly enlightened people believe in evolution? How can one defend the scriptures against critics when so many quotes and incidents from Jesus' ministry contradict each other across the different gospel writers' accounts? How can a church that has supported slavery—and defended that evil practice with Bible quotes—still have a credible voice in the modern world?

The battles for denominational control were taking place in general assemblies and judicial commissions across the land. In the Presbyterian Church in the U.S.A., when Union (N.Y.) Seminary professor Charles Augustus Briggs challenged in 1891 the Princeton theology of biblical inerrancy, he was tried for heresy. Even though he still affirmed such essential teachings as the virgin birth of Christ, he was found guilty and the subsequent General Assembly vetoed his appointment to the chair of the seminary's Biblical Studies department. The 1892 Assembly then affirmed the doctrine of inerrancy, and the 1893 Assembly suspended the professor from the ministry. Lane Seminary professor Henry Preserved Smith, who had defended Briggs, also was defrocked. "In no uncertain terms, the Presbyterian Church had placed itself squarely on the side of biblical inerrancy."[1] For the next thirty years, under repeated attempts to broaden the interpretive framework for biblical interpretation, the church held its line through legislative and judicial means. In particular, the General Assemblies of 1910 and 1916 declared that all candidates for ordination must affirm "five fundamentals," namely, the inerrancy of scripture, the virgin birth, substitutionary atonement, bodily resurrection, and the miracles of Christ.

In June 1922, Harry Emerson Fosdick, a Baptist minister serving in the First Presbyterian Church in New York City, preached a sermon, "Shall the Fundamentalists Win?" In those days, leading preachers' sermons often were printed in Monday's newspapers, and that particular sermon set off one of the hottest controversies in the country. At the 1923 General Assembly, the fundamentalists, led by William Jennings Bryan, condemned Fosdick's doctrine and tried to force his congregation to maintain loyalty to the Westminster Confession of Faith. Failing that, the following Assembly pressed Fosdick to transfer ordination from Baptist to Presbyterian and to subscribe to the latter's doctrinal standards. He chose instead to resign that pulpit and to take his energy to Park Avenue Baptist Church, which he soon developed into the Riverside Church.

Also in 1923, J. Greshem Machen published *Christianity and Liberalism*, titled intentionally to draw an unambiguous distinction between what he considered to be two mutually exclusive sets of beliefs.

The controversies raged; the 1925 General Assembly appointed a special committee to investigate two ordinations, carried out by the Presbytery of New York, of candidates who did not affirm the virgin birth of Christ. The 1927 Assembly adopted the commission's report, which declared the fundamentals to be nonbinding on the church. In the process, the Assembly put forth the clear message: "Theology divides and mission unites."

In the midst of all these ecclesiastical controversies, the Scopes Trial brought the general population on board with a resounding support of the modernist, open-minded ideas of Fosdick and others, along with a shunning disapproval of the fundamentalism promoted by Bryan and Machen.

In the years that followed, Machen turned his sights to the purification of theology at Princeton Seminary. Convinced that both the church and the seminary truly had crossed their orthodox theological boundaries, and confident that the vast majority of Presbyterians supported his commitment to conservative, biblical faith, he called for the organization of Westminster Seminary in Philadelphia and a new Independent Board of Presbyterian Foreign Missions. Conflicts and controversy soon engulfed the new board; Machen spoke out against the leadership of Robert Speer, the beloved statesman of Presbyterian missions, and at the P.C.U.S. General Assembly of 1936, Machen and several other clergy were suspended.

But they quickly realized their dreams of forming a new Presbyterian Church of America, at whose first General Assembly Machen declared: "On Thursday, June 11, 1936, the hopes of many years were realized. We became members, at last, of a true Presbyterian Church; we recovered, at last, the blessing of a true Christian fellowship. . . . With that lively hope does our gaze turn now to the future! At last true evangelism can go forward without the shackle of compromising associations."[2]

Convinced that the vast majority of Presbyterians shared his biblical convictions, Machen became a grand marshal, leading a parade of faithful Presbyterians into a whole new church. But nobody showed up for the parade, or more accurately, a scant few thousand communicants joined the new church. Within six months he had been ousted as president of the Independent Board for Presbyterian Foreign Missions, and "his infant church was torn by dissent over premillennialism and the use of alcoholic beverages."[3] Machen soon contracted pneumonia, and he died on January 1, 1937.

The Division You Have with You Always

The tragedy of the fundamentalist-modernist controversy is that a profoundly rich Christian faith, perhaps the most highly educated faith expression the world had seen, was being boiled down to a few simplistic definitions, a few essential litmus tests, which in turn polarized people subscribing to such a sound-bite faith against those questioning such sound bites. Theologian John Leith's book, *Crisis in the Church*, has laid siege on the liberal theological establishment currently leading many seminaries, but nevertheless concedes,

The fundamentalist-modernist controversies of the first half of this century fixed for the most part on many secondary doctrines. . . . The church's existence has never been dependent on a particular doctrine of verbal inerrancy, nor has it been dependent on the affirmation of the virgin birth as a historical fact. There could be a million virgin births without an incarnation. No serious person can believe Christian faith depends on an axhead floating or a talking serpent.[4]

Sadly, such secondary issues did emerge as polarizing catalysts; conflict soon escalated to the point of no return. Moreover, the ensuing split in the church demoralized the thousands of conservative Christians whose theological sympathies were with Bryan and Machen but who could not split from the church, either because of a genuine commitment to church unity or out of concern for the spiritual, emotional, and financial costs involved. For Machen, one conflict begat another—as has been the case time and again when churches have adopted schism as its vehicle for advancement. Most tragic of all, the inability of the leaders to work through the enormous issues they were facing led to an untenable resolution of the battle: the choice simply to unite around a common *mission* to the neglect of a common *theology*. "Theology divides, mission unites" became a refrain sung again and again and again.

In effect, many of the issues raised in the fundamentalist-modernist controversy never have been solved. In some cases, like the challenge that probably faced the Jewish community in Beth Alpha, every generation must wrestle with Jesus' prayer that his disciples be "in the world" but not "of the world" (John 17). Neither the Bryan-Machen answer nor the "mission over theology" answer provided a sufficient conclusion.

Given that the Presbyterian Church of America (later renamed the Orthodox Presbyterian Church) has continued to hover in relative obscurity, one would expect one's peers to avoid making the same mistakes that Machen and his allies made. One might imagine that the lessons of history would teach us to exercise great caution when tempted to ignite fires of conflict, but that lesson apparently is not an easy one to learn.

In the 1960s, as the general assemblies of the Presbyterian Church were implementing a policy of gender equality and were writing new confessions, which were perceived by some as softening the authority of scripture, a band of Southern Presbyterians felt alienated from such initiatives. They formed the Reformed Theological Seminary in Jackson, Mississippi (following the pattern of Machen forming Westminster Theological Seminary). In 1973, they left to form the Presbyterian Church in America (a different denomination than Machen's Presbyterian Church *of* America). Again, they expected a large exodus, but again only a small portion of the disaffected actually took the action to depart.

In 1978 some Northern Presbyterians also felt disaffected by a particularly heavy-handed approach to forcing the ordination of women on all congregations, as well as to the renewed perception of a drift toward the left. They seceded to form the Evangelical Presbyterian Church. Yet again, what threatened to be a mass exodus turned into a small collection of congregations, far flung from one another, trying to exercise a connectional relationship as a more "truly" reformed body of believers.

Still many conservative and/or evangelical and/or moderate Presbyterians remain in the mainline church in spite of their running arguments with the "liberal hegemony" (an expression used honestly and self-confessingly by Laird Stuart, comoderator of Covenant Network of Presbyterians, whose leaders long have led that liberal hegemony) that has managed to dominate church policy development and implementation. Their alienation from the national offices has led many to channel their best energy into programs outside the national church. In fact, the landscape is dotted with nondenominational, parachurch organizations that have been formed primarily by disaffected mainline church leaders (many of them Presbyterians), from Campus Crusade to InterVarsity Christian Fellowship, from World Vision to Bread for the World, from Young Life to Christianity Today, from Fuller Theological Seminary to David C. Cook Publishing House.

So why do they stay?

Lessons from a Very Early Church History

As said earlier in this chapter, we have been here before, not only in the twentieth century, but also in the first century . . . in Corinth, to be exact.

Where are we? We are thick in the battle of defining proper limits for sexual expression. In Corinth, one of the men of the church was enjoying a sexual relationship with his mother—incest! And many were bragging that Christ set them free for such pleasures!

Where are we? We are hotly contesting a proliferation of worship styles, musical forms, and outward expressions of praise to God that some people find exhilarating and others deem offensive, even repulsive. In Corinth, the worship services had become a cacophony of shouting voices, competing prophets, noisy gongs, and clanging cymbals. Agape feasts turned into gluttonous, drunken parties.

Where are we? We are continuing to wrestle with the role of spiritual gifts, including the working of miracles in our midst—somewhat jealous that Pentecostal and Charismatic churches seem to be bursting at the seams. In Corinth, speaking in tongues had become the badge of true spirituality, with many in their company parading it before others like Pharisees showing off their eloquent prayers on street corners.

Where are we? We are battling for the Bible. The whole question of authority ("Who has the final word on what the church believes and teaches?"—with accusations of "literalist!" and "relativist!") rings out from various groups in the church. In Corinth, Corinthians were disregarding, discrediting, and damning the very person who had brought them the gospel and had planted their church, the very one so inspired by God that he became the most prolific author of the New Testament letters.

Where are we? We are debating all kinds of issues around the matter of Christian liberty vs. standards of practice. In Corinth, they were battling over kosher foods and sabbath laws.

Where are we? We are rethinking so many essential teachings of the church . . . questioning the meaning of the atonement, the significance of the miracles, the finality of Jesus' promises, and the applicability of his teachings. In Corinth, they were denying the resurrection of Christ.

Where are we? We are arguing with one another. In Corinth, they were taking their fights to the secular courts.

How did the apostle Paul treat the troubles that were foaming at the mouth of the Corinthian church? He confronted those problems. He scolded the Corinthians for their immorality. He redirected their disorderliness in worship. He commanded them to recognize the body of Christ for what it is. He told them to settle their disputes in the church and not in the courts. He defended his apostleship. He proclaimed Jesus' resurrection. But Paul's longest discourse and most eloquent words were directed to another subject: church unity in the midst of its diversity. After his words of greeting, he states the thesis of the letter: "Now I appeal to you, brothers and sisters, by the name of our Lord Jesus Christ, that . . . there be no divisions among you, but that you be united in the same mind and the same purpose" (1 Cor. 1:10). After recounting the reports he has heard, he asks, "Has Christ been divided?" (1 Cor. 1:13). The folly implied in such a rhetorical question sets the tone for the lengthiest teachings in the First Letter to the Corinthians. This tone carries through the first chapter into the second and continues in the third chapter where he scolds them for remaining people of the flesh, mere infants in Christ. ". . . For as long as there is jealousy and quarreling among you, are you not of the flesh, and behaving according to human inclinations?" (1 Cor. 3:3). He continues his words with an additional question, "Do you not know that you ("all of you"—the Greek pronoun is plural) are God's temple (singular) and that God's Spirit dwells in you (plural)? If anyone destroys God's temple, God will destroy that person. For God's temple is holy, and you (plural) are that temple" (1 Cor. 3:16–17).

He picks up similar issues in the eighth chapter, where he reorients the believers' values by saying, "Knowledge puffs up, but love builds up" (1 Cor. 8:1b). He recasts the kosher and sabbath laws by the effect one's own behavior is having upon others: "But take care that this liberty of yours does not somehow become a stumbling block to the weak" (1 Cor. 8:9). This discussion is revisited in the tenth chapter, with the one loaf and one cup of Christ reminding us that "we who are many are one body" (1 Cor. 10:17). Then he affirms Christian liberty but with an important caveat: "'All things are lawful,' but not all things are beneficial. 'All things are lawful,' but not all things build up. Do not seek your own advantage, but that of the other" (1 Cor. 10:23–24). Then he considers their unruly, thoughtless worship and points them to the damage they are causing the poor among them due to their lack of discernment of the body of Christ, of which they are a part (11:29). Then at great length he expounds that the only dividing line between true believers and unbelievers is whether or not they declare, "'Jesus is Lord,'" for doing so can happen only as empowered by the Holy Spirit (12:1ff), whose presence evidences one's election as a child of God. He explains how the diversity of gifts that challenge the church's unity also multiply the body's effectiveness in ministry. The great love chapter eloquently declares what is the more excellent way of love—not romantic love between spouses but gutsy love toward unlovely folk in the church. And then he recasts the whole worship experience as doing that which will build up one another. After proclaiming the good news of Jesus' resurrection, he sends personal greetings interspersed with such reminders as, "Let all that you do be done in love" and "Greet one another with a holy kiss" (1 Cor. 16:14, 20).

Get the point? The unity of the church is not an expendable commodity, or just a nice by-product of theological unanimity. On the contrary, this unity exists first by the creative power of a God who has worked long and intensely to bring disparate elements together to make unified composites. *And* this unity exists only as the participants resolve to allow nothing to break them apart. How does the line go? "What God has joined together, let no one tear asunder."

John Calvin took a long look at the Corinthian problem. He bemoans the fact that "There was not one kind of sin only, but very many; and they were no light errors but frightful misdeeds; there was corruption not only of morals but of doctrine." But what does the apostle do? "Does he seek to separate himself from such? Does he cast them out of Christ's Kingdom? Does he fell them with the ultimate thunderbolt of anathema? He not only does nothing of the sort; he even recognizes and proclaims them to be the church of Christ and the communion of saints [1 Cor. 1:2]."

Calvin highlights Paul's call to exercise discipline and urges the same upon the contemporary church, and he also admits that many churches tend to indulge such evils. "But," he says, "even if the church be slack in its duty, still each and every individual has not the right at once to take upon himself the decision to separate."[5]

Let there be no doubt about the apostle's message. The unity of the church must be fought for, not against. The division of the church is equivalent to the unthinkable division of Christ himself.

To be honest, proving one's passion for unity is difficult while participating in a church that at its inception five hundred years ago did secede from the one, holy, catholic, and apostolic church. Does not the past history of the church discredit one's call for unity? Well, the truth be told, most historic Protestant denominations were organized not by insurrectionists but by excommunicants. Neither Luther nor Calvin nor Wesley had any desire to divide from others. They were forced out of a church that had no room for their biblical messages. Most later denominations were formed not by theological division but by language disparities. As immigrants from Europe exported their faith experience to the New World, new congregations were organized around common languages. For example, Dutch Reformed and Scottish Presbyterians believed the same, but they worshipped separately in familiar language congregations, even when living nearby. Given the blend of many of those languages today, ecumenical initiatives are helping erase such divisions, and denominations are forming new language-specific, immigrant congregations within those denominations, thereby avoiding the proliferation of denominational divisions that marked earlier American history.

The unavoidable fact of the matter is that the call to unity, regardless of differences, is an essential, core requirement of the New Testament. The only ultimate basis for division—says the apostle Paul—is if a person or group of persons saying, "Jesus Christ is Lord" changes that affirmation to "Let Jesus be cursed" (1 Cor. 12:3).

History is the essential teacher in this case, because its best lessons do not indulge divisiveness but challenge it.

Recent History Teaches, Too

One reason this pastor has taken to writing this type of a volume is the painful set of church divisions that I have observed in only a half-lifetime. Given a multidenominational experience in earlier years, coupled with my relatives' participation in a variety of faith traditions, I have seen a lot . . . a lot more than I wish to report. From the split of a church after the pastor left his wife, to a church whose charter members all pulled away when the new minister took the congregation in a contrary direction . . . from my father-in-law's retirement days watching his final congregation fight so intensely over their new pastor that they finally closed their doors permanently, to the Presbyterian congregation that divided over the proposal to move to the Evangelical Presbyterian denomination . . . history has not been pretty.

Every one of these battles, and so many other battles reported by other participants, has created untold pain in many lives. When passionate believers on one side of a battle separate from passionate believers on the other side of the battle, most of the combatants will ultimately settle into a fellowship of their choosing that will better suit their convictions. But at least two other things will happen, too. Many of those people involved suddenly find themselves with a whole new challenge: to turn their angry, wall-building energy into creative, bridge-building energy. Such channeling, however, seldom happens. Usually one conflict begets another. One split begets another. The self-emancipated congregants who now are free to build the church of their dreams discover that—behind the expressed anger toward their former fellow parishioners—they have neglected to formulate many aspects of the dream. Instead of arguing about sexual moral standards—now unanimous since such a battle is what galvanized their angry movement—they now are poised to battle over worship styles, curriculum choices, budget priorities, new denominational affiliations, program activities, mission spending, or a host of other issues. Church splits beget other splits.

The second and greater tragedy of church conflict is the *shrapnel effect*. Those passionate battle leaders—who have been tossing grenades at one another in the heat of ecclesiastical battle—ultimately land on their feet, participating in a church of their choosing. But many others, such as young teenagers or new believers, catch the shrapnel of the others' rhetorical weaponry. Too many conclude, "If this is what Christianity is all about, I'll have nothing to do with it." They fade away.

The late Clayton Bell, a leading champion of evangelicalism for forty years, once reflected, "the damage caused by division is too devastating." In 1989 lines were drawn by staff members and lay leaders who proposed taking their eighty-three-hundred-member Highland Park Presbyterian Church (Dallas, Texas) out of the mainline denomination. After an eighteen-month battle to stay put, a sufficient block of votes was amassed in order to keep the church where it was. However, a large minority still left to form a congregation in the conservative Presbyterian Church in America. "As folks on both sides tried to accumulate votes, deception overwhelmed honesty, false accusations flew, and mistreatment of one another nearly broke us," reflected Bell. As if that was not costly enough, he added, "Families were divided over the vote. Years later, some relatives still are not on speaking terms." Worse yet, Bell continued, at least one thousand members simply dropped out of church altogether. "As best we can tell, most of them have not returned to any church. Many have given up on God."

Is that not reason enough to join with the apostle Paul in fighting for the unity of the church? Must we keep learning again and again that, given all the conflicts in the church and given the appearance of an "easy-out" solution of splitting, no such easy solution is available? Can we not learn from our forebears that the antidote—division—is worse than the poison—ridding the church of others' influence?

I say, given the choice between the potential horrors of schism and the existing tension of disagreements, let the tension continue. Then again, we need more than tension. We need insight; we need understanding; we need wisdom; we need grace; we need to grasp just what is going on among us. Why do so many issues confront us? Why do we find ourselves at odds so frequently, even constantly? What is driving us to such anger? Are we believing in different gods? Or, perhaps, are we seeing God going in different directions to accomplish different things through different kinds of ministries to reach different kinds of people and make different kinds of impact in their lives? Perhaps we are looking at and bringing service to the same God, but we are doing so from such different perspectives that they hardly resemble one another.

Many noble, godly people seeking to serve God have run headlong into others aiming for the same purpose. But they have run into each other ironically because they were running in opposite directions. Repeatedly, they have gravitated into two camps, two contrary positions, two party affiliations—all in pursuit of doing the right thing. Perhaps such a division is unavoidable, even advantageous. Perhaps we ought to simply allow everybody to join their preferred party and let the contest begin. Then again . . .

Chapter 3

The Two-Party Church?

*I*n Mr. Warnaar's fifth-grade class we learned the hard way how easy it is to divide into two parties. We learned our lesson by rewriting American history, and doing so—aided by the humble pie it served me—left lasting insights for me to remember.

In order to help his Yankee students delve inside the conflict known as the Civil War, and to focus our imaginations on the greatness of one Abraham Lincoln, Mr. Warnaar decided to have his students restage the Lincoln–Douglas debates. Gregory Smith was assigned the role of Stephen Douglas. The role of Abraham Lincoln was assigned to me, if only because one of my more flattering nicknames was "Honest Habe." The assignment seemed simple enough. I read the *World Book Encyclopedia* article on the subject. I discussed with my mom the importance of abolishing the practice of slavery from the nation, which was reinforced by the almost-daily reports of news from down South, where Martin Luther King Jr. and the Civil Rights Movement were working to rid the nation of racial prejudice. I memorized a few of Lincoln's greatest quotes.

When the day came to present our positions, Greg and I were seated behind the teacher's desk in the front. I gave a three-minute speech, reminding the students that a "kingdom divided against itself cannot stand." Greg followed with a seven-minute speech, promoting the notion of "popular sovereignty" to his fellow Americans. He pressed them to allow for states' rights, for all localities to self-determine the course that they should take. He did well. I had a sinking feeling inside. Questions were solicited from the class. We both did our best to field them, but he did better. Finally Mr. Warnaar directed the students to vote by secret ballot who they believed should prevail: Lincoln with his appeal for unity or Douglas with his plea for local option. My stomach was in knots as he announced the results: Lincoln drew eleven votes; Douglas garnered fourteen.

Ten-year-old children do not quickly forget those times when their mediocre performances effectively overturn great moments in history. This Lincoln wannabe has never forgotten. More significantly, though, a greater lesson has not been forgotten. Greg's arguments for states' rights, local control, and self-determination proved more compelling to our fellow students than did my arguments for peace, unity, and equality.

The pattern of conflict in history, as outlined in the previous chapter, seems to strike a chord with something deep in the human psyche: a driving need to separate and go different ways. Whether we are children of the 1960s saying, "Do your own thing," or children of the 1970s saying, "Look out for number one," whether we are postmodernist, deconstructionist academics, or simply rebellious teenagers, something about independence compellingly attracts us.

No doubt, we Americans have been lulled into quiet confidence by the general absence of global conflict in our day. Not for decades have we needed to unite as one people and contribute everything each one could give in order to surmount an overwhelming obstacle, such as was posed by the Nazism and fascism of the 1940s. We rest secure in the expectation that today's calm shall continue to be a lasting peace. When the big picture is peaceful, we are free to indulge the luxury of cultivating more close-at-hand competitions and skirmishes. Why else would so many millions of us tune in to the more ignominious skirmishes depicted in soap operas, reality TV, and Jerry Springer–type television programs? We expose our penchant for fighting when we clap more loudly for the political candidate who makes character attacks on the opponent, and when we shout "Amen" in response to the fervent preacher who boldly takes on the "enemy," however that may be defined.

We do indulge such competitions and conflicts, but not only as spectators; we live them out in our own lives, where our dreams of permanence are replaced with proclamations of liberation. Where once the promise "for as long as we both shall live" clearly meant something, divorce parties now are celebrated. "Irreconcilable differences" has become the blanket explanation for breakups. To add more rationale to support such divisions among us, we have created euphemistic oxymorons like "amicable divorce," "holy war," and "necessary evil."

Do you remember that poignant question, "Why can't we all just get along?" The question was asked with tears but often receives the response of a cynical laugh that seems to imply a rejoinder question, "How stupid can you be that you'd ask such a question?" We all know the real response is, "Of course we can't all get along. Life just doesn't go that easily." In the process we sell our peace for a few gold coins of autonomy.

Two-Party Divisions

Particularly striking along this vein is the common contemporary practice of dividing into categories—two categories, to be exact. Whether black or white, Republican or Democrat, capitalist or communist, liberal or conservative, paper or plastic, fresh or frozen, eat-in or take-out, we almost invariably offer just two options. In its simplest form, such binary thinking boils down to "us" versus "them." Two-party thinking helps organize life clearly, if somewhat simplistically. Binary thinking provides clearly defined choices and simple categorizations, relieving us of the responsibility to deal with uncomfortable issues, undesirable ideas, unattractive options, and unappealing persons.

Binary thinking also provides a great way to win an argument. Effective salespersons, trial lawyers, and debaters long have understood that one way to try to win an argument is to pose just two options to the person or persons that one is aiming to sell to, persuade, or outdebate. "The choice is clear," we say. "It's either this or that. One or the other. Choose now, or forever hold your peace."

So-called conservatives and liberals use each other in this binary system to situate themselves and define their own positions as "the opposite of those other people." Utilizing the opponents' most negative caricatures allows each party to present its own positions in the most positive light. Further, utilizing these two favorite labels—liberals and conservatives— empowers the people using them to align themselves with all others who have used such labels in the past; one's own significance is enlarged by taking the mission's mantle that such past heroes supposedly have passed to oneself and one's own peers. The eyes of all great good people wait for us to save the world![1]

Let there be no doubt that binary thinking provides a great way to win a war. When a leader can identify a singular, visible, and tangible enemy, and at the same time clearly portray the one issue worth dying for, that person can recruit an army and convince many to risk life and limb to fulfill the righteous cause. On the other hand, declaring such a war and recruiting such an army produces collateral damage that the world should never need face. When categorizing another band of people as *them* to be opposed by *us,* we invariably look for reasons to blame them, to demonize them, and to drive them away. Such a categorization colors all our perceptions of them, finding hidden agendas behind everything they say or write. The us-them dynamic finds conspiracy theories behind all actions and sets up self-fulfilling prophecies. As Salim Munayer, the founding director of *Musalaha,* the Palestinian Christian ministry of reconciliation, says, "We behave and talk to others in a way that provokes them to fulfill the very behavior we expect from them."[2] In the process, everybody is damaged. The others, our opponents, are dehumanized by our treatment of them. At the same time, we take on a siege mentality, arming ourselves to the teeth to protect our rights, and in the process, we become infected by the cancer of power-mongering. Just as economically divided countries drive the poor into crime and the wealthy into self-defensive postures (buying guns and installing alarm systems), so, too, a two-party church brings out the worst in all.

One problem arises when categorizing differences into two neat camps. The categorizations almost invariably are incomplete and inaccurate. The world is not just black or white; it also comes in every shade of gray, not to mention red, orange, yellow, green, blue, indigo, violet, and all the shades of color in between. Political parties are not limited to Republican or Democrat but also Reform, Green, Libertarian, nonaffiliated, and a host of others. Governments come not just as capitalist and communist but also monarchies, anarchies, socialist, and so forth. Even fruit comes not just as fresh or frozen but also canned and even rotten! Two-party thinking almost invariably is too simplistic to be meaningful.

While binary thinking makes life simple, helps win arguments, and is a great way to win a war, it also misrepresents the truth and, accordingly, is a godawful way to run a church.

Impasse?

When well-intentioned evangelical Christians overtured the Presbyterian Church General Assembly of 2000 to declare that the church had reached an impasse, they were following this pattern of casting the parties into two camps. The evangelicals carefully catalogued two contrasting sets of theological and ethical beliefs that they believed manifest a line of demarcation standing between the classical, orthodox faith practiced by the overture's authors and the more newfangled, heterodox faith practiced by the others. Urging the General Assembly to acknowledge that the differences were too clear to deny, the evangelical Christians suggested that a healthy dose of reality was needed to provide at least the first step to curing the ills within this branch of the Church.

What is so wrong with declaring an impasse? First, the implication is that today's church is so much more divided than were the churches in the apostolic era as to warrant an ecclesiastical divorce that was unthinkable to the apostles. "Is Christ divided?" was Paul's response to such impasse arguments in ancient Corinth. That response still sounds right today.

Second, the declaration of irreconcilable impasse implies that Christ is incapable of healing his church. If the design, construction, and maintenance of the church ultimately falls into Christ's hands, and if his promise is never to allow the gates of hell to prevail against it, and if the manifest intention for the church is that it be unified under the headship of Christ, then a declaration of impasse would declare Jesus' own promise to be null and void. To be blunt, such a declaration is a faithless cry of faith-loyal believers.

Third, inviting those people unwilling to maintain existing standards to be granted the freedom to leave with church property feels disingenuous. For an unhappy congregation to petition to be allowed to transfer to another Christian fellowship with which it many unite is one thing. For the larger body to invite the dissidents to leave is an entirely different thing. Here stands a related irony. The evangelical, conservative writers of the overture err by thinking that their opponents think as they do. If one expression—simplified as it is—summarizes well the differences between Christian conservatives and Christian liberals, consider the one offered by Rev. Harry Hassall, former director of Covenant Fellowship of Presbyterians, the Southern Church forebear of Presbyterians for Renewal. "Liberals err in the direction of heresy, and conservatives err in the direction of schism." Underlying that assessment is the long-standing difference in practice between the sense of mission pursued by conservatives and that pursued by liberals. Conservatives try to change the world "one soul at a time," and liberals seek to transform the culture one institution at a time. The individualistic focus of conservatives has long fed the tendency to withdraw from denominational affiliations in order to be liberated to do ministry unimpeded by the weight of an uncooperative organization. The more corporate structure of the liberal movement, with its recognition of both the potential power for good that comes from positive organizations and the wretched impact for evil generated by corrupt organizations, has built a powerful resolve that has outlasted conservatives' impatience. Indeed, apart from the Unitarians' split from the New England Congregationalists, every significant theological division in American Protestant church history resulted from conservatives leaving the liberals or, on a couple occasions, excommunicating liberals.

For conservatives to invite liberals to leave the denomination thrusts a freedom upon them that only conservatives would want. It reminds me of the Christmas that my little brother gave me a gift of army men, one of his favorite kinds of toys, which he knew I did not enjoy (Yes, I've forgiven him, but not before I countered by making him feel guilty for a few decades!). The giver is giving a favorite gift to a recipient who has no interest in it.

Moreover—and most germane to the subject at hand—the division of the house into two neatly packaged sets of beliefs does not match reality. Faithful Christians' beliefs don't line up to party lines.

The very first thesis statement in the impasse overture claims that some believe that "the Bible is accurate and the Word of God speaks to His entire Church with absolute authority," while others believe that "biblical authority is determined by personal feelings or various academic disciplines." To be honest, very few Christians would bluntly attribute biblical authority to be what feels right, but most Christians do grant a greater import to texts of scripture that "speak to me," a phenomenon of insight generally attributed to the Holy Spirit. Most Christians also take seriously the scholarly research that helps determine the original intention of the inspired authors, if only to provide a hedge against the human tendency to read one's own preferences into the text. Moreover, even the most conservative Christians who boldly declare that the Bible is accurate and absolutely authoritative certainly give greater importance to some texts; scriptures declaring the good news of salvation by grace through faith certainly are emphasized over those that prescribe kosher foods and proscribe the sewing of different kinds of cloth together.

From there the overture divides the church into people who hold to proclamation watchwords of "grace alone, faith alone, scripture alone" and people who prefer the ethical exhortations of "justice and love." Since when should the church choose between its central proclamation and its central ethic, as if they were mutually exclusive?

The impasse overture proceeds to caricature the beliefs of its opponents as rejecting Jesus as the unique source of salvation in favor of a diversity of religious traditions; understanding the gift of salvation as purely a political, social, and economic recovery; the setting of sexual norms by societal standards or motivational intentions, etc. In the process, the two-party outline as offered collapses on its own reductionistic simplification of realities. Tragically, not only do such oversimplifications misrepresent one another, they also paralyze the very communications that could help correct such misrepresentations.

The two-party approach does not fit the realities. Sociologists of religion, Bill Trollinger and Doug Jacobsen, express it well: "When we ask individuals to which party in the culture war they belong, we are typically met with either a blank stare (what war?), [or] a vigorous denial of personal partisanship, or a qualified agreement with only part of the total platform of one side or the other."[3]

Indeed, while Richard G. Hutcheson Jr. and Peggy Shriver utilize the two-party model as a way of describing life in the Presbyterian Church, they do concede the ambiguities surrounding such a scheme. In fact, when asking interviewees whether they acknowledge themselves to be liberal or evangelical, "most accepted the perceived label, but usually added some modifiers, such as 'I am a moderate liberal' or 'I am a moderate evangelical.' Only one claimed 'I am a conservative evangelical.'" The authors add, "Clearly, neither camp is monolithic. Within each group can be found not only a spectrum of positions from moderate to cutting edge, but also internal controversies and disagreements."[4] Indeed, the majority of Presbyterians, they found, were located toward the middle, helping to stabilize the church amid the currents of controversy.

The most obvious support for the two-party theory in contemporary Presbyterianism is the emergence of articulate voices from two different camps. The Presbyterian Coalition has effectively formed a large constituency of evangelical and conservative Presbyterians who intend to stand for truth, tradition, and the gospel of salvation. The Covenant Network has emerged, giving voice to more progressive ideas as typified by their support of changing the current standards for ordination that exclude active gay and lesbian persons. These two organizations have provided voice, energy, resources, and hope to many who share some common aspirations and fears. But these two organizations are not monolithic. They are not political parties, comprised of undifferentiated, single-minded allies engaged in groupthink. Speaking from the perspective of a former moderator of one of the organizations, more energy is spent wrestling and juggling the differences within the organization than in combating the flaws of the outsiders. The same is the case in the other organization. The primacy of the internal battles has taken place since the inception of these groups, and the future promises to exacerbate further the internal conflicts.

Christians simply do not categorize so neatly. Presbyterians are too diverse—in political visions, in personal experiences, in educational influences, in spiritual gifting, in biblical studies, in geographical roots, in spiritual shaping—to fit into such simple categorizations.

Amicable Divorce?

What if the church actually splits into two particular camps? Would not the cause of Christ be better served by allowing them simply to go their separate ways? Cannot a level-headed group of leaders plot a course for the church, once and for all, to undergo an amicable divorce?

Such plots have been hatched before. Most recently, when the northern UPCUSA merged back with the southern PCUS 120 years after the

Civil War, allowance was made for southern congregations to vote for dismissal to other reformed denominations. Article XIII of the Articles of Agreement provided the steps that any congregation that wished to investigate such a possibility could undertake. Each such church would engage in a season of study in order to weigh more carefully its options. On a date well-known by all involved, the congregation would hold a vote by silent ballot, and if two-thirds of the present voting members so chose, the congregation would be dismissed to the other denomination. Several dozen churches initiated such a process. A few voted overwhelmingly to go, but many other bodies discovered that their congregations were more divided than they had expected. Academic discussions turned into vitriolic accusations. Bible study classes and choir rehearsals degenerated into shouting matches. Friendships and even families were divided. Eventually, two factions split apart, one remaining within the PC(USA) and the other transferring to another church. With few exceptions, the experience turned ugly.

Could an amicable divorce be planned and executed for a whole denomination of more than eleven thousand congregations and 2 million members? Seldom do you find a divorcing couple who are capable of undergoing such an amicable parting of the ways. It flies in the face of human nature even to pose such a possibility, even if we *could* neatly divide into two parties, two categories.

How Shall We Then Categorize?

Not all categorizations are irrelevant and meaningless. Quite the contrary. Martin Marty writes generally about the two streams of American Christianity, typified by the liberal movement and the fundamentalist movement. Those categories—if kept pliable—certainly summarize some different ways of approaching the faith.[5] Avery Dulles suggests the existence of six major models of contemporary Roman Catholic and Protestant churches, namely, the church as institution, mystical communion, sacrament, herald, servant, and community of disciples. Such categorizations help assess the "feel" of different ministry styles.[6] Richard Foster categorizes the whole American theological landscape according to their different traditions, i.e., the contemplative, the holiness, the charismatic, the social justice, the evangelical, and the incarnational.[7] William Westom posits the notion that the mainline churches, and the Presbyterian Church (U.S.A.) in particular, are made up of three parties, with the centrist, loyalist party being the mediating, decision-making party that arbitrates between the proposals offered by the liberal and conservative parties.[8]

Helpful as these categorizations are, they all leave something missing. Marty's two-party theory admittedly articulates a framework for understanding American churches that unabashedly adopts stereotypes as perceived in the larger media culture. In reality, he constructs two polarities between which most churches locate themselves within a wide range of latitudes. Dulles draws heavily upon Roman Catholic terms to adopt categories that fit more naturally within the catholic, liturgical traditions. Foster summarizes the contributions of historic traditions, which help the reader to locate one's own church, but he does not address the internal conflicts and convergences dynamically working out within the church. Westom's insights into the Presbyterian Church help break out of the troubling binary thinking that typically prevails, but he does so by proposing the notion that a huge loyal center exists. While many centrist moderates are out there somewhere, at last count the number of truly loyal Presbyterians had dropped to about seventeen (okay, so I'm exaggerating a little bit). On the other hand, if one renames that group by the label "moderates," then suddenly 90 percent of all mainline Christians wear that tag, although many moderates would not recognize others as their allies.

None of these frameworks approaches the heart of what is happening within historic, mainline Protestant denominations—and more importantly, what is happening within the individual Protestant Christians who are seeking to fulfill God's calling upon their lives. To put it simply, the words of this book, the message of a sermon, and even the content of scripture are all processed by your unique intellect and emotions. You are not simply a part of a historic tradition, a simple categorization of movements, or a participant in a liturgical drama written, directed, and choreographed by some other church professional. While you may identify with and feel a kinship toward others who seem to share a similar vision for ministry and similar concerns for the church's future, the greater question for you is not, "What movement defines me?" but "What do I believe God's will is for the world?" and more specifically, "In what type of service is God calling me to participate?"

The way you answer those questions probably will lead to a comfortable categorization alongside a cluster of other persons who answer those questions similarly. In the process you will be able to locate yourself according to your GodView.

Chapter 4

GodViews

We hold these truths to be self-evident." Upon those noble words a nation was born. As Thomas Jefferson penned, some values are so essential and foundational that every person in every place and in every time ought to know them, believe them, subscribe to them, submit to them, and promote them. The values of human equality, life, liberty, and the pursuit of happiness—inalienable rights endowed by the Creator—were proclaimed by Jefferson and the others signing the Declaration of Independence. With such a declaration, this new national experiment was birthed.

With those words a brutal war was joined, too. Since the beginning of time, many wars, feuds, and crusades have been waged to satisfy purely selfish expansions of power and wealth, and even just to unleash unbridled rage. But many more conflicts have emerged from persons pursuing noble causes. Millions of warriors have spent incalculable amounts of time praying for God to grant courage, wisdom, and success in fulfilling their righteous military cause. Whether it be the Israel of Joshua's day, the Western Europeans of the Crusaders' day, or the colonists of Jefferson's day, their personal ambitions at the very least were undergirded by the high purpose of serving a greater good. In fact, most conflicts that escalate to the level of outward warfare are fueled by what all the principal parties believe to be a cause worth dying for.

Noble causes do drive the church to fulfill the loftiest of purposes and protect the most essential values. But such noble causes can also decimate the church by the conflicts they unleash. Convictions drive us and divide us, especially when we believe that they are supported by God-evident truths. Truths revealed by God can and must be known, believed, subscribed, obeyed, and promoted.

As historian Bradley Longfield says, Christians fight so intensely because of their very confession that Jesus Christ is Lord. Making such a confession immediately obligates a person to do the will of

Christ, no matter how much opposition one encounters, no matter how nontraditional one's convictions may be, or even no matter how much one may be accused of heresy, ignorance, or bigotry. "If Jesus is Lord, and Christians believe that faithfulness to Christ calls them to a certain position on particular issues, then they are compelled to respond. Jesus is Lord. Not just over part of life but all of life, and this will, sooner or later, tend to push individuals and groups to conflict."[1]

Is it any wonder that the nonreligious John Lennon would pen the lyrics of "Imagine," which link religious belief to greed, hunger, and war? Listen to that song and you too might say that he is a dreamer. Christians would probably want to say that he is putting too much blame on religion, when in fact many other institutions, belief systems, and disbelief systems contribute to things that people "kill or die for." Nevertheless, nobody can deny that people's commitment to the truth as they know it—including religious beliefs—drive many people and groups to declare holy wars.

Convictions drive us to do good, and they divide us to the point of evil.

Getting to the Root Issues

But why do convictions make us act this way? Must this continue? Cannot the convictions that drive us also unite us? Certainly any hope of turning the pattern around must begin with understanding the convictions themselves. What beliefs drive and divide us? If Christ is undivided and the church as the body of Christ is united by the head who is Christ himself, should not unity result automatically as we join around the convictions that Jesus taught?

Even a cursory look at today's church suggests that something is amiss; the tendency to balkanize appears to overwhelm the spirit of unity. In the previous chapter we challenged the notion that the church is divided into two parties. While the two-party model is fraught with misrepresentations, only Polyanna would deny that the church is divided nonetheless. The reality of the divisions is obvious when considering the many special-interest groups that have arisen in recent decades. Pro-lifers have organized, as have pro-choicers. Twelve-steppers have incorporated, as have re-imaginers. Sociologists of religion have formed their own guild to match those of biblical scholars and pastoral counselors. Pro-gay groups proliferate, and sexual healing ministries multiply. Why do so many folks put so much energy into what so many other folks consider to be minor, even peripheral, issues or ideas? What's going on here? What drives believers to express so much passion about so many different causes?

Perhaps categorizing such divisions is not so bad after all. Indeed, while challenging the two-party categorizations of beliefs in the previous chapter, one ought not assume that all categorizations are misguided. Our belief structures have not become so complex and individually driven that they defy categorization. Quite the contrary. The sheer fact that so many Christians cluster together into groups identified by common interests and shared passions begs for analysis. What has drawn some to the Witherspoon Society or to Presbyterians for Renewal? Why have large-church pastors formed covenant groups? Why do some clergy attend the same summer institute at Princeton or Union Seminary every year? Obviously, baits of different flavors are drawing fish of different breeds to schools of different interests.

Cliff Kirkpatrick calls them "affinity groups." At one time the *Book of Order* called them "Chapter Nine Organizations." Laird Stuart calls them "enclaves of agreement." Call them what you will, but they exist because well-intentioned individuals who feel called to serve God in particular ways tend to find one another and form organizations that encourage, facilitate, and promote their shared sense of call. The question that begs asking is, "Can we possibly understand and identify those particular calls?"

The growing field of the sociology of religion keeps positing different categorizations for such groupings. In *The Heretical Imperative*, Peter Berger observes, "The regrettable fact is that nobody trying to make sense of modern theology . . . can fail to attempt some sort of typification; otherwise the sheer diversity and complexity of the phenomenon will frustrate any effort at understanding."[2]

As mentioned earlier, categories of denominations and traditions can help individuals locate themselves on the theological map. But most of today's church conflicts are being waged not *between* those denominations and traditions but *within* them. The worst fights seem to occur when one individual Presbyterian fights with another individual Presbyterian, when one particular Baptist overpowers another particular Baptist, when one Methodist prosecutes another Methodist. In other words, the convictions that drive and divide are ones held in each individual heart, mind, and soul.

In this fragmented age, individuals would logically be the locus of conflict. The century-old message of modern psychology—for better and for worse—has impressed upon us all the need to find ourselves, to know ourselves, to actualize our potential, to fulfill our dreams, to stand our ground, and to follow our calling. With the avalanche of print and broadcast media providing us everything we could possibly want to know about any one of those dreams or callings—or, for that matter, impediments in the form of opponents and enemies who must be overcome—we are picking our own battlegrounds. We don't simply follow the party platforms written by our denominations, our curricula, our pastors, or even our Sunday school teachers. While we subject ourselves to the voices coming from the pulpits and read the editorial pages, when all is said and done, nobody but ourselves will decide who are our prophets and who can be dismissed as cranks. We think for ourselves.

Church and tradition categories help explain the religiocultural landscape. They help explain why the Pentecostal church down the street has developed such a strong Sunday school, why so many lapsed Catholics think visiting a Protestant church is more sinful than sleeping in on Sundays, and why Presbyterians evoke less denominational loyalty than Baptists. But why do people respond to the same sermon with such diverse comments as the following:

- "I feel so much closer to God now—the pastor had me in tears."
- "I now know God is calling me to teach a Sunday school class."
- "I felt so excluded by the constant references to God as a man."
- "The preacher played fast and loose with the scriptures."
- "I'm going right home to call my mother to tell her how much I love her."

Why do we perceive values-emphasizing, theology-driven, Christ-centered preaching in such different ways? Why do we gravitate to affinity groups or enclaves of agreement within our denominations, and why do we throw down the gauntlet on the fight-to-the-finish battle lines that keep being drawn over hot-button issues? Why the divisions, and what purpose do they serve?

The divisions exist because of the passionate beliefs we hold. The passions can be so intense as to beg for new categories for our understanding. This new, balkanized world demands that we formulate different ways to analyze our belief systems. Some categories must be legitimate, because the fragmentation of our convictions has not become so individualistic that we cannot find anybody with whom we agree. In order to balkanize as we have, points of agreement are as necessary as points of disagreement. Identifying both enemies and allies is important. When drawing lines in the sand, the implied points of separation demark both excluded outsiders and included insiders. What brings the allies—the insiders—together?

A New Vocabulary Word

While studying for an undergraduate degree in religion and philosophy, I often wondered if college was not little more than a costly, painstaking vocabulary class. I had no ax to grind. I loved college and grad school, too! But sometimes it seemed that the sum of learning—especially in my major fields of study—boiled down to understanding the meaning of such terms as *dialectic* and *existentialism, soteriology* and *exegesis*. The proof of your knowledge of a particular subject was to be found in your ability to define and use that discipline's key vocabulary words.

In the present case, the need to explain the balkanization of the church may also boil down to learning a new vocabulary or perhaps just one specific word. Perhaps we can just invent a word. What term would you use to express that internalized, passionate conviction that drives you to serve God in a particular way, and yet, at the same time, differs with the inner passionate conviction that drives other believers to serve God in different ways? Given that such a drive seems to function automatically, instinctively, and almost precognitively, you might call it an impulse. Since this presupposition arises with so much passion that it causes many to throw all their proverbial eggs into that one basket—risking friendships, reputation, and sometimes even physical safety to follow it—perhaps the presupposition ought to be called an ideology or an ideological impulse. Then again, since for the Christian this unconscious drive arises out of and in response to one's perceived call from God, it begins and ends with one's theological framework. How about calling it a "theo-ideological impulse"? *Theo-ideological impulse* is a bit of a mouthful. Let's explore another term: "GodView."

GodView. Think about it: Our view of who God is, our view of what God is doing in the world, our view of what God is calling the church to do, our view of what God is calling us to do. A view that finds its basis in the revealed word of God. A view that has been proclaimed in some, if not all, of the church's confessions. A view that has been pursued—albeit in different ways and to different degrees—through the history of the church. A view—or to borrow the philosophical term, an *a priori assumption* upon which our other values are built—that is so deeply dyed into the lens of one's eyes that it colors everything one sees and predisposes us to tap our toes to the rhythm of particular beats of scripture and tradition and to tune out altogether other beats of scripture and tradition. These presuppositions are so essential to one's internal belief structure that they resist all criticism, and perhaps even perception. As one pastor put it, "It's what you *know*."

A GodView differs from the more familiar expression "worldview." The various worldviews generally provide more sweeping possibilities, like "the world is under God's direct control," "the world knows no sovereign apart from laws of nature," "God wound up the world like a clock and then abandoned it," or "God may or may not exist, but God is now irrelevant to human existence." Whereas worldviews may or may not have a religious base, all the GodViews presume belief in a God who has called humans into partnership. Whereas some worldviews oppose Christian belief, all the GodViews arise because of Christian belief. Whereas some worldviews subvert Christian practice, all the GodViews reflect a significant aspect of the church's ministry. But like worldviews, GodViews differ from one person to another.

Whence Cometh These GodViews?

GodViews arise from many sources. Rooted in our temperaments, they are shaped by our environments, "converted" by our faith experiences, empowered by our spiritual giftings, reinforced by our affiliations, and magnified by our sense of call. Let's take a closer look.

An individual's GodView is founded upon one's own psychological makeup. That fact alone implies an infinite variety of mind-sets. Theologian Miroslav Volf captures in complicated terms the enormously complicated way we humans form our own mind-sets:

> Psychologists tell us that humans produce and reconfigure themselves by a process of identifying with others and rejecting them, by repressing drives and desires, by interjecting and projecting images of the self and the other, by externalizing fears, by fabricating enemies and suffering animosities, by forming allegiances and breaking them up, by loving and hating, by seeking to dominate and letting themselves be dominated—and all this not neatly divided but all mixed up, with "virtues" often riding on hidden "vices," and "vices" seeking compensatory redemption in contrived "virtues." Through this convoluted process the center of the self is always reproducing itself, sometimes by asserting itself over against the other . . . , at other times by cleaving too closely to the other . . . , sometimes pulled by the lure of throbbing and restless pleasures, at other times pushed by the rule of a rigid and implacable law.[3]

Whew!!! What a maze of influences! Let's untangle it.

A person's psychological self builds upon a foundation of one's temperament. While geneticists, sociologists, and psychologists all claim that their own disciplines explain root causes for temperament, we all have one, regardless of its source or sources. As the Taylor-Johnson Temperament Analysis Test summarizes, at least nine polarities exist wherein one's temperament may be measured. We all are more or less nervous or composed, depressive or lighthearted, socially active or quiet, expressive or inhibited, sympathetic or indifferent, subjective or objective, dominant or submissive, hostile or tolerant, and self-disciplined or impulsive. The introverted, self-disciplined person is more likely to adopt a GodView that can be fulfilled by an introverted, self-disciplined person—like becoming a scholar. The extroverted, expressive, compassionate person more likely will sense God calling to serve in the Peace Corps.

Building upon temperament, one's GodViews have been shaped through life experiences—both good and bad. Behavior that has generated guilt or injected shame, catastrophes that have left one terrorized or resolute to "never let it happen again," losses that have left one heartbroken, and triumphs that have overwhelmed with joy . . . these circumstances all shape one's GodViews.

GodViews also come from one's present status in life vis-à-vis the meeting of needs. To borrow from Abraham Maslow's hierarchy of needs, a person who is lacking the basic essentials of food and shelter will not likely become absorbed in theological debates regarding predestination and free will. All the more, the person of faith whose community has just been decimated by a tornado will more likely throw herself into rebuilding damaged homes than into street evangelism. Self-actualizing, the pursuit of one's highest potential, always defers to the more immediate, tangible need.

Given the variety of influences, a person's identity will foster either the formation of a healthy GodView or a neurotic, grandiose exaggeration. In fact, speaking about GodViews and their ideological center brings one close to the edge of a psychological precipice. That is, the visionary nature of our "theo-ideological impulses" easily can become distorted by confusing one's ideals with one's idealized self-image. A person's self-realizing process becomes jumbled up with a self-idealizing neurosis. Psychoanalyst Karen Horney explains that a person "under the pressure of inner distress reaches out for the ultimate and the infinite which—though his limits are not fixed—it is not given to him to reach; and in this very process he destroys himself. . . ."[4]

What does that say about our GodViews? Are they implicitly neurotic? Of course not. To abandon ideology is to become apathetic. The value of *apatheia* may have been promoted by Seneca and the Stoics in first-century Rome, but the passionate Christians and Jews never subscribed to the emotionless disinterestedness that later would be modeled by *Star Trek*'s Mr. Spock. The believers expressed great passion in their service to Christ and the church. But as the contemporary inheritors of the faith they proclaimed, we also have inherited temperaments, circumstances, and dreams; we have been shaped by our nature and our nurture, through the assessing and meeting of needs, through the formation of our personal identities, through our enrolling in causes with others who share our temperaments and ideals, and through many other factors that shape our psychological selves.

At the same time, our GodViews are molded all the more by our spiritual formation. Believers witness to beginning their faith journeys at the starting lines of church cradle rolls and college philosophy classes, at Billy Graham crusades and youth campfire sing-alongs, and at mothers' funerals and at nephews' baptisms. Through one's years in faith, our GodViews are shaped by the formation of our Christian minds, with credit going to Sunday school teachers and graduate-school professors. Is it any surprise that when clergy meet one another they immediately ask, "What seminary did you go to?" Clergy can quickly pigeonhole their colleagues who attended Yale Divinity School and Dallas Theological Seminary; they know what influences are present in those seminaries known as McCormick, Fuller, Princeton, and Louisville. Most clergy know that their seminary experience profoundly shaped their own vision of ministry and that their choice of seminary may well have been shaped by the Christian experience they already had embraced.

The process of spiritual formation also is powerfully influential in the various ways believers are gifted by the Holy Spirit. "Now there are varieties of gifts, but the same Spirit; and there are varieties of services, but the same Lord; and there are varieties of activities, but it is the same God who activates all of them in everyone. To each is given the manifestation of the Spirit for the common good" (1 Cor. 12:4–7). In this short paragraph, the apostle preached a simple, three-part sermon to the Corinthians. Part one, all ministry gifts, services, and activities come from the one, triune God. Part two, God has distributed gifts, called forth services, and organized activities of an almost infinite variety. Part three, every believer has been given a manifestation, i.e., a Spirit-empowered gift, service, or activity for the greater benefit of all. This variety of gifts and ministries accounts for one person's call into Bible translation and another's call to music ministry. This variety unleashes the gift of preaching and the passion for intercessory prayer ministry, and explains why some instinctively respond to the call to paint a church classroom, while others love junior-high ministry.

Above all else, one's GodViews are shaped by the direct influence of God, who through Jesus Christ established a New Covenant that promised to shape all the thinking of the people called to be a part of Christ's church. As promised by the prophet Jeremiah, the laws written on tablets of stone now have been written—in the New Covenant—on the tablets of our hearts. The writer of Hebrews proclaims the fulfillment of Jeremiah's promise in 8:10:

> "I will put my laws in their minds,
>   and write them on their hearts,
> and I will be their God,
>   and they shall be my people."

That promise is echoed by Ezekiel in 36:26–27: "A new heart I will give you, and a new spirit I will put within you. . . ." And according to Paul (2 Cor. 3:2–6), that promise is fulfilled in the gospel: "You yourselves are our letter, written on our hearts, to be known and read by all; and you show that you are a letter of Christ, prepared by us, written not with ink but with the Spirit of the living God. . . . [O]ur competence is from God, who has made us competent to be ministers of a new covenant, not of letter but of spirit; for the letter kills, but the Spirit gives life."

In other words, one of the marks of the Holy Spirit's work in the New Covenant cut by Jesus Christ is the inner transformation of one's thinking—the laws of God being inscribed on one's heart and programmed into one's mind. Paul describes this internal work as nothing less than God being "at work in you, enabling you both to will and to work for his good pleasure" (Phil. 2:13).

However, as the multiplicity of Christian traditions demonstrates and as the apostolic era manifests, that internal work of God expresses itself in a diversity of mind-sets among us. In fact, as we noted earlier, that diversity is nowhere more obvious than among the Corinthians, to whom Paul expressed the radical assertion, ". . . but we have the mind of Christ" (1 Cor. 2:16). How can that be? Obviously, by the Spirit of God customizing the message of God's heart to each individual. The internal work of the Spirit, in effect, directs each one of us toward different GodViews.

Lest you misunderstand, the variety of legitimate GodViews is not infinite. Some perceptions of God and some truth claims about Jesus Christ clearly violate the revealed word of God given for all time. Some believers—indeed, all believers—understand that some ideas are in error. Just as the church through history has from time to time condemned some ideas as contrary to scripture, so, too, heresy still exists outside and within the church, and we ought to resist its deceptions. However, the variety of GodViews does reflect the creative hand of God having formed them.

How Much Variety?

Suggesting that the number of GodViews is equal to the number of believers would be easy. The God who made all fingerprints different surely has made our minds all the more complex and unique. But if we were totally unique in every possible way we would not—indeed, *could* not—associate with one another except in the most cursory, perfunctory ways. That so many of the faithful have gravitated into affinity groups—prayer groups, lobby groups, Bible study groups, recovery groups, support groups, and mission groups—indicates that some common denominators form magnetic fields that draw together birds of a feather.

At closer inspection, and with careful listening, one can perceive that a few particular kinds of fuel propel the GodViews of faithful Christians. Some obviously are fueled by a passion for the essential, traditional message of the gospel. Sometimes sounding dogmatic and judgmental, their readiness for debate issues from a passion for truth. Some other believers are passionate about people and are unable to sleep on cold nights knowing that homeless children are huddled around junkyard fires. The compassion of Christ pushes them out of their comfortable climes to make a discernible difference in the lives of the destitute. Other believers seem driven by a simple hunger for God, a spiritual longing for closeness, a celebration of oneness, a joy in worship, and a discipline of prayer. Still others find themselves aggravated over injustice and provoked by prejudice; they cannot sit back passively while others are denied basic human rights. Some GodViews find expression in more subtle ways that are every bit as energetic as the rest. Certain people just happen to show up whenever their church needs someone to mop floors, lead a youth group, serve on a committee, or usher or drive or visit. GodViews drive these people to work hard at many tasks that often go unnoticed by others. Then again, you'll hear from such individuals when controversies tear at the fabric of church unity.

Five GodViews

When you listen to the hearts of believers throughout the church—at least through the mainline Protestant churches of European descent—you can hear five kinds of voices expressing passion for Christ's service: the voices of five GodViews.

One cluster of believers has adopted what we will call the *Confessionalist* GodView. They are committed to discerning, proclaiming, and preserving the truth.

Another cluster of believers follows a *Devotionalist* GodView. They are hungry for God; they love to pray; they worship, meditate, and study. They want to know God, and they want others to know God, too.

A third cluster of believers embodies an *Ecclesiast* GodView. These folks are known not so much for their advocacy as for their action. They serve on committees, teach church school classes, sing in choir, attend community-wide ecumenical events, and give generously. They provide the backbone of healthy church ministries.

A fourth block of believers does ministry under the influence of what we will dub the *Altruist* GodView. They see human tragedies that others overlook, and they do something about them. They give to the needy, serve in local soup kitchens, build community-wide homeless shelters, and serve on the boards of charitable organizations.

The fifth group identified here also sees human need but responds as directed by an *Activist* GodView. This group addresses far-reaching realms: systemic evils, racial prejudices, gender exclusion, power-mongering, and injustice in every form. The activists join protest marches, demonstrate against polluters and political machines, advocate for policies of inclusion and compassion, and raise their voices for those silenced by unjust structures in society.

One or More?

Each of the GodViews as outlined above is founded upon a large body of biblical teaching and can cite a long list of champions who have established exemplary role models throughout church history. Each GodView can claim a proud heritage and a visionary calling. Also, as over against the liberal-conservative or liberal-loyalist-conservative categories, these five GodViews truly do fuel particular passions for ministry that arise within believers to varying degrees. A healthy denomination pursues all five GodViews. Most local churches pursue all five to varying degrees. Most believers can discern at least two—and as many as all five—at work within them. Then again, at the end of the day, most believers find that one of the GodViews stands above the rest; their primary sense of call to Christ's service rises out of its force field. One kind of sermon hits home more than others because it affirms or prods the fulfillment of that one GodView. When it comes time to join a committee or sign up to participate in a mission project, one particular kind of service will just *feel* right, because it resonates with a particular GodView. In other words, the five GodViews reside within the human spirit like a college student's major fits within an overall academic program. To have a complete education, one will learn a little something about a broad range of subjects, but the student will also specialize in one major field and possibly minor in another.

The major GodView—and, possibly, the minor GodView—resides within the human spirit like a neutron at the core of a hydrogen atom. Just as that neutron clings to a positively charged proton, the GodView draws its creative energy in the dream of what God longs to accomplish in the world. Also, just as that neutron-proton core is counter-energized by the electron that revolves around it, one's GodView is mobilized into action by fear or anger over what could befall or indeed already is violating what one perceives to be God's plans. In other words, the Confessionalist dreams of the world being filled with the knowledge of the Lord "as the waters cover the sea" and grows angry with and fearful of those forces of deception and misinformation that squelch the proclamation of the liberating truth. The Devotionalist dreams of the day when that knowledge of the Lord is not just a head-knowledge but a heart-experience of God; at the same time, the Devotionalist weeps over how distracted, busy, and preoccupied fellow believers have become. The Ecclesiast yearns to see the church exercising quality pastoral care, informed Christian education, God-glorifying worship, and significant world mission, but the holder of this GodView weeps over church divisions that are wrecking the fulfillment of that vision. The Altruist dreams about the eradication of poverty, ignorance, and abuse; that same Altruist cannot understand why so many other so-called Christians won't lift a finger to help meet the needs of the hungry and needy. The Activist dreams of wolves lying down with lambs, of a day when justice rains down over all the earth, when the chains of prejudice are no more, when the environment is rejuvenated, and when the peaceable kingdom is pervasive in every corner of the earth. That same Activist shudders with anger over the church's failure to rise against the evils of injustice, indeed when the church shelters and even creates such injustices.

Like a neutron within an atom, each GodView draws upon the positive energy of a dream and is equally empowered—sometimes super-powered—by the negative energy resident in that dream's frustration.

So whence cometh your vision, your dream, your fear, your anger—as you seek to serve God, the church, the world? Which GodViews fuel your mission? What other believers drive you crazy as they live out their respective GodViews?

Chapter 5

The Confessionalist GodView:
A Passion for the Truth

*D*riving a car is like riding a bike. Once you've mastered the skill, even if you've been away from the habit, you don't need someone to reteach you how to ride or drive. You never really forget how.

You would think that would also be the story for commercial airline pilots. Once they learn and practice and are certified to take hundreds of passengers on their jets, you would think that they would know the instructions like the backs of their hands. But no. When they—into whose hands have been the entrusted the survival of up to hundreds of lives—climb into the cockpit of their jets, do you know what they do? They pull out the instruction book and, line by line, relearn how to fly. Once airborne, if anything out of the ordinary should occur, they bring out the instruction book again to guide them through its resolution. In fact, if they don't read through the instructions and go through the required checklist, they'll be fired. Their career is over.

Airline pilots do it by the book. So do Christians.

To the outsider, Christian devotion understandably looks really strange. Out of the millions of books that have been written, over 1 billion humans order their lives according to the directives contained in one particular book. Just one book is granted a devotion and finality that equates to that which is accorded the Eternal.

Perhaps that overstates the matter. We do live in a day when the proliferation of books, magazines, Internet communications, plays, movies, and other forms of entertainment has collectively distracted Christians—virtually all Christians—from the disciplined reading of that book, which many of their forebears exercised. We live in a day when leaders of the faith—pastors and Christian educators especially—frequently decry the biblical ignorance that has become pandemic in the churches. We live in a day when scholarly skeptics write book after book that seem to discredit the historical accuracy of the Bible and call into question the classical interpretations of the Bible; frankly, many of those books sell quite well.

Nevertheless, if you were to ask the billion-plus Christians why they believe what they believe, most would say, along the lines of the children's song, that they believe "for the Bible tells me so."

The Thrill of Discovery

Intrinsic to this devotion to the Bible is an energy born out of a passion for the truth, growing out of the thrill of discovery. The mystery of the ages has burst forth like light from a new sun, like a live broadcast from another planet. God has made known the ultimate mystery in the person of Jesus Christ.

The apostle Paul testifies, "I became [the church's] servant according to God's commission that was given to me for you, to make the word of God fully known, the mystery that has been hidden throughout the ages and generations but has now been revealed to his saints. To them God chose to make known how great among the Gentiles are the riches of the glory of this mystery, which is Christ in you, the hope of glory" (Col. 1:25–27).

Paul's discovery was akin to that testified to by the apostle John, expressed in the opening words of the fourth Gospel. "In the beginning was the Word, and the Word was with God, and the Word was God. . . . And the Word became flesh and lived among us, and we have seen his glory, the glory as of a father's only son, full of grace and truth" (1:1,14). The writer of Hebrews begins on a similar note: "Long ago God spoke to our ancestors in many and various ways by the prophets, but in these last days he has spoken to us by a Son. . . . He is the reflection of God's glory and the exact imprint of God's very being, and he sustains all things by his powerful word" (1:1–3).

In these passages, as in many others in the New Testament, the essential starting point of all our beliefs comes down to the great news that the God who had been revealed through the ages only in brief glimpses has become a living revelation in the person of Jesus Christ, the only begotten Son of God. Then again, God's revelation in Jesus is not simple and static, like a stick-figure drawing or a mathematical calculation. Every visual image and eye-opening explanation provoke even more questions, curiosities, and mystery.

The mystery surrounding ultimate things fascinates the multitudes. The popularity of mystery novels attests to that fact. Skilled as authors are at raising all kinds of questions in the minds of their readers, the writers just as skillfully tie all the questions together in the closing pages of those novels, as the protagonist solves every question, leading the reader to utter, "Aha! Now I get it!"

In a similar way, the receptive reader of scripture finds one question after another begging for answers. When finally encountering Jesus of Nazareth, following him through his life stories, one also can anticipate that this protagonist will answer every question. That dramatic pursuit of answers certainly eludes his closest followers throughout their years with him, but then as he hangs on a cross, one of his crucifiers, a Roman guard, finally utters the answer, "Truly this man was God's Son" (Matt. 27:54). The mystery is solved. But then again, more mystery follows: the resurrection, visits with his band of followers, their continually dumbheaded questions ("[I]s this the time when you will restore the kingdom to Israel?" [Acts 1:6]), the sudden ascending disappearance, the outpouring of the Holy Spirit, and on and on. One can't help but wonder, "What's the point if the answer itself is a mystery?"

At closer inspection, we find out that when the apostle says that in Jesus the mystery has been made known, he is not thinking like a typical mystery writer, for whom the perplexities are all solved by the brilliant protagonist. Jesus functions not only as the brilliant protagonist; he is revealed as the author as well! To encounter Jesus Christ does not mean that the questions have all found a simple, "How could I have missed it?" answer. Rather, encountering Jesus is like meeting the novel's author him- or herself. You may not know all the elements of the story, but you now know the story's author. Knowing him allows the reader—that is, the participant in life's drama—to approach the author with questions, some of which will be answered, others left unanswered—at least for the moment. Nevertheless, the participant in the story hears those words of assurance from his or her savior, "Trust me. I am writing the story. It will have a good ending." Surprisingly, we realize we are part of that story as it is yet being written.

Jesus' role as the mystery writer shows forth in the story of the transfiguration. He takes aside his three closest disciples, Peter, James, and John, and leads them up the hill. Suddenly he turns aglow like white-hot steel. Moses and Elijah materialize on the scene as if from thin air. Note that we don't really know how the three apostles recognized the two visitors; they did not have the benefit of Renaissance artists to show them what their visitors looked like. Perhaps Moses was carrying a replica of the tablets of stone and Elijah was accompanied by a fiery chariot—who knows? Regardless, the apostles found the whole experience to be wondrous and mystifying, like children seeing their first display of fireworks. "If you wish, I will make three dwellings here," blurted Peter. At that a bright cloud overshadowed them all, and a voice rang out from heaven, "This is my Son, the Beloved; with him I am well pleased; listen to him!" (Matt. 17:4–5).

Did the transfiguration solve the mysteries of the ages, or did it raise more questions in the minds of the apostles? Well, the transfiguration offered hints about a few issues. First and most obviously, it revealed that Jesus is above and beyond anything they had yet conceived. Of major importance was his elevation in significance by the father of the Law, Moses, and by the father of the prophets, Elijah. In the process, all the teachings about God communicated in the Hebrew scriptures were now finding their embodiment in the message, the mission, and the person of Jesus. Indeed, he was being singled out above his two forebears.

The twin reality of both the presence of these Old Testament leaders and the manifest superiority of Jesus as the Son begs for more explanation. The presence of the fathers of the law and the prophets highlights the importance of the theological and ethical content of Jesus' message. One can be easily caught up in the thrill of a spiritual happening, all the while missing the message that is being conveyed. Whether through high liturgy or quiet contemplation, through charismatic enthusiasm or interpersonal interaction, one can become so caught up in the glow of experience that the glow is all that remains. In Jesus, the Christian discovers not only the experience of God, sometimes even with phenomenal happenings; one also encounters a message that at once proclaims good news and exhorts faithful response.

The thrill that captivates Christians with a passion for truth is in discovering that in Jesus Christ all truth converges.

In fact, the passion for truth animates life for so many Christians not simply because of the intellectual information that has been made understandable through him, but also by realizing that his truth has changed one's own life. While "The Battle Hymn of the Republic" is sung most often at patriotic services, its final verse captures a sense of the impact of such a transformation:

> In the beauty of the lilies Christ was born across the sea,
> With a glory in his bosom that transfigures you and me:
> As he died to make men holy, let us die to make men free,
> While God is marching on.

In the second line the songwriter expresses well the experience shared by so many members of the Christian community, whose encounter with

Jesus in faith has transfigured them. Not everyone has had a Mount of Transfiguration or Damascus Road–type experience. Some have. Most have encountered Jesus in quieter ways, within the context of a life lived in faith over time. But so many people testify of a change. Where they knew guilt, they now know forgiveness. Where they knew estrangement, they know they have been reconciled. Previously known fear has been cast out by perfect love. Once overwhelmed with despair, they now live in hope and confidence. Where they were caught in a maze of doubt, they are now led by faith. Having wandered aimlessly, they now pursue a higher purpose in life.

The thrill of that discovery has made many a Christian irrepressibly passionate for the truth of the gospel of Jesus Christ.

The Need to Broadcast

The discovery of truth has also given so many budding Confessionalists a good reason to want to promote that truth to others, which takes us back to the story of the transfiguration. When the glow faded and the vision of Moses and Elijah disappeared, Jesus began to lead his friends back down the hill to rejoin the other nine apostles. Glibly, "Jesus ordered them, 'Tell no one about the vision until after the Son of Man has been raised from the dead'" (Matt. 17:9).

Can you imagine their response when, upon their reunion, the other nine disciples must have asked, "So what have you all been up to?" The impetuous, energetic, revolution-sparking James and John had earned the nickname the Sons of Thunder (Mark 3:17). Can you imagine these brothers having to stifle their excitement? Then there is Peter, the disciple with perpetual foot-in-mouth disease. Can you imagine him containing his wonderment? They had just seen a vision like few ever see in a whole lifetime, and Jesus tells them to keep quiet about it.

Their inevitable struggle to contain themselves hints of the struggle we all have in such circumstances. Deep within the human psyche a voice longs to express itself. When something exciting befalls, when a controversy erupts, when disappointment crashes, most people find themselves saying, "I've just got to tell somebody!" Every human, at least once in a while, needs to broadcast whatever excites them.

We all do need to publish and proclaim whatever is newsworthy to us, because we all want to share what we know. Joe Donaho, when writing a book on personal evangelism, fittingly titled the book, *Good News Travels Faster!*[1] Indeed it does. Christians thrilled with the discovery of the transforming, transfiguring truth about Jesus Christ naturally want to share that news with other people so that they may also make the discovery and fuel a passion for truth for themselves.

As he was preparing to ascend to heaven, Jesus reversed his earlier order of silence—which had been repeated on many occasions—by commanding the apostles to broadcast the good news. "'All authority in heaven and on earth has been given to me. Go therefore and make disciples of all nations, baptizing them in the name of the Father and of the Son and of the Holy Spirit, and teaching them to obey everything that I have commanded you. And remember, I am with you always, to the end of the age'" (Matt. 28:18–20). In expressing the Great Commission, he was commanding them to proclaim the truth he had taught and modeled for them. By implication, he was also commanding them to study, protect, and manage that truth judiciously.

The Concern to Protect

Startlingly wonderful as the truth is, people of faith have seldom done a good job of maintaining it. Throughout the Old Testament the people of the covenant and the law often forgot the God who had called them into faithfulness. Repeatedly they strayed from the clearly revealed words of God. They can be excused, given the somewhat sketchy ways God's will was sometimes conveyed to them. However, in the New Testament, given the benefit of having known Jesus and having received the presence of the Holy Spirit and all the benefits of salvation, one would think the early believers would have naturally held clearly to the truth.

Not so.

The early believers repeatedly were drawn into false ideas by misguided propagandists. From the Gnosticism of those denying Christ's humanity to the skeptics denying Jesus' divinity, from the Corinthians' penchant to break the rules to the Galatians' practice of adding to the rules, the church strayed from the truth again and again. Conflicts arose immediately. Apostles spoke out, even to the point of excommunicating some who were purveying false teachings. The need to protect the truth became a major preoccupation of the believers. (Read Gal. 1:6–12, for example.)

Throughout history the church has struggled to remain faithful to the truth. That fact might seem strange; the church simply ought to stick to the essentials taught throughout its history, and leave it at that. However, that option is easily followed only if Christians can be content to live hermits' lives. The church has continually wrestled with the meaning of its faith because the church throughout history has continually faced new, daunting questions. So often, beliefs once held dear must hold up under a new level of scrutiny, and the people holding the faith must find the capacity to consider if perhaps they have been wrong all along. The church has pursued this process in reconsidering its positions on slavery, women, divorce, the environment, and war, to name just a few. The list will grow until Christ returns. But truth continually teeters in the balance, and the church rocks with each new controversy.

Why do churches fight so much among themselves? Why do arguments among Christians wax so intense? Three reasons emerge: (1) because believers perceive new questions as assaults on beliefs held dear, (2) because confronting critics seem to be threatening the faith once delivered to the saints, and (3) because the struggle to discern truth runs headlong into the concern to protect truth.

The Confessionalist Imperative

Some people within the church enjoy testing the boundaries of the faith, taking on the role of iconoclasts. Provoking controversy and stirring up the ire of traditionalists become sport. Others feel compelled to promote counter-traditional ideas as they become sensitized to voices previously silenced or dismissed. For others, the need to challenge old assumptions comes as a drudgery, a necessity that forces itself upon them only when a perceived inconsistency or prejudice compels them to speak out. Regardless of the cause, the church continually finds itself conflicted and troubled. Inevitably, many people rise up to protect the church from foreign ideas, like white blood cells fighting off infection. Often the responses exaggerate the problem and leave the church worse off than when the questions were raised.

The instinct to protect the truth gives rise to the Confessionalist God-View. Having been taken captive by the grace of the gospel and by the powerful truths of scripture, the Confessionalist enlists in God's mission to proclaim and promote the truth. Sensitized by a lucid memory of the many times the gospel has been mutated and by the damage that a deformed faith has exacted upon the church, the Confessionalist is driven to stand up for scriptural truth. Joining the great theologians, the Confessionalist happily affirms the core doctrines elucidated in the great creeds and catechisms of the Church and, when facing challenges to the truth, puts the declaration of truth above maintaining comfortable relationships within the Christian community.

The Confessionalist certainly faces more than a few challenges today.

The spirit of academic inquiry fostered in the modern era challenges the scientific and historical accuracy of biblical claims. As science-driven modernism has given way to pluralistic postmodernism, the resulting relativism has called into question any truth claim, suggesting that all ideas stand equal to one another.

Vagueries aside, denials of Christian truth come from every direction. The traditional belief in the one Bible being the one authoritative, written source of God's revelation has given way in some quarters to the notion that the Bible is just one inspired book among many. The salvation proclaimed in the Bible—granted by the power of grace received through faith—is subtly disregarded in favor of a universal salvation wherein grace is redefined as indulgence. The one Savior, Jesus the incarnate Son of God, by whose death sin is atoned and by whose resurrection new life is given, is portrayed as just one of a number of religious leaders whose "similar" messages all lead to heaven. Indeed, the one God, who in the first commandment excludes the existence of other gods and who repeatedly warns of the perils of idolatry, is redefined to be whomever they reimagine God to be.

If these assaults on the historic faith were coming merely from secular universities or from antireligionists, perhaps they could be overlooked. But the assaults are also heard from leaders in church, seminary, and denominational bureaucracies.

The Confessionalist who hears such assertions speaks out in no uncertain terms. Does the Confessionalist enjoy the fight? Perhaps a few do. Conflict does energize. But most Confessionalists speak out only when necessary in order to put down the brushfire of heresy, always with an eye to returning to the essential work of ministry, the proclamation of the truth.

Obviously, the Confessionalist GodView almost always resists change. Change disrupts the status quo, and that status quo—particularly in a culture that still emanates the spirit of traditional Christendom—usually looks at first blush to be more truly Christian than the new idea being introduced.

Ironically, many changes that have come to the church in the past century have enhanced the church's quality of biblical proclamation. The practice of ordaining women more truly aligns with the radical feminist initiatives of Jesus and Paul in the first century. (While Paul often is accused of misogyny, many positive statements he made regarding male-female equality, when taken within the context of first-century Mediterranean culture, qualify as revolutionary, exceeded only by Jesus' equal treatment of women.) The church's more compromised position on divorce, including the elimination of the automatic prohibition of all divorcees from ordained ministry, better reflects the complex approach to divorce and marriage modeled in scripture—and manifests the forgiving and reconciling grace that stands ready to redeem past failings. The widespread abandonment of jealous defensiveness toward the theory of a literal seven-day creation has helped Genesis scholars to comprehend better the more topical intentions and poetic style utilized in the writing of Genesis 1. The focus upon literary interpretative methodologies has helped seminarians and preachers more readily engage the content of the message of any particular scripture text, finally inviting people in the congregation truly to hear the text on its own terms.

The list of recent gains in biblical study goes on and on. Rather than threaten the Confessionalist GodView, those very challenges have validated and fulfilled it again and again.

On the other hand, the irrepressible creativity of heretics continually assaults Confessionalist sensibilities. The resulting impatience of Confessionalists is understandable. Unfortunately, that impatience becomes further exasperated by the many times church leaders fail not by taking radical departures from the faith but by subtly diverting from the core values that have defined the faith. John Leith elaborates:

> The primary source of the malaise of the church . . . is the loss of a distinctive Christian message and of the theological and biblical competence that made its preaching effective. Sermons fail to mediate the presence and grace of God. Many sermons are moral exhortations, which can be heard delivered with greater skill at the Rotary or Kiwanis Club. Many sermons are political and economic judgments on society, which have been presented with greater wisdom and passion at political conventions. Many sermons offer personal therapies, which can be better provided by well-trained psychiatrists. The only skill the preacher has—or the church, for that matter—which is not found with greater excellence somewhere else, is theology, in particular the skill to interpret and apply the Word of God in sermon, teaching, and pastoral care. This is the great service which the minister and the church can render the world. Why should anyone come to church for what can be better found somewhere else?[2]

A renewal of biblical preaching and a recentering of the church's proclamation stand at the heart of the Confessionalist GodView.

The basic job description for the Confessionalist GodView was written centuries ago, particularly in the words of the Great Ends of the Church, found in the opening chapter of the Presbyterian Church's Book of Order. The Great Ends are "the proclamation of the gospel for the salvation of humankind; the shelter, nurture, and spiritual fellowship of the children of God; the maintenance of divine worship; the preservation of the truth; the promotion of social righteousness; and the exhibition of the Kingdom of Heaven to the world."[3] Why is the "preservation of the truth" a great end of the church? Because from the time of Christ's ascension, the church has been entrusted to convey faithfully the truth of God to the world.

Shall the church be effective in communicating the promises and claims of Christ to the world? Only if she states its message as Christ would have it spoken. Thankfully, ever since the Reformation put the Bible back into the hands of its laity as well as clergy, the church has seldom lacked a strong cadre of Confessionalists ready to speak the truth with passion. They have not always spoken it in love, but that subject will be considered a bit later. Nevertheless, Confessionalists have held forth before the church the continual need to be a discerning people, contemplating new questions, considering new truth claims, and relentlessly testing all such ideas against the revelation of God in Christ, as conveyed to us through scripture.

Does this sound a bit arrogant, a bit too self-assured? One elder commissioner to the PC(USA) General Assembly in 2000 commented, "What bothers me this evening is that there seems to be such a lack of self-doubt among us." The Confessionalist certainly can sound that way at times. Any claim to the truth carries the subtle implication that all nonconforming ideas are erroneous, maybe even evil.

Jerry Andrews, the moderator of the Presbyterian Coalition, helps temper that understanding: "While it is obviously true that we do not have a complete hold on the truth, we do affirm that the truth does have a hold on us."

Leith shares a humble expression of such a claim:

The task of the Christian witness is on the one hand to proclaim the message with integrity and, on the other hand, to help those who believe to understand how Jesus Christ answers the deepest questions of their lives and illuminates and makes sense of their experience within the church. The Christian witness is both proclamation and explanation. However, it must be underscored that preaching is not moral exhortation, not therapy, certainly not entertainment. It is the very solemn endeavor in a fragile and human way to proclaim the Word of the Creator and of the Redeemer to the people whom God has made and to help those who believe understand their lives in the light of this faith.[4]

The endeavor to proclaim God's word holds forth a wonderful prospect: the opportunities to transform lives, to refocus goals, and to engage the living God in human lives. Like the pilot who carefully "does it by the book," so, too, when the Christian directs one's life according to the Bible, the aim in view is that the will of God be accomplished in the person's life. God's will may be carried out by taking stands on issues of justice or by caring generously for the hurting. God's will integrates the individual within the community of faith and leads the person into a deepening, expanding, vital relationship with God.

We now turn our attention to the building of that relationship, which is most keenly pursued by people who hold a Devotionalist GodView.

Chapter 6

The Devotionalist GodView:
Hungry for God

*N*ow as they went on their way, he entered a certain village, where a woman named Martha welcomed him into her home. She had a sister named Mary, who sat at the Lord's feet and listened to what he was saying. But Martha was distracted by her many tasks; so she came to him and asked, "Lord, do you not care that my sister has left me to do all the work by myself? Tell her then to help me." But the Lord answered her, "Martha, Martha, you are worried and distracted by many things; there is need of only one thing. Mary has chosen the better part, which will not be taken away from her." (Luke 10:38–42)

The church has had a running argument with Jesus about Mary and Martha. We take him at his word when he says, "Mary has chosen the better part," but we don't really believe him. Perhaps a few do, like the monks that gather in their monasteries, practicing the discipline of silence. Lacking televisions, stereos, and conversation, they have cultivated an ethos of awe-filled serenity. They appreciate the value of sitting and listening. Quakers, the Society of Friends, also support Jesus' alignment with Mary against Martha. They gather in their unadorned meeting houses, and in silence they listen for the "inner light" to speak God's word and to guide their way. In so doing, they are emulating the example set by Mary and affirmed by Jesus.

Most of us aren't inclined "to go there." Most of us feel an acid-burning, gut-grinding revulsion when hearing this story. Some protest Jesus' odd favoritism. "He was really unfair to Martha," they protest. Some try to help Jesus interpret himself. "He obviously didn't really mean what he was saying," they explain apologetically. Others, looking to rationalize their own instincts, say with a shrug, "I guess I'm just more of a Martha than a Mary."

These two sisters, along with their brother Lazarus, were probably Jesus' closest friends outside the twelve disciples. Jesus stops by Martha's house—where Mary had already arrived for an afternoon visit—and Martha goes about the business of picking up the clutter, preparing tea and bread. In the meantime, sister Mary simply sits at Jesus' feet and, all agog, takes in his every word (in modern terms, the label "groupie" comes to mind). Martha, feeling miffed over her sister's laziness, mutters her suggestion that maybe Jesus ought to hint to Mary that she should join in serving their famous friend.

Jesus turns the tables on the two sisters, and indeed on the modern reader. "Martha, Martha, you are worried and distracted by many things; there is need of only one thing. Mary has chosen the better part, which will not be taken away from her."

How could he say such a thing? How could he discount the servant spirit in Martha and endorse the truancy of Mary? What kind of a message is that sending to the younger generation?

Why Such Difficulty?

Why do we have such a hard time accepting the import of this story? Why is it hard to imagine that Jesus was just as intent—perhaps more intent—to draw out of people their adoration of God than their service to humanity? Why is it hard to believe Jesus when he says, "I do not call you servants any longer, . . . but I have called you friends" (John 15:15)? Why is it hard to take seriously Psalm 46 when it says, "Be still, and know that I am God"? Why do we become squeamish when we stop and really ponder that first great commandment: "You shall love the Lord your God with all your heart, and with all your soul, and with all your mind, and with all your strength" (Mark 12:30)? Face it. As J. Mary Luti muses, "We know we are supposed to love God, but the idea can seem strange and a little flaky, In love with God?"[1]

Most Christians have a cooler, more professional relationship with God than this story would allow. Most of us experience a coolness toward God we have come upon honestly. We have inherited the American Protestant work ethic. That ethic teaches us that if we work hard six days in a week, we will earn for ourselves a day off. If we work hard fifty weeks in succession we will earn a two-week vacation. If we study hard for twelve to twenty years, then work hard for forty to fifty years, and if our health sustains us, we will then be deserving of a relaxing retirement. All along the way, we must never forget that our worth to family, to society, and to God is measured by the quality of the work we do and the quantity of pay we earn.

Many Protestants, especially those in the Lutheran and Reformed traditions, have inherited a proud intellectual bias. "Low church" Protestants may express enthusiastic outbursts in their worship, but we stay away from such displays of emotion. Other "high church" Protestants, Catholics, and Orthodox may utilize icons, statues, symbols, and rituals in their worship, but we stay away from ornamentation. We are reasonable and intelligent. We do all things "decently and in order." In fact, if anything can't be done decently and in order, then we just won't do it at all.

The typical, middle-class, Anglo-Protestant church has also inherited a guilt-driven mission of charitable service. Its logic is direct: given our privilege of prosperity and given others' burden of poverty, our obvious life's mission is to become servants of the underprivileged.

Anyone who has inherited the Protestant work ethic, a proud intellectual bias, and a guilt-driven mission cannot help oneself bristling over the Mary and Martha story. Jesus has sided with the wrong person!

Reasons to Redirect

Lest we be misunderstood, let nobody cast dispersions on those teaching a strong work ethic. Paul did set the standard for the Thessalonians, "Anyone unwilling to work should not eat" (2 Thess. 3:10). However, God has called for something more than all that. God has called us to begin more deeply than all that and to end more deeply than all that. In an article reflecting on the Protestant spirituality experienced in the communities of Iona and Taize, Belden Lane reflects, "If we are transfixed by a common vision of God's astounding beauty, then every aspect of our ecclesial, theological and liturgical life should flow from this center— from the praise of God's glory revealed most tellingly in the cross of Christ." He concludes, "If the church lacks clarity about its first love, then it has little to offer (from therapy to charity) that can't be better provided by others."[2]

Lest we forget, that expression "first love" also comes from scripture, this time from one of the brief letters written in John's Revelation. "To the angel of the church in Ephesus write: These are the words of him who holds the seven stars in his right hand, who walks among the seven golden lampstands: 'I know your works, your toil and your patient endurance. I know that you cannot tolerate evildoers; you have tested those who claim to be apostles but are not, and have found them to be false. I also know that you are enduring patiently and bearing up for the sake of my name, and that you have not grown weary. But I have this against you, that you have abandoned the love you had at first" (Rev. 2:1–4).

First love. The expression paints such vivid pictures in the mind's eye for anybody who has fallen in love. It also captures images in many a memory of a youth retreat when "Kumbaya" or "Alleluia" or "Awesome God" was ringing out lustily around the campfire from otherwise "cool kids." Many a believer has experienced the first love, that first blush of affection for God. Too many believers have subsequently taken it all in stride as a nice, past phase of growth—but one not to be repeated or renewed.

Renewing that first love for God ought to be priority number one, or so Jesus is implying in his affirmation of Mary. Doing so simply acknowledges the way God made us. Howard Rice says it clearly: "To be human is to be created for relationship with God, and anything other than such a relationship leaves us unsatisfied, even when we cannot name what we want."[3] Or as St. Augustine says, "Thou awakest us to delight in Thy praise; for Thou madest us for Thyself, and our heart is restless, until it repose in Thee."[4]

Fortunately, the contemporary church provides many resources to facilitate such an endeavor. Just a generation ago, if one wished to cultivate the contemplative side of one's discipleship, one would need to attend a church in the Catholic, Orthodox, or Quaker traditions. They major in contemplation. On the other hand, if one wanted to cultivate an enthusiastic practice in worship, one would have had to go to the Pentecostal church, or perhaps an African-American congregation of Baptists or Methodists. If the intellectual side of the faith were the goal, then the Presbyterian-Reformed church would suffice. But if one wished to pursue a spiritually disciplined, holiness-seeking lifestyle—that is, to love God with all one's strength—then the Methodist or Holiness or Baptist church would be the church of choice. Something wonderful transpired through this past century: these different church traditions discovered one another. Oh, they knew of each other's existence before, but geographical and cultural distances kept them at a prejudicial arm's length. In time, the civil rights movement brought racial integration, the ecumenical movement brought ecclesiastical dialogue, the mass communications proliferation brought variegated publications and recordings into unfamiliar studies and studios, and as the twenty-first century dawned, the determination to love God with heart and with soul and with mind and with strength was being encouraged in sanctuaries of all kinds of Christian traditions.

Particularly within Presbyterian and Reformed churches, books on spirituality have proliferated. In related seminaries, ministerial preparation has turned from being a purely academic exercise to being one of

spiritual formation, if only because local churches began refusing ministerial candidates who were prepared in their heads but not in their hearts.
"These seminarians may know their theology, but they don't know God,"
protested search committees. "If we have to choose, we'd rather they
know God." In response, theological scholars turned their attention to
developing a theology of the Christian life—going well beyond the purely
academic exercise of traditional systematic theology. "For me the key
word is devotion," writes theologian Donald Bloesch. "Indeed, the first
fruit and decisive mark of grace is 'a sincere and pure devotion to Christ'
(2 Cor. 11:3). Service in the world must be grounded in heartfelt devotion
to the Savior, Jesus Christ. Ethical action cannot long maintain itself
apart from spiritual passion."[5]

Methodist theologian Thomas Oden agrees: "Spirituality in the New
Testament sense is not a moral program, not a set of rules, not a level of
ethical achievement, not a philosophy, not a rhetoric, not an idea, not a
strategy, not a theory of meditation, but simply *life lived in Christ*."[6]

Such ruminating about spirituality certainly was not invented in the
twentieth century. Jonathan Edwards established himself as perhaps
America's greatest theologian during the Great Awakening, but his
preaching pressed not only the academic understanding of God but also
the personal experience of the Holy Spirit.

Even the writings of John Calvin were rediscovered. As Calvin himself put it, "True piety consists," he wrote, "in a pure and true zeal which
loves God altogether as Father, and reveres him truly as Lord, embraces
his justice and dreads to offend him more than to die."[7]

The mix of traditions has been particularly evident in the introduction
of new music into worship. Every generation in the past has introduced
its new forms, but most new forms have also met formidable resistance.
The old way with its familiar hymns has been baptized in the minds of
worshipers as the only godly way to worship the God of the ages. Resistance to such changes in the twentieth century has followed the pattern of
earlier generations. However, with the accelerating pace of change in the
culture in general, the intermixing of traditions addressed above, and the
stark reality that a generation lacking denominational loyalties is following what "feels good," a new energy is being generated in worship that in
past years largely was not cultivated. Presbyterians have drawn heavily
from the ecumenical mix of music offered by the Iona community in
Scotland and the Taize community in France—both of which were
founded by Presbyterian/Reformed leaders. At the same time, the popularity of contemporary praise music, born in the charismatic movement
but spread through the pan-denominational Christian recording industry,

has injected new music into most mainline denominational churches in the United States.

Such trends have fostered one end in view: the personal and corporate experience of God. Loving God, adoring God, honoring God, glorifying God, and even enjoying God—as the Westminster divines urged—has come into fashion in the church. Many Christians are effectively sitting at the feet of Jesus, listening to him. Mary is finally getting the credit she is due. She did indeed choose the better part.

Two Paths: Two Kinds of Devotion

The devotion being expressed toward God follows on two tracks that alternate between running parallel and crisscrossing one another. The one is commonly labeled evangelical piety and the other contemplative mysticism.

Evangelical pietism as a movement was born during the century following the Protestant Reformation, as an attempt to reform hearts as Luther and Calvin had reformed theology and the church. While the pietistic movement has cycled through periods of surging and subsiding ever since, it has flowed in and out of many Protestant church traditions. This style of devotion is called evangelical because it stresses the evangelical doctrine of justification by grace through faith, thereby leading believers to a confident security regarding their status before God. It is called pietist because like Michelangelo's breathtaking statue the Pieta—which depicts the adoring mother of Jesus holding his dead body on her lap—it engenders a deep and pious affection for God. The movement has fostered among its adherents a passion to move beyond eternal security to internal purity. Wanting to cooperate with the sanctifying work of the Holy Spirit, the Pietist has engaged two central disciplines: repentance and the pursuit of holiness. Those disciplines require a person to confess as sin all acts of rebellion committed against God and to express remorse for all ungodly thoughts, words, deeds, and oversights. In so doing the person seeks Christ's forgiveness and aims to amend one's lifestyle in the hope of becoming more truly conformed to the image of Christ himself. The payoff for such cross-bearing is an "immediatism of faith"[8]—a direct, unmediated relationship with God. It is not unusual for the evangelical pietist to testify glibly, "the Lord showed me . . . the Lord told me . . . ," or to sing boldly, "He walks with me, and he talks with me, and he tells me I am his own. . . ."

In contrast, the contemplative mysticism movement dates back to the early centuries of the church, having been born in wilderness monasteries. The Desert Fathers and other church leaders in the early centuries withdrew from the cities and metropolitan areas in order to pursue a more perfect, undistracted devotion toward God. They enjoyed an ascetic luxury, enduring the hardships their primitive settings brought but reveling in the simplicity such a setting afforded them. In the quietness, they gave meaning to such expressions as *detachment, renunciation, transcendent prayer, illumination, solitude, dark night of the soul, centering prayer,* and *Imitatio Christi (the imitation of Christ)*, all amid an emphasis upon the immanence of God. While the mystics shared the later Pietists' pursuit of holiness, theirs was one that was less centered upon the certainty of salvation, or for that matter, upon the already revealed word of God, and all the more, upon a relentless search for the yet-unrevealed mysteries of God. In such a pursuit they developed a model of devotion that begins by withdrawing from daily activities, invests large blocks of time into quiet reflection upon the wonder of God, and manifests itself in a commitment to a simple, unadorned lifestyle.

Both of these devotional styles have experienced a resurgence in the twentieth century, evangelical pietism having a heyday in Pentecostal, charismatic, evangelical and fundamentalist churches, and contemplative mysticism thriving in Catholic, Episcopal, and Orthodox churches. In middle-of-the-road Protestant churches, such as Presbyterian, Disciples of Christ, and Methodist, both styles have surged in popularity, although most faith communities have promoted one to the exclusion of the other. These two styles need not be mutually exclusive. Both offer much to the church.

The Devotionalist GodView

This chapter began by claiming that the church has long disputed Jesus' priority of Mary's devotion over Martha's service. In reality, not all of the church has carried forth that dispute. Some people within the church jump for joy whenever reading this story. Some find that nothing thrills them more than to sit or kneel in silence, pondering the wonders of God. Others cannot wait for a church service where they can sing loudly the praises of the God whose joy floods them like spring rains. These Christians can't imagine bustling around a kitchen while Jesus is sitting in the living room. Any moment, every moment with God screams with excitement. They are Marys in their hearts.

These Christians hold to a Devotionalist GodView. They have adopted a vision for God and a commitment to God's mission that calls people into a direct, vital, and dynamic relationship with God. For some, this vision has been birthed deep within, having been taken captive by a hunger for God. Others have adopted this GodView by associating with people who also promote such priorities. In evangelically minded churches, "accepting Christ as Lord and Savior" provides the natural port of entry into Christian faith. The clear proclamation of the completeness of Christ's cross and resurrection, and of the believer's experiential embrace of such grace, fosters a spirit of celebration in such churches' worship. The relational emphasis in such a proclamation also helps the believer to nurture a personalized faith encounter in ways similar to any human relationship. Humans typically come to know one another through conversations; these Christians come to know God via prayer. Humans tell each other their personal stories; these believers read the Bible to learn God's story. Humans grow closer by coming to know one another's families; believers come to know God better by communing with God's family, the community of faith. Persons—particularly those in love—express their love by giving gifts and expressing words and acts of endearment; Christians engage in tender and passionate expressions of worship to their loving Lord. Simply put, for the Devotionalist, all disciplines, all service, all faith-based activities grow out of and lead back to the core value of hungering for God.

The contemplative also organizes religious activities around the spiritual experience of God but in a less triumphalistic way than the evangelical pietist. Valuing a more open-ended, less explicit set of beliefs, the Devotionalist always keeps open the possibility of God speaking a new word, granting a new insight, painting a fresh image in the mind's eye. All beliefs, all practices, and all convictions flow from the central conviction that the experience of God is to be revered as of the highest value and central significance.

Whether of pietistic or contemplative style, Devotionalists will eschew the more political ways people often relate to one another in the church. They will urge other "churchians" to become more personally engaged in spiritual exercises and classical disciplines. They often wonder why others seem so content to live a spiritually shallow existence when God's invitation to a relationship is so inviting, so welcoming, so intimate. Like New School Presbyterians they likely will find Confessionalists to be too Old School, unnecessarily fretting about the letter of the law while missing the vital spirit of Christ's good news.

Mutually Exclusive?

Apart from Mary, the one New Testament figure who most truly modeled the Devotionalist lifestyle was the apostle Paul. In his letter to the Philippians, he puts his own life's priorities into that kind of perspective.

If anyone else has reason to be confident in the flesh, I have more: circumcised on the eighth day, a member of the people of Israel, of the tribe of Benjamin, a Hebrew born of Hebrews; as to the law, a Pharisee; as to zeal, a persecutor of the church; as to righteousness under the law, blameless.

Yet whatever gains I had, these I have come to regard as loss because of Christ. More than that, I regard everything as loss because of the surpassing value of knowing Christ Jesus my Lord. For his sake I have suffered the loss of all things, and I regard them as rubbish, in order that I may gain Christ and be found in him, not having a righteousness of my own that comes from the law, but one that comes through faith in Christ, the righteousness from God based on faith. I want to know Christ and the power of his resurrection and the sharing of his sufferings by becoming like him in his death, if somehow I may attain the resurrection from the dead. (3:4b–11)

Nothing was more important to Paul than his hunger for God, his passion to know Christ more and more deeply. Like Jacob of old, he wrestled with God, determined to receive the blessing of the Lord. Like King David, he was a man after God's own heart. Like the hemorrhaging woman in the crowd, he was determined to touch the hem of Christ's robe. And like Mary, he was content to sit quietly to listen at the feet of his Lord. He "chose the better part."

What's particularly striking about Paul's Devotionalist priority is that it comes from the greatest Confessionalist of all time. Paul's theological writings, especially his letters to the Romans and the Galatians, set the theological high mark of the New Testament. Was he a Confessionalist or a Devotionalist? He was both. In fact, he also was a passionate Ecclesiast. He happily joined Peter and the whole company of people to whom Jesus said, "I will build my church . . ." (Matt. 16:18).

Chapter 7

The Ecclesiast GodView:
I Will Build My Church

*I*n our childhood, my brother, sisters, and I suffered a disadvantage endured by few other children. Our mother was a college professor of child psychology. We often found ourselves second-guessing her, wondering which relational hat she was wearing: mother-to-child or psychologist-to-guinea-pig.

On one occasion, when I was about fifteen years old, Mom successfully roped me into cleaning the kitchen after supper—a major achievement considering my track record for doing chores. As I worked, Mom joined in and waxed chatty. I was in a talkative mood, too. After the dishes were complete, I jumped up onto the counter, and after a pregnant pause, she looked me squarely in the eye and asked, "Who are you?"

The question seemed straightforward, not critical, so I responded simply, "Me."

She asked again, "Who are you?"

Again, I responded, "Me."

"Who else are you?"

The second-guessing began. *Have we moved into the psychologist-and-guinea-pig mode?* I wondered silently. But I responded, "Jack."

Again she quizzed me, "Who are you?"

"A child of God."

"Who are you?"

"Your son."

The questions continued. The responses followed, "A Haberer . . . a brother . . . a student . . . a football player . . . a piano player. . . ."

When, after a few minutes, the answers were no longer coming quickly, she broke off her inquisition and commented, "That's good. Those were good answers. Healthy answers."

As I had suspected, she *had* morphed into psychologist-to-guinea-pig mode. She added, "Your answers were positive and secure. It is sad how some people answer this question, 'a loser,' 'a failure,' 'hopeless,' 'ugly,' and the like."

We talked a little about the issue of identity and self-esteem, affording me one of Mom's many impromptu psychology classes, which really proved to be a great advantage that my siblings and I had as her children.

Life's Most Pressing Questions

So who are *you*? The question is one of life's most pressing. Schoolteachers ask it. So do guidance counselors, college admissions officers, job placement directors, and discussion group leaders.

The question has a corollary, a follow-up question. My responses to Mom's questions point to the corollary, insofar as every response I gave after the first two could answer the second. It asks, "*Whose* are you?"

Americans have become deluded into thinking of themselves as rugged individualists, masters of their own fate, captains of their own ship. The Robinson Crusoe ideal may turn the pages of great fiction, but when we go out on a search to "find" ourselves, we discover that our identities are unavoidably shaped by our relationships. Indeed, our personal value largely comes from a sense of belonging to others. We all need to belong, to be able to say whose we are.

Take, for example, the initial experience of belonging provided by one's family of origin. Mother, father, brother, sister: they provide a place of belonging and a role to play. Doubtless, many people endure troubled childhoods, broken families. But such cases highlight all the more the importance of family. When a television magazine report recounts the tear-filled reunion of an adult offspring with her natural mother twenty years after being given up for adoption, the value of family identity becomes obvious.

The Family of God

In the plan of God, the nuclear family relationship does not constitute the most essential human experience of belonging. The essential family experience in the kingdom of God is the community of faith, the people of God.

In today's church context, not every Christian revels over his or her membership in the community of faith. When asked, "Whose are you?" what believer responds, "I am a part of the body of Christ, one of the living stones in the temple of the Spirit, a citizen in the kingdom of God, a child of Abraham and Sarah, a member of the house of David, one of

Jesus' band of disciples, and a part of the brotherhood and sisterhood of the church"? The title "body of Christ" suggests that the church is supposed to embody and reveal Jesus' character to the world, but discerning Christ's character is not easy when one considers the misdeeds of known religious leaders and their fleecing of fortunes out of gullible believers. Christ's character escapes observation when we witness radical religious leaders advocating major departures from what seem to be self-evident moral and ethical principles.

Perhaps more tragically, though Jesus embodied God's love, today's church does not display a lot of love. If the church is supposed to be God's agent of inclusion, welcoming the kinds of people Jesus welcomed, why does the church look so exclusive? How can it be that the eleven o'clock hour on Sunday morning is the most segregated hour in America's week? How has the church become so divided, denomination against denomination?

Moreover, given the church's commission to be Christ's ambassadors of reconciliation in the world, why all the church fights? Why is virtually every national gathering of denominational governing bodies now reported in the media, providing the fireworks of conflict that qualify as "newsworthy"? One can defend some of today's religious leadership by remembering that in previous eras, the debates were engaged behind closed doors; the public nature of today's arguments more reflect the media explosion than a conflict escalation. Nevertheless the religious community certainly has not demonstrated even a modicum of self-control that would better convey to the larger public the graciousness of God's love. Frankly, too many of today's battles seem to reveal a greater hunger for power and control than for reconciliation and peace. In the process, church conflicts too often look like Custer's lieutenants arguing over mess privileges before the Battle of Little Big Horn. For this reason alone, many Christians would just as soon distance themselves from any identification with the church of Jesus Christ.

For Christians though, such distancing is not an option. When Jesus said, "I will build my church," he was investing himself totally and completely in this endeavor, and for good reason. God had been engaged in this construction project through all of Israel's history. From the initial call of Abram and Sarai through the exodus, from the formation of the nation of Israel through the era of the prophets, the people's identity was built upon God's call to be the set-apart people of God and upon God's promise to be their God. As Roman Catholic theologian Hans Kung says, "The concept of the people of God is at the heart of Judaism. Fundamentally the whole faith of Judaism can be summed up in the single phrase: Yahweh is the God of Israel and Israel is the people of Yahweh."[1]

The covenantal formula, "You shall be my people and I will be your God" (Ezek. 36:28), provides Israel the defining vision and self-identification to guide her throughout her unfolding biblical history. Again and again, God utters these words as either the appeal of a lover to the beloved or as a promise assured by divine faithfulness. This promise explains why God calls Israel into covenant, motivates the people to obey God's revealed law, accounts for why God blesses Israel with the divine presence, and discloses why the prophets equate the people's sins with infidelity.

When turning to the New Testament, one cannot mistake the reality that the church sees itself in continuity with and in fulfillment of such a plan from God. The church saw itself as the new Israel, the new people of God. These believers took seriously the confession that the church was Jesus' creation. They confirmed that confidence by dubbing the church with many vivid metaphors: "people of God," "body of Christ," "temple of the Spirit," "family of God," "chosen race," "holy nation," "remnant," "flock," "new humanity," and the list goes on. One cannot miss the note that each such label is both singular and plural. Grammatically speaking, each is a singular noun that is made up of many components: one people—hence many persons united; the body of Christ—hence many body parts interconnected; one temple—hence many living stones built together; one family—hence many family members of common blood; one race and nation of many citizens, one flock of many sheep, etc. As the saying goes, *E pluribus unum*: out of many, one.

Jesus certainly had such a oneness in mind when he prayed "that they may be one" (John 17:11, 21a, 21b, 22, 23). Sadly, typical of the church's penchant for controversy, the modern church long has taken his intention and turned it upside down. Returning to Jesus' words to Peter, for hundreds of years we have debated not Jesus' promise but the prepositional phrase leading up to it, i.e., "on this rock . . ." (Matt. 16:18). What did he mean by that? Peter the rock? A papacy to follow? Or Peter the pebble with the confession of faith as the real rock? A repudiation of the papal structure? Much ink has been spilled arguing over the meaning of the prepositional phrase, all while the heart of the sentence—the subject, verb, and direct object—has been neglected. "I will build my church." That was his point. This entity, this gathering of believers is not a voluntary gathering of like-minded religious individuals sharing a nonprofit corporate status. This church is the creation of the creator Jesus. It is the property of Lord Jesus. It is the ongoing project of the contractor Jesus.

It is the guarantee of the sovereign God, Jesus. And lest one should doubt, not to be overlooked is the other independent clause, "the gates of Hades will not prevail against it" (Matt. 16:18). The church is what Jesus is up to, and he has guaranteed its success.

Yes, for some the church is too imperfect for their taste, but for others the church is the mission of Christ, and they love it. They take a philosophical and practical tack; they invest themselves in the imperfect institution, the injured body of the Christ. They cuddle infants in the church nursery. They sing in the choir. They mow the church lawn. They teach Sunday school classes. They visit the elderly in nursing homes. They usher worshipers to their pews. They accept the call to become ministers of Word and sacrament. They accept nomination, election, and ordination to the church's bodies of governance and service.

The Ecclesiast in Action

Recognizing Christ's enormous investment in the church, many believers have adopted an Ecclesiast GodView. They have enlisted in his program of church-building and are providing the leadership and service that have built countless churches worldwide. Each such Ecclesiast has discovered that church service entails lots of messy work. While one can hold high values and pure theological concepts in a sterile, ivy-covered context, one can relate to the church only in tangible ways . . . in concrete, albeit complex relationships. That is, one cannot be a church member in principle without being a church participant in practice. The regular gathering of a particular community of faith for worship, for sharing in sacraments, for study, for mutual care, and for service is essential for the church to live into its calling in Christ.

The Localist Ecclesiast

Church-builders usually begin close to home. The most immediate context for enlisting in Jesus' church-building program is that of the local congregation. Whether it be the Antioch or Galatia of the apostolic era or the Downingtown or Omaha of modern America, church happens when people gather for worship and nurture. The majority of American Christians gather in relatively large congregations (250 or more), while the majority of congregations are relatively small (100 or less). The vast majority of Christian service takes place within such smaller congregations.

While much writing in church circles through the twentieth century focused on either big-picture theological and ideological concepts or immediate personal and individual practices of faith, the 1990s saw a revival of interest in that intermediate zone, the local church. Within mainline circles such interest was fueled by Loren Mead's *The Once and Future Church*[2] and by Stanley Hauerwas and William Willimon's *Resident Aliens*.[3] Both books finally exposed what was so late in being recognized: America has reached a post-Christendom era, and the church's mission now begins with the congregation rather than with the national, global missionary–sending administration. America had become a mission field and, as Jack Rogers summarizes, "Congregations do not exist to fund the mission agendas of national denominational bureaucracies, but those bureaucracies should exist only to support the mission agendas of local congregations."[4] As those writers pushed the national bureaucracies to rediscover the local churches, thousands of everyday Christians within evangelical circles were reading Rick Warren's *Purpose-Driven Church*.[5] Warren, a Baptist pastor of one of America's largest megachurches, somehow elevated church ministry strategizing from the realm of paid specialists to that of every church member. Thinking together, planning together, ministering together, growing together, and doing substantial theological reflection together all have become marks of churches following the purpose-driven model. Taken collectively, these books and the many others written in their wake have revived the call to be Ecclesiasts, church-builders.

Church-building entails a few key activities to be pursued effectively. Regardless of size, every church needs to be engaged in four particular tasks, which can be summarized as the *Ministry CODE*: *Caring, Outreach, Devotion,* and *Equipping*.

First, the vital church *cares* for the flock. From infants to the feeble elderly, one of the wonderful tasks of ministry is simply that of caring for people whom God has called together into the common fellowship. The sacrament of baptism wonderfully announces the unwitting infant's inclusion into the family; the child's ignorance powerfully illustrates the work of God's grace that precedes and empowers our faith response to the gospel. In that sacrament, the congregation accepts the role of godparents, promising to partner with the parents in the Christian nurture of the child. Over the years, the child, teen, young adult, middle adult, and older adult all can fully expect the community of faith to continue to embrace them, teach them, and support them in their growth in God. Toward such an end, many congregants are raised up to exercise spiritual gifts of service and nurture. Three particular kinds of care come to mind. The *"Great Wedding Banquet" model of care* draws upon Jesus' parable that invites all to come from highways and byways to join in the celebrations and growth events of the faith community. The largest share of caring ministry occurs simply as the people of God gather for the worship of God, hear the Word of God, and enjoy the feast of God. The *Mary Magdalene model of care* brings to mind that particular follower of Jesus who, having numerous troubles in her life, kept coming to Jesus, where she could appropriate not only his affirming support but also his healing touch. The vital church provides resources of healing, counseling, and personal prayer for people who make their needs known. The *Good Shepherd model of care* emerges from Jesus' teaching about the good shepherd, who will do everything possible to protect even a single sheep from straying away from the flock. The caring ministry of the church determines to watch over the flock, to keep wanderers from straying too far, and especially to keep them from danger. Perhaps the world has become too sophisticated and cynical to think that such care can really take place, but the Ecclesiast knows it can and works to make it happen.

Second, the Ecclesiast leads the church into ministries of *outreach*. The local church can never allow its vision to be turned inward. Like a bathroom mirror whose range of sight is limited by the proximity of the walls, some churches have become shortsighted by erroneously putting all their attention into caring for their own flock to the neglect of the many wanderers nearby . . . and far away. Vital churches commit a significant level of funding and service to ministries beyond their doors. At a minimum, such believers aim to share the love of Christ with the needy in their communities. While more will be said at length in the next two chapters regarding people driven by the Altruist and Activist GodViews, the Ecclesiast knows that a disciple cannot grow simply by filling one's mind with the Bible, one's quiet times with prayer, and one's worship with song. Like the lungs in the body, one's spirit needs both intake and outflow to oxygenate one's spiritual health. The primary activities involve acts of service to people in tangible need and communications of the gospel to people in spiritual need. The welcoming ministry of the church is particularly critical here, given that the Ecclesiast knows that "apart from the church there is no salvation" as Augustine said.[6] The vital church will unabashedly search out the unchurched, provide many ports of entry for them to feel welcomed into the church's fellowship, and introduce them to a discipling process into which they may engage their efforts.

Third, the Ecclesiast seeks to nurture its members' lives of *devotion*. As you may hopefully have inferred from the previous chapter, the vital church cannot allow its daily tasks to overshadow its call to lead the people into an intimate knowing of God. Through worship expressed in God-centered services and by prayer in small circles, the church must cultivate the vertical relationship between its members and its God.

Fourth, the Ecclesiast recognizes that one of the particular privileges of ministry is that of *equipping* its members for service to God. Ephesians 4:11ff. says that God has raised up specialized leaders in the church, i.e., apostles, prophets, evangelists, pastors, and teachers, in order to "equip the saints for the work of ministry." Realizing that "saints" means not deceased heroes but living members, the real work of the ministry in the church shall be carried out by the members in any given congregation, with the task of the clergy and other specialists being the equipping of the real ministers, the laity. Such a task entails the Christian education of the members, so they may be informed of God's will and ways. The task entails intentional efforts to help members discern God's gifting and calling for their ministries. Equipping the laity requires leaders to challenge the members to be good stewards of the resources of time, treasure, and talent entrusted to their utilization. This task also requires leaders to invade the creeping complacency of the culture by sensitizing members to the needs of the society and creating avenues for believers' service to God and community.

While a basic thesis of this book is that Christians operate out of one of five GodViews, the majority of Christians probably operate out of this localist Ecclesiast GodView. For this reason, so many Christians do not identify with either the religious right or the liberal left. Contrary to common accusation, the localists are not just the "muddled" or "mushy" middle. They do not lack character or conviction. Quite the contrary, many people who are unwilling to engage in right-to-left or left-to-right conflicts simply think that such battles dissipate energy and distract from what matters most. The local church—with its call to caring, outreach, devotion, and equipping—is the locus of God's primary activity of building the church, and these members of the local church give sacrificially to fulfill that calling.

The Connectional Ecclesiast

Some Ecclesiasts would beg to differ with the prior, localist view. They share the commitment to build up the church, but they exercise their ministry in a larger context, in the governing bodies and agencies that oversee and serve the local church.

By design, the Connectional Ecclesiasts make up a small minority of the overall church while exercising a large influence upon many local churches. These governing-body Christians provide an essential, albeit largely invisible, linkage within the whole church. The value of such linkage becomes evident whenever nondenominational ministers join together to form ministerial alliances or mutual accountability groups. While one may pour all energy into building the local church, most ministers and many laity sense an internal need to connect with other believers in other communities. Even the congregationalists, who have developed a strong apologetic for local church autonomy, find themselves in need for each others' partnering in order to be able to send missionaries overseas, to develop curricula and other publications, and to develop fellowships of mutual support for their leaders. Ironically, given the availability of clergy to develop such affiliations, such groups often end up looking like clerical hierarchies in the Anglican-Catholic tradition, as evolved in the early centuries of the church in Europe and Asia.

In contrast to such evolving (devolving?) movements, the reformers, especially John Calvin, determined to reform not only the beliefs but also the practices of the church, which entailed developing connectional structures of accountability. The resultant Presbyterian system produced a parity of leadership between clergy and lay leaders that is most in evidence when the local church board of elders gathers to exercise oversight of the ministries of the church. Such oversight does not end with the governance of the local church. It carries over to the organization of regional bodies of oversight, presbyteries (known as *classes* in Reformed churches) and synods, as well as national General Assemblies (in the Reformed church, General Synod). As regional and national bodies, these groups—which at all points share authority equally between lay and clergy leaders—exercise many checks and balances of oversight and implement combined efforts in mission.

As intimated in the earlier quote from Jack Rogers, recent trends have complicated the actual relation of governing bodies to local churches. The post-Watergate era has promoted a general distrust for authority figures, and that distrust pervades the church. No longer do local congregations easily take orders from national governing bodies. Instead, they expect the national and regional bodies to serve their vision for ministry. Whenever the regional and national bodies fail to meet local bodies' expectations, the larger organizations are fair game for criticism and even defiance. While post-Christendom realities do imply the need for mission to begin at and from the local congregation and for the whole nation to be seen as part of the mission field, the need to coordinate and oversee local ministry still is needed.

The Connectional Ecclesiast is caught in between. Having both a love for the local church and a desire to empower effective ministry invites a passion for facilitating that ministry. At the same time, that person still wants to exercise oversight, to exercise veto power when a congregation wishes to call an incompetent or irresponsible minister. Tragically sometimes, troubles spin out of control, requiring a higher governing body to seize "prior jurisdiction," overruling erring and rebellious local governing bodies.

The Connectional Ecclesiast often finds him- or herself torn over the seemingly reckless disdain other people hold for the larger church, whether the criticism comes from radicals to the left or right or simply from localists. The connectionalist will spend great energy to keep the church united together, even when very real differences of opinions look irreconcilable. In the light of Ephesians 4:1–6, such effort takes on the role of a high calling:

> I therefore, the prisoner in the Lord, beg you to lead a life worthy of the calling to which you have been called, with all humility and gentleness, with patience, bearing with one another in love, making every effort to maintain the unity of the Spirit in the bond of peace. There is one body and one Spirit, just as you were called to the one hope of your calling, one Lord, one faith, one baptism, one God and Father of all, who is above all and through all and in all.

The Ecumenical Ecclesiast

If the Connectional Ecclesiast finds oneself required to study the peace of the church, the Ecumenical Ecclesiast is absolutely driven by that passion. Jesus' prayer "that they may be one" (John 17:11) rolls off the tongue of the ecumenist, to whom the division of denominations stands as an unacceptable scandal that must be eradicated.

As the nineteenth century dawned, tremendous optimism gripped the new ecumenical movement. In what promised to become the "Christian Century"—this optimism launched a magazine by that name—determination to undo the shame of our divisions captured many people's imaginations. Then the Fundamentalist-Modernist controversy erupted, and the unity sought became a fragmentation realized. Not to be deterred, the modernists, who now were leading most mainline churches, set about the process of reuniting the different denominations. The World Council of Churches and the Federal (later National) Council of Churches were formed. What began in 1960 as a call for unity between Presbyterians and Episcopalians grew into the Consultation on Church Union (COCU), formed in 1962. Community-wide ecumenical services were being organized all around the country, and a feeling of inevitable success permeated the air.

Then the bottom fell out. While church executives negotiated and organized new models for ministry, proposing what seemed to them to be minor tweaks to respective polities in trade for reunions that history could only commend, the grass roots balked. The COCU proposal was rejected by presbyteries in the Presbyterian Church (U.S.A.). Treating that defeat as an aberration, another modified version was proposed, but the presbyteries rejected it, too—even though every other participating denomination apart from the Episcopal Church had already approved it. Presbyterians clearly were not willing to compromise their commitment to the parity of lay elders with clergy. At the same time, the Episcopalians could not find room in their definition of ministry—whose validation comes from the apostolic succession of bishops—to approve those ordained apart from bishops' laying on of hands.

Momentum was gone and finances were fading (at the time of this writing the National Council of Churches faces possible extinction due to a huge drop in funding), the Ecumenical Ecclesiasts were not to be deterred. Some bright successes in the 1990s pointed in a positive new direction. The easy and near-unanimous adoption of the Formula of Agreement between the Lutherans, United Church of Christ, Reformed Church in America, and Presbyterian Church (U.S.A.) signaled a new model for ecumenical accord. Its less grandiose approach of "Mutual Affirmation, Mutual Admonition" allowed these four churches to recognize the validity of each others' ordained ministries and administration of sacraments (this approach will be elaborated upon further in chapter 14). The COCU proponents followed that lead by offering a similar model, even changing their name to Churches Uniting in Christ (CUiC, pronounced "quick"), which found a resonant response among the participating denominations. Above all these developments, the accord signed by the Roman Catholics and World Lutheran Federation in 1999 effectively brought the Roman Catholic Church to the affirmation of salvation by grace through faith as Luther, Calvin, and the other Reformers proclaimed. For the mainline churches, the twentieth century did not fulfill all their dreams, but persistence did pay.

At the same time, the conservatives also made ecumenical progress of their own. The first half of the century brought fragmentation of every conceivable variety as the independent-minded conservatives—particularly the pentecostals and the neo-evangelicals—created new movements and literally hundreds of denominations. But the formation of the National Association of Evangelicals (NAE) in 1942 provided a point of connection for the conservatives. Moreover, evangelicals in mainline churches, lacking a voice and influence in denominational offices, poured enormous energy into the formation of major parachurch organizations such as Billy Graham Evangelistic Association, Christianity Today, World Vision, Young Life, Campus Crusade for Christ, and Inter-Varsity Christian Fellowship. At the dawn of the twenty-first century, under the leadership of Kevin Mannoia, the National Association of Evangelicals and the National Council of Churches (NCC) began exploring the possibility of a broader range of ecumenism among churches represented by both the NCC and NAE.

Who cares? The Ecumenical Ecclesiast cares and even thrills over the possibilities for union in Christ—in any shape or form. The church's identity as a fragmented collection of separate enclaves scandalizes the church's witness to the world. The possibilities of uniting in fellowship, sharing in worship, or combining efforts in mission scream with excitement.

So Whose Are You?

Moreover, a united—or at least, uniting—church and a broader, diverse fellowship could make a difference for any believer responding to that child-psychologist-to-guinea-pig question, "Who are you?" and its corollary, "Whose are you?" Just as the child whose dysfunctional home life has made identity formation a daunting ordeal, a dysfunctional church family has made identity formation difficult as well. But the one who sees the reconciling, nurturing, strengthening hand of God at work in the contemporary church may experience a new sense of identity. As Dietrich Bonhoeffer put it, "Christian brotherhood is not an ideal which we must realize; it is rather a reality created by God in Christ in which we may participate. The more clearly we learn to recognize that the ground and strength and promise of all our fellowship is in Jesus Christ alone, the more serenely shall we think of our fellowship and pray and hope for it."[7] It has happened before. At one time Jews and Gentiles hated each other. But as the Letter to the Ephesians tells us, unity brought not only peace, but also a whole new sense of identity:

> So he came and proclaimed peace to you who were far off and peace to those who were near; for through him both of us have access in one Spirit to the Father. So then you are no longer strangers and aliens, but you are citizens with the saints and also members of the household of God, built upon the foundation of the apostles and prophets, with Christ Jesus himself as the cornerstone. In him the whole structure is joined together and grows into a holy temple in the Lord; in whom you also are built together spiritually into a dwelling place for God. (2:17–22)

Take note: In the Apostolic era, the proclaimed peace welcomed the many who were far off, as well as those who were near. Today peace is needed not just for these nearby—that is, within the church—but also for those far away, outside the church. They need to be loved, and the church is called to be Christ's hands, Christ's instruments to extend that love. At this point, the Altruist GodView steps up to lead us.

Chapter 8

The Altruist GodView:
To the Least of These

*W*WJD? Millions and millions have read a nineteenth-century novel that put that acronym into circulation. The novel, *In His Steps*, written by Charles M. Sheldon, opens in a pastor's study as he prepares a sermon on the scripture text found in 2 Peter 1:21: "For even hereunto were ye called: because Christ also suffered for us, leaving us an example, that ye should follow his steps" (KJV). As he works, a homeless man appears at his office seeking help. The pastor sends the man away, but the man shows up to church that following Sunday. In fact, this uninvited guest speaks up in the worship service commenting on the sermon, "The minister said . . . that it is necessary for the disciple of Jesus to follow His steps, and he said the steps are 'obedience, faith, love and imitation.' But I did not hear him tell you just what he meant that to mean, especially the last step. What do you Christians mean by following the steps of Jesus?"[1] After some more elaborating thoughts, the man collapses on the altar steps. The minister takes him back to his own home to nurse him to health, but he sinks. Six days later he dies. After a week of the whole town buzzing over the Sabbath surprise, the stunned minister enters the pulpit and asks the congregation all the more pointedly what it really does mean to follow the steps of Jesus. Finally, he concludes the sermon by challenging members to commit themselves to taking no actions and making no decisions for a full year without first asking themselves that life question made up of just four words, "What would Jesus do?"

To the pastor's happy surprise, fifty members meet with him in the church study following the service to make such a commitment, and gradually others follow. What also follows is a transformation of the whole community as believers become doers.

Millions of readers later, that question has been rekindled in the form of its acronym, WWJD. Worn as a bracelet, necklace, or T-shirt art, WWJD is the question for a new generation of believers.

Bible study groups and Sunday school classmates are holding one another accountable to take the question seriously in each participant's daily activities, and for good reason. WWJD changes things.

The Christ of the Creeds
Becomes Jesus of the Needs

This question changes the way we answer that ultimate question, "Who is Jesus Christ to you?" How one answers that question defines so much of how one lives. In the early centuries of the church, church leaders felt compelled to settle theological controversies by clearly defining the identity of the Jesus Christ whom people were following. The Nicene Creed and Apostles Creed were articulated to answer that most pressing question. The Apostles Creed begins by placing Jesus in the trinitarian godhead: "I believe in God the Father, maker of heaven and earth; and in Jesus Christ his only Son our Lord." It then summarizes the essential moments of his earthly sojourn: "who was conceived by the Holy Ghost, born of the Virgin Mary, suffered under Pontius Pilate, was crucified, dead and buried . . ."

Do you notice something missing there? ". . .born of the Virgin Mary, suffered under Pontius Pilate . . ." That's right. What's missing is thirty-three years. The content of the life of Jesus, especially of his three-year public ministry, reported not just once but in four forms by the inspired Gospels . . . missing! Between birth and death, Jesus lived a life! The Nicene Creed enlarges its definition of Jesus' divine attributes but still overlooks entirely that life. The reason? The early church leaders were fighting controversies regarding Jesus' identity as fully human and fully divine. They needed to articulate Jesus' identity, especially as it relates to God's redemption of humanity. In the process, they theologized Christ, as was needed. They addressed the large, theological issues: the virgin birth, the atoning crucifixion, the bodily resurrection. But they distanced Jesus from the everyday life.

What would Jesus do? The question reverses that tendency, taking the questioner back to his life and making it the central subject of consideration. WWJD reintroduces us to the religious leader who ate and drank with sinners, the holy man who defended prostitutes against their accusers, the rabbi who criticized the hypocrisy of other religious leaders, and the teacher of scriptural law who liberated sinners by grace. WWJD presses us to treat just as seriously the Jesus presented in the Gospels as the Christ taught in the epistles.

Stanley Hauerwas and William Willimon underline this point in *Resident Aliens*:

Early Christians, interestingly, began not with creedal speculation about the metaphysics of the Incarnation—that is, Christology abstracted from the Gospel accounts. They began with stories about Jesus, about those whose lives got caught up in his life. Therefore, in a more sophisticated and engaging way, by the very form of their presentation, the Gospel writers were able to begin training us to situate our lives like his life. We cannot know Jesus without following Jesus. Engagement with Jesus, as the misconceptions of his first disciples show, is necessary to understand Jesus. In a sense, we follow Jesus before we know Jesus.[2]

In other words, to really know the Christ of the creeds, we need to know the Jesus of the needs. It helps to ask, "What would Jesus do?"

Gift Discernment Shifts to Needs Assessing

For all the time we spend looking at ourselves, the question of "What would Jesus do" presses us to see ourselves differently, too. Consider the field of literature on vocational choices. Consider the books that help you find the right mate. Consider the marketing of products ranging from makeup to automobiles. The singular standard upheld for all such decisions boils down simply to choosing *what fits me*. The church is just as inclined in this direction as the secular culture. Choosing the church that worships they way I like, choosing a Christian education class that teaches what I want to learn, choosing the committee that matches my interests, and doing ministry that fits my spiritual gifts—all these mindsets are promoted widely in American churches.

Consider in particular the process of cultivating lay ministries within the church. In so many sectors of the church, the working formula is "you need to discern your spiritual gift" or, in other words, "you need to hear God's call." While this approach certainly is not entirely wrong, neither is it complete. When focusing on one's gifts or calling, the determinant for one's service is internal and subjective, deriving from our perceptions of what God wants us to do. Many people exempt themselves from doing unpleasant forms of service, at least any and all activities that do not mesh with their particular callings.

That approach, or lack of approach, is apparent in one of the parables that Jesus told. As a man lay on one side of the road bleeding and dying, two religious leaders passed on the other side, no doubt motivated by their own need to fulfill their gifts and callings. God had called and employed the priest and Levite to provide worship leadership in the temple, especially in the presentation of sacrificial offerings. But one thing would disqualify them for such service: touching human blood. Any contact with blood made them ceremonially unclean for seven days. Accordingly, providing assistance to the dying man would have prevented them from providing their needed services to God's people at the temple. They kept themselves clean. They walked on the other side of the road. Were they just before God? Not according to Jesus. The responsibility at the moment was not that of following one's calling but of assessing and addressing others' needs.

In fact, when we ask, "What would Jesus do?" we can easily recognize that Jesus did know what his gifts and callings were. He was on a mission. Jesus the teacher had teachings to teach. Jesus the healer healed the sick. Jesus the Savior died for sins. He stuck to his mission. Then again, he didn't. At least, he seemed so easily distracted along the way. Whether it was the woman touching the hem of his garment or the lepers staying outside the city, Jesus had an eye for people in need. Whether it was the children others shushed or the drunkards others scorned, Jesus repeatedly turned away from his mission at hand to give the greater priority to their need.

Such distractibility is seldom found among people who have struggled to be self-sufficient, self-relying, self-propelling, self-defining, self-helping, self-respecting, self-improving, and self-sustaining—all of which inevitably lead most people to become self-serving, self-indulging, and just plain self-centered and self-absorbed. When asking, "What would Jesus do?" one is forced to move outside that subjective, internally driven self-absorption, forced to turn attention to the kinds of people who continually were distracting Jesus and still finding him wondrously available to address their greatest needs.

John Buchanan, pastor of Chicago's Fourth Presbyterian Church, summarizes the church's role this way:

> Any important part of being the church of Jesus Christ is to know the world, to be a part of the world. And the way to do that is to observe our communities carefully and to ask our neighbors to tell us about their needs, hopes, fears, aspirations. Being a church in the middle of the human community means joining the search for authentic spirituality, the quest for meaning, the hunger for truth. Being the church means being in the world, thoroughly and unapologetically. And it means serving; giving something of life away in order to live fully and authentically. There is something about the mission—the intentional outreach, the consistent asking after the needs of the community, the neighborhood, the world—that authenticates and celebrates and communicates the message of the gospel.[3]

WWJD changes things.

Turning Context into Community

You and I live within a context. We live in a physical environment comprised of home, work, and school. We live in a relational environment made up of parents, siblings, children, neighbors, classmates, teachers, fellow employees, store clerks, phone solicitors, and strangers— including car drivers who change lanes without warning. All these people create a context for our lives. Some people in that context carry demands and requirements: jobs to do, laws to follow, lessons to learn, and responsibilities to fulfill.

Some aspects of the context carry a lot of freight. The "world" often is depicted in scripture as an enemy of our soul. The apostle Paul lists it with the flesh and the devil as the unholy trinity. Jesus himself warns the disciples that the world will hate them (John 15:19), and he prays that God will protect them from that hatred (John 17:15). In response many Christians have retreated from the world, whether into desert monasteries or simply into congregational enclaves. But Jesus really doesn't recommend Christians to relate to the world in that fashion. In the high priestly prayer, his intention for his followers is elaborated: "I am not asking you to take them out of the world, but I ask you to protect them from the evil one. They do not belong to the world, just as I do not belong to the world. Sanctify them in the truth; your word is truth. As you have sent me into the world, so I have sent them into the world" (John 17:15–18). This passage parallels the Great Commission, "Go therefore and make disciples of all nations . . ." (Matt. 28:19). The world is not a trap to be avoided but a mission field to be reached. One's context is one's community.

When asking "What would Jesus do?" one is pressed to see that Jesus would have us dignify our surroundings by pouring God's love into every available vessel. Knowledgeable believers who ask what Jesus would do cannot help but hear the Great Commission ringing through the air and can't help but see the world as the community of Jesus' family. They know what their calling is: Simply to express Jesus' love to all whom they encounter.

Inasmuch . . .

In that kind of light Jesus presents one of his most wonderfully alarming parables, in Matthew 25:31–46, with its memorable phrase, "Truly I tell you, just as you did not do it to one of the least of these, you did not do it to me."

The Jews of Jesus' day expected someday to be standing before God's throne of judgment. They were prepared to be scrutinized according to two standards. First they would be asked their race. As Jews, they could claim insider status as among the chosen people. The Gentiles would cower, disadvantaged by being outsiders. Second, the Jews would be judged by their performance of the Ten Commandments. If they had been obedient, especially in resisting temptation to rebel against the prohibitions within those laws, they would be ushered into their eternal reward.

Jesus' words turned everything upside down. He disrupted the Jews' confidence. The only issue of status that will ultimately matter in the judgment will be that of the "least of these." And the performance that most matters will not be the sins committed but the virtues overlooked. The sins of omission will matter more than the sins of commission.

This message startled his Jewish followers and still has the same impact on Gentiles today. We who follow the teachings of the apostles can happily shout to the rabbis of Jesus' day that matters of race or legalism do not save us. Rather, when we stand before God's throne of judgment, we can declare with confidence that we stand on grace alone! Grace received by faith grants one the sure salvation provided by our Savior in his cross and resurrection. This parable throws us a curve, though. In it Jesus, the very one who brought the message of grace and purchased its benefits by his suffering, seems to be saying that grace demands a response that goes beyond beliefs to the performance of service. He calls us to a higher level of accountability, one that takes behavior seriously. At the end of the day, he seems to be suggesting, God will divide the so-called believers themselves as a shepherd divides his flock (at night, sheep enjoy the open night air, whereas goats need to be sheltered from the elements). How shall the royal Shepherd distinguish the sheep from the goats? The measure will be whether each one's faith has become an event in the life of the hungry, the thirsty, the naked, the stranger, the sick, and the imprisoned. In other words, Jesus' last question will not be, "Who did you believe?" but "What did you do?" It will not matter what you owned, where you lived, or how you felt. The only thing that will matter will be, "What did you do?"

James makes this exact point: "What good is it, my brothers and sisters, if you say you have faith but do not have works? Can faith save you? If a brother or sister is naked and lacks daily food, and one of you says to them, 'Go in peace; keep warm and eat your fill,' and yet you do not supply their bodily needs, what is the good of that? So faith by itself, if it has no works, is dead" (2:14–17). When trying to comprehend essential theology, we all tend to go to extremes. When hearing the call to holiness, many become legalists. To them the apostle writes Galatians, Romans, and Ephesians, all declaring clearly, "For by grace you have been saved through faith, and this is not your own doing; it is the gift of God—not the result of works, so that no one may boast" (Eph. 2:8–9). On the other hand, when hearing of the free gift of grace, many people become antinomian, liberated from all standards of morality. To such readers James writes his corrective, declaring that faith—if genuine—will naturally lead to doing good works. He illustrates his point by highlighting the plight of the "least of these" and the believer's obligation to address not only their spiritual needs, but also their substance needs. Faith becomes an event in another person's life.

Lest the point be missed, the apostle John adds his flavor: "Those who say, 'I love God,' and hate their brothers or sisters, are liars; for those who do not love a brother or sister whom they have seen, cannot love God whom they have not seen" (1 John 4:20).

Put simply, the true believer finds it natural to ask in any given situation or facing any particular decision, "What would Jesus do?"

The Altruist GodView

The enormous popularity of *In His Steps* has fueled many believers who live instinctively by the Altruist GodView. To be as Christ to others, particularly as one sharing one's privilege of prosperity and good health, seems the only obvious thing that we ought to do! For a considerable body of faithful Christians, altruism toward the needy is the most obvious, most essential expression of their gratitude toward God. The Altruist GodView drives many a Christian's service, because, as Jesus put it, what God is up to is caring for the least of these: feeding the hungry, refreshing the thirsty, sheltering the stranger, clothing the naked, caring for the sick, and visiting the imprisoned.

Of course, Charles Sheldon did not invent Christian charity. The analytical theology of the Puritans led them to ask in substantive terms, what does it mean to love my neighbor as myself? By daring to ask categorical questions, quantifying neighbor-love in economic terms, medical terms, nutritional terms, etc., the Puritans determined that the Golden Rule requires every Christian to ensure that all one's neighbors, near and far, are assured that all life's necessities are provided. If my necessities are being met and my neighbors' needs are not, then I must share what I have to bring the other to my level of provision.

In the early part of the twentieth century, Walter Rauschenbush revived such thinking by launching the "social gospel" movement. He found in Jesus' teaching on the kingdom of God a call to all believers to be transformers of society for the common good. "Wherever the Kingdom of God is a living reality in Christian thought, any advance of social righteousness is seen as a part of redemption and arouses inward joy and the triumphant sense of salvation."[4]

The social gospel movement burst on the scene along with turn-of-the-century optimism. After enduring a Great Depression, a Holocaust, two world wars, and other smaller-scale wars too numerous to count, that optimism found itself chastened, but a new determination took hold. As a post-Depression General Assembly declared, "We believe that the time has come when the Church should address itself, not merely to the relief of poverty, but to its prevention and cure."[5] The post-WWII church, fueled by the baby boom, grew rapidly in numbers and influence. Many social programs formed in the 1950s came to characterize mainline Protestant churches as the altruist servants and the moral conscience of American society. Although the number of long-term foreign missionaries began to decline, the actual participation in missions continued to grow. Protestant missions were extending the message of the gospel by embodying it in the formation of hospitals, the building of educational institutions, and the organization of programs for agricultural and technical training, as well as economic development. Closer to home, Protestant missions took the lead in forming programs to feed the hungry, shelter the homeless, reclaim the victims of dissipation, and heal the sick.

However, outreach to others has run into some roadblocks. The booming prosperity accompanying the turn of the millennium has pushed the poor out of sight. The appearance of increased racial integration has concealed the economic segregation that still prevails. The failure of some costly programs formed during the eras of the New Deal and the Great Society left a sour taste in many mouths and fostered greater resistance to venture into new projects. The secularization of many religiously-based social organizations, often fueled by limitations imposed by granting foundations (both private and governmental), has distanced existing organizations from the church and discouraged churches from launching new endeavors. Further, the radical theologies promoted by some "social gospellers" has pushed some hard-working supporters to the ecclesiastical fringe. Also, the collectivist and institutional message implicit in the call to address social evils has not struck the same chord with the general population as has the more individualistic call to salvation and family values promoted by fundamentalist and evangelical churches. Frankly, those churches have experienced a boom in growth while the more socially focused churches have tended to shrink. Volumes of writings attempt to explain these phenomena—not much additional light can be shed on these pages—but suffice it to say that the social gospel movement is struggling to find its way.

Nevertheless, the impulse, the deep passion, the GodView that pulsates with compassion for the needy still rises up in the hearts of many faithful believers. Thousands of Christian missionaries serve the poor around the world. Leaders like the late Mother Teresa of Calcutta still capture the imagination, serving as role models for a generation and invoking a commitment from many to "give my all to Jesus." That's because the question still begs for a response that activates action. What would Jesus do?

Don't forget that acronym: WWJD. It will continue to sell books, bracelets, and T-shirts. More importantly, for many Christians it will continue to provide a guiding light for a life that matters. But don't be surprised if fellow believers come up with some different answers. The Altruist is sure that Jesus would help the needy by addressing their substantial needs. The Ecclesiast has no doubt that Jesus would be building and uniting the church. The Devotionalist is confident that Jesus would be deepening the faith experience of each believer. The Confessionalist knows that Jesus would be proclaiming and defending the truth. But one other group of Christians sees all those actions as, well, a bit weak, somewhat insufficient, and truly too easy. They are sure Jesus would make a more decisive and radical mark. Their service to Christ is driven by a GodView you might call Activist.

Chapter 9

The Activist GodView:
Breaking the Chains of Injustice

*C*lichés come and go. Some emerge as the "questions of the day"; that is, they pop up in conversation after conversation and, in the process, highlight a pondering that seems to pervade the culture's ethos. One such cliché question seemed to be in constant use in the 1990s. Repeatedly one would hear the query, "What's wrong with this picture?" Whether it appeared as the caption in a Sunday newspaper comic, in a complaint lodged by a student over the seeming unfairness of a test score, or as a rhetorical response in a White House news conference, "What's wrong with this picture?" seemed to summarize a curious aspect of the ethos of the times. "What's wrong with this picture?" hints of irony, paradox, and contradiction.

That caption could easily be printed in picture Bibles under the scene where Jesus is surrounded by the children. Proud parents would be looking on while disgusted apostles would be scolding the parents for bringing their children to the Savior. "What's wrong with this picture?" To the modern mind the apostles are what's wrong. They should never be shunning the children, deterring them from Jesus' embrace. But in the culture of the day, they were actually the only thing about the picture that was right. In that place and time, children were neither to be seen nor heard. In a culture that was strictly hierarchical, the men would gather in public for social intercourse, the women would gather in homes for fellowship, and the children would be expected to stay out of sight. They could play quietly on the roofs of the houses or out in the open fields, but their presence in public was unacceptable. Their status ranked along with that of slaves. So when parents brought the children to Jesus, as if he were a modern politician kissing babies to solicit votes, they were stepping way out of line. The apostles appropriately tried to direct the children back where they belonged. But Jesus broke with social convention. He did the unthinkable, scolding the apostles for their exclusiveness. He welcomed the children, hugging and loving them right out there in public.

In the view of the whole story of Jesus' public ministry, this incident would not seem to be a big deal, taking up only two verses where the story is told. But it stands as just one of many incidents in which Jesus overturned commonly accepted social standards. Surrounding himself with the "sinners" of the day—as the religious people labeled them (akin to today's labels of "immoral" or "heretical")—Jesus repeatedly disrupted social standards, offending the good people of faith. A streetwalking woman bathes his feet in ointment while he reclines at table. Drunkards share a boisterous meal with him—with the wine pouring. Lepers are allowed into his company, and he actually touches these quarantined pariahs. Wealthy tax collectors, hated as they are for their systematic extortion of the masses, become close friends with him.

Jesus disrupted the social order because he was a social transformer, a revolutionary. His revolution was outlined in the language of the Great Reversal, as scholars have catalogued his teachings. "The first shall be last," he proclaimed, "and the last shall be first." He proclaimed a reversal of hierarchies, power management, wealth, and prestige. He mapped out a journey of faith that ultimately would arrive in glory but would travel an unscenic route through such out-of-the-way places as self-sacrifice, self-denial, and persecution. His tender words turned harsh when encountering those who ranked high on the hierarchy.

> "The Scribes and the Pharisees sit on Moses' seat; therefore, do whatever they teach you and follow it; but do not do as they do, for they do not practice what they teach. They tie up heavy burdens, hard to bear, and lay them on the shoulders of others; but they themselves are unwilling to lift a finger to move them. They do all their deeds to be seen by others; for they make their phylacteries broad and their fringes long. They love to have the place of honor at banquets and the best seats in the synagogues, and to be greeted with respect in the marketplaces, and to have people call them rabbi. But you are not to be called rabbi, for you have one teacher, and you are all students. And call no one your father on earth, for you have one Father—the one in heaven." (Matt. 23:2–9)

> Then he looked up at his disciples and said: "Blessed are you when people hate you, and when they exclude you, revile you, and defame you on account of the Son of Man. Rejoice in that day and leap for joy, for surely your reward is great in heaven; for that is what their ancestors did to the prophets. But woe to you who are rich, for you have received your consolation. Woe to you who are full now, for you will be hungry. Woe to you who are laughing now, for you will mourn and weep. Woe to you when all speak well of you, for that is what their ancestors did to the false prophets." (Luke 6:22–26)

Certainly Jesus' stance drew a great following among the poor and disenfranchised, while also drawing the ire of the powerful and the wealthy. That's what social transformers do. They make enemies for themselves, because they pose a threat to the people who possess the world's goods, the people who enjoy the power and prestige that their position provides.

Jesus really did make enemies, although you would not understand that if the Jesus you know looks like the figure who has played his role in most movies on the life of Christ. The warm, tender, blue-eyed, brown-haired, European-American image of the nice guy portrayed in most Jesus movies does not match the Jesus proclaimed in the gospels. Face it. When watching those movies, does it not seem to be a *non sequitur*, a startling turn of momentum, when suddenly the crowds are shouting for the crucifixion of the truly nicest person in the whole movie? The biblical Jesus does have tender moments, but he also has many incendiary encounters with people whose power he has come to dismantle. The real Jesus made many enemies, and many people wanted to kill him, just like many people came to want to kill Abraham Lincoln, Martin Luther King Jr., and Anwar Sadat.

In particular, Jesus threatened the religious power and authority of the Jewish religious elite, the priests and Pharisees, and he threatened the political power of puppet politicians of the Romans. When he marched into Jerusalem to a palm-waving crowd, the power elites hatched their conspiracy to kill him, lest his popularity wield a power that might disrupt theirs.

Obviously, their success was short-lived. The resurrection conquest was followed by the church's prolific growth. Christians infiltrated the masses. Although Rome successfully vanquished the Jewish leaders in their march upon Jerusalem a generation after the founding of the church, they could not hold back the spread of the Christian faith. In time they concluded, "If we can't beat them, then let's co-opt them." The Christianizing of Rome domesticated the church, utilizing the bishops and priests just as the earlier Romans had used the Sadducees and other Israelis to tame their religious convictions for the empire. Faith again became a tool of the powerful to extend their power.

Some of the Reformers, familiar only with a church-state partnership, perpetuated the practice. Other Reformers broke rank. The Anabaptists, in particular, promoted the notion of an autonomous church, one that challenges the power of the established order. The pacifist convictions of the Mennonites continue that tradition, in particular when the government extends its power by violent methods. Working within the government, revived Christians of the Great Awakening became a force for the dismantling of the institution of slavery, the key to Western prosperity. Although Americans would ultimately settle this issue via its most destructive war, in England the faith of William Wilberforce and his friends led to the emancipation of slaves without drawing blood. As a member of the British Parliament, he wrote in his diary one morning in 1787, "God Almighty has set before me two great objects, the suppression of the slave trade and the reformation of manners."[1] In 1807, Parliament passed by an overwhelming majority a bill to abolish slavery. The government purchased the slaves' freedom, compensating the slave-owners 20 million pounds. W. E. Lecky called that event "one of the three or four totally righteous acts of governments in history."[2]

Like Wilberforce, many other Christians have been set aflame by an Activist GodView. Following Christ, they have sensed God's call to become social transformers, fighting racial segregation, gender inequality, imperialism, industrialization, urban blight, and environmental exploitation. In the process, the vision for activist Christian service has sharpened and intensified. At the same time the call to do social transformation has been blurred by an ongoing difficulty felt by those trying to sort between their faith and their politics. The willingness of some people to simplify their Christian convictions by saying, "I'm a Christian, so of course I support the Democratic platform" has been matched by those saying, "I'm a Christian, so of course I support the Republican platform." One set of political ideologies becomes the prima facie summation of the activist faith.

All the while a clearer biblical basis begs to be considered. Where does this biblical basis begin? A good place to start is by asking, "What's wrong with this picture?"

What's Wrong with This Picture?

It's not hard to see some of the things that are wrong with God's world. Corruption, exploitation, abuse, greed, hatred, war, and poverty desperately need to be addressed. What is not clear is, "Why?" So many of these evils arise as a kind of shadow of a bright part of the culture. An open democratic government of, by, and for the people is manipulated by the corrupting powers of politicians on the take. An open economy that encourages entrepreneurial creativity often leads to money-mongering greed. An open immigration system can cultivate a life-broadening multiculturalism but it also produces social prejudice. Should the good be dismantled simply because its light casts dark shadows? The answers are not clear. Nevertheless these systems and others not so meritorious all participate in larger structures that weave webs of "systemic sin."

Systemic sin is the committing of evil and abusive acts against people and creation that are perpetrated not so much by particular individuals as by structures of society, commerce, government, and sometimes also by the church. Such sin can wreak enormous damage to persons' lives, but by the very nature of the sins nobody is likely to be held accountable for them either. Nobody is likely to feel any guilt over them. "It's just the real world," we say. "That's reality," we justify. Accordingly some people call these "anonymous sins."

The most obvious systemic sin is the system of slavery. Modern sensibilities label slave trading and ownership an evil, a sin, but many Christians—including notable leaders in the church—once justified the structure of slavery as simply a part of the world system, a necessary component of a healthy economy. Today we have seen clear to eradicate the system—or at least, most of the system. Yet other systemic sins continue. When an employer seeking to be competitive tries to hire the best employees for the lowest competitive wage and chooses women because they will accept lower pay for their services, the sinful system wins. When a nation suffering the impact of an economic blockade chooses to invade its neighbor in search of foodstuffs, the sinful system wins. When communities subscribe to antisegregation laws but then enact zoning ordinances that prescribe segregation according to income levels, the sinful system wins again.

The gains and losses caused by such systems are decidedly difficult to measure and assess. Should a given system be dismantled wholesale? Can it be modified and redeemed?

Jesus clearly confronted such systems, along with the individuals complicit in producing them. "Woe to the world because of stumbling blocks! Occasions for stumbling are bound to come, but woe to the one by whom the stumbling block comes!" (Matt. 18:7). Note the fact that according to Jesus the world system is guilty of producing stumbling blocks. At the same time, individuals are guilty for producing those stumbling blocks. He condemns both the individual participant as well as the overall structure of sin. Accordingly, the Christian disciple is called to a life of sanctification in matters both individual and systemic. In other words, in addition to confessing personal sins and striving for Christlike behavior in individually chosen words and deeds, so, too, each believer is commanded to confess corporate sins and to influence corporate structures to be more godly in their actions as well.

What Can I Do about It?

If asking, "What's wrong with this picture?" provides a good place to start, the next step might be asking, "What can I do about it?" Typically people do one thing or the other. The one thing? They look the other way.

"It's not my issue."

"It doesn't affect me."

"It's not my gift."

So the responses go. Worse yet, some people do not even recognize the existence of the problems. "It can't be that bad," one insists. Another sheepishly shrugs, "I didn't know." To paraphrase the song by Bob Dylan, how many times can you turn your head and pretend not to see?

In my home growing up, I discovered early that "I didn't know" would not buy me a pardon. "You may not have known, but that is because you chose not to know. You are too smart to be as stupid as you claim." We were taught the principle of culpable ignorance, never plausible deniability.

One of the causes of culpable ignorance is the opiate that religious practice can provide. In this regard, Karl Marx was not completely wrong. The Book of Isaiah says so:

> Shout out, do not hold back!
> Lift up your voice like a trumpet!
> Announce to my people their rebellion,
>   to the house of Jacob their sins.
> Yet day after day they seek me
>   and delight to know my ways,
> as if they were a nation that practiced righteousness
>   and did not forsake the ordinance of their God;
> they ask of me righteous judgments,
>   they delight to draw near to God.
> "Why do we fast, but you do not see?
>   Why humble ourselves, but you do not notice?"
> Look, you serve your own interest on your fast day,
>   and oppress all your workers.
> Look, you fast only to quarrel and to fight
>   and to strike with a wicked fist.
> Such fasting as you do today
>   will not make your voice heard on high.
> Is such the fast that I choose,
>   a day to humble oneself?
> Is it to bow down the head like a bulrush,
>   and to lie in sackcloth and ashes?

> Will you call this a fast,
> a day acceptable to the LORD?"

(Isa. 58:1–5)

Religious Jews were endeavoring to do God's will. They delighted to study the law of God. They prayed for God to exercise judgment upon them. They prayed and worshipped, aiming to glorify God in their devotion. They humbled themselves before God and even quelled their earthly appetites by fasting. Yet the prophet excoriates them. He declares them to be rebels. Their fasting and worship were aiming not for God's creative purposes in the earth but for their own prosperity. In fact, as he points out, they were even complaining that their sacrifice was not bringing a good return on the investment. Though they certainly would have accused the prophet of demeaning their sincerity, the prophet clearly saw what they were missing: the real kind of service God seeks from the faithful is not such as serves one's own self-interests but the interests of others. And to be blunt, they would be better off sounding the benediction to get out of the worship center so they could get to the work God really seeks from them, out where the world needs to be changed.

Truth be told, traditions of the faith often gloss over injustice in ways that obscure the believer's sight. Implicit in the work of the Activist God-View is the need to challenge long-standing assumptions, to open blind eyes, and to force issues to the surface where others can finally be awakened from their dull slumber. The resulting revisionist approach to theology has long provided the fodder for much influence exercised by the Activist GodView. Relevancy became the central agenda of Activist Christians in the first half of the twentieth century and, though the language adjusted through the next fifty years, Activists kept asserting without embarrassment that the church must draw its agenda from the culture, learning from it as much as possible, influencing it as effectively as possible, and encouraging it to reach its highest potential as genuinely as possible.

Looking the other way is not acceptable. Pie-in-the-sky dreams of heaven cannot encompass the promises of the gospel. Or, as Martin Luther King Jr. said, "Any religion that professes to be concerned about the souls of men and is not concerned about the slums that damn them, the economic conditions that strangle them and the social conditions that cripple them is a spiritually moribund religion awaiting burial."[3]

Jane Hanna, president of the Activist Presbyterian organization, The Witherspoon Society, cites a 1966 *Christian Century* editorial stating that "'the heart of Christianity is not concern for the soul but concern for the world.' It was this Biblical interpretation that motivated the founders of the Witherspoon Society and continues to shape its agenda."[4]

No, looking the other way is not acceptable. The right response to systemic sin is to get angry . . . angry not in the sense of being out of control or violent, but in the sense of being riled enough to do something. Some of the angriest persons in the world have been the prophets of Holy Scripture. Amos, Jeremiah, Zechariah, and Malachi all excoriated the people. They cut with a sharp knife, dissecting the excuses and avoidance techniques of the people. "Something is wrong with this picture," they would begin. "You need to do something about it," they would continue.

Prophets often are called "seers" because they see things others miss. For example, while the nation is celebrating its prosperity, a prophet likely will indict the rich for trampling the poor underfoot in order to accumulate wealth. While businessmen multiply their investments, the prophet accuses them of denying would-be businesswomen the right and opportunity to prosper as the men do. While the white-collar workers gather for their Sunday afternoon church dinners, the prophet threatens disaster upon them, since the blue-collar workers are being forced to work till sundown and are thereby kept away from the Table of the Lord. That is exactly what was going on in first-century Corinth. The eloquent summary of the Lord's Supper is set into an argument by the apostle Paul as he scolds the wealthy for going ahead and eating the church potluck dinner, while the servants and slaves are still out in the fields working. People who were going ahead and eating without being cognizant of fellow members in the body of Christ were eating and drinking "judgment against themselves." Tragically, a food shortage had brought skyrocketing inflation and with it poverty for some of those workers. "For this reason many of you are weak and ill, and some have died" (1 Cor. 11:30). The seer Paul warned them of the judgment of God that they were bringing upon themselves. He commanded them, "When you come together to eat, wait for one another" (1 Cor. 11:33).

Prophets see things others miss, and they get angry. In response to their Corinthian-like self-serving religiosity, Isaiah offered a better alternative:

> Is not this the fast that I choose:
>   to loose the bonds of injustice,
>   to undo the thongs of the yoke,
>   to let the oppressed go free,
>   and to break every yoke?
> Is it not to share your bread with the hungry,
>   and bring the homeless poor into your house;

> when you see the naked, to cover them,
>> and not to hide yourself from your own kin?
> Then your light shall break forth like the dawn,
>> and your healing shall spring up quickly;
> your vindicator shall go before you,
>> the glory of the LORD shall be your rear guard.
> Then you shall call, and the LORD will answer;
>> you shall cry for help, and he will say, Here I am.
> If you remove the yoke from among you,
>> the pointing of the finger, the speaking of evil,
> if you offer your food to the hungry
>> and satisfy the needs of the afflicted,
> then your light shall rise in the darkness
>> and your gloom be like the noonday.
>
>   (Isa. 58:6–10)

Motivated by a godly anger, a righteous indignation, the right response
can come forth. That response rises more appropriately when one catches
the best of God's heart.

Perceiving the Activist Heart of God

God is the ultimate social engineer, history's most radical social justice advocate. Consider the defining moment in the Hebrew scriptures.
Given that the defining event in the New Testament is obviously the resurrection of Jesus from the dead, the defining event in the Old Testament
is just as obvious. Ask any Jew what is the most important story in biblical history, what act constitutes the Israelites as the people. The answer
will always be the same: the exodus. Or to put it in summary terms,
God's great act of history intervention prior to the incarnation of Jesus
was that of leading a slave rebellion (see Exod. 3:7–10).

Throughout Israeli history the people are reminded of their identity as
the people God redeemed from slavery. Truly one of the greatest acts of
justice in the ancient world, this escape from slavery carried their identity
through wilderness journeys and into the land God had promised them.
To this day, the celebration of Passover marks their identity as a rescued,
emancipated people. What motivated God to deliver them? Mercy, justice and the promise of *shalom.*

God's heart is well-expressed in the frequent use of these three words
that dot so many pages of the Hebrew scriptures: *justice, mercy,* and
shalom. Justice (Heb.: *mishpat*) speaks from the world of forensics to the
issue of sin and righteousness. However, *mishpat* is not limited to the

retributive justice pursued by "law and order" candidates for public office. Biblical justice is both retributive and distributive, working both to eradicate lawbreaking and to promote fairness, equality, inclusiveness, and sharing. *Mishpat* punishes and promotes, corrects and creates. The justice of God is one that builds.

Mercy (Heb.: *hesed*) is used interchangeably by translators with loving-kindness, steadfast love, and covenant love. *Hesed* expresses God's unwavering compassion for people, expressed particularly in the covenant relationship introduced by the call upon Abram and Sarai to parent a special people "whose God is the LORD" (Ps. 33:12). This love also extends to the nations to be blessed through Abram and Sarai.

Shalom, or peace, envisions a completeness, a wholeness and community that simply has it all. Richard Foster reminds us that "the great vision of shalom begins and ends our Bible. In the creation narrative, God brings order and harmony out of chaos; in the Apocalypse of John people from all the nations form a loving community in 'the holy city, the new Jerusalem,' which has no temple, 'for its temple is the Lord God the Almighty and the Lamb' (Gen. 1, Rev. 21)."[5]

When these three words, justice, mercy, and shalom, all merge, one captures the heart of God. God yearns to bring such realities to bear in all creation. The person truly seeking the heart of God will share in that yearning and participate in bringing about its realization. As Micah says,

> "He has told you, O mortal, what is good;
> and what does the LORD require of you
> but to do justice, and to love kindness,
> and to walk humbly with your God?"
>
> (6:8)

Deciding to Take Action

So what does it take to be the activist that Jesus was? How can we join in God's program of social transformation? To turn back to the words of Jesus, the simple task is to "love the Lord your God with all your heart, and with all your soul, and with all your mind, and with all your strength" (Mark 12:30) and to "love your neighbor as yourself" (Mark 12:31). Dumb question department: "Is it possible to love your neighbor as yourself without being concerned with the neighbor's well-being?" Of course not! Your commitment to love your neighbor, to extend justice toward all, and to cultivate *shalom* for all creation naturally means that you will attend to the well-being of all.

As suggested in the previous chapter, Puritan Christians articulated the real implications of the Great Commandment by cataloging the things they considered essential for their own well-being and then ensuring that every one of their neighbors had access to those same necessities. They dared to take that notion to the next level of implications: If I am obligated to ensure my neighbor's access to basic necessities, then the neighbor has a right to expect those needs to be met. The notion of "human rights" was born in the church as a way to make tangible Christian love.

Like the Puritans, we need to undergo a values transformation. History has commended the Puritans for their thriftiness and Protestant work ethic, and no doubt it will remember Americans at the beginning of the twenty-first century as prosperous above and beyond any culture in any other era or any other place. But those Puritans transformed their prosperity into compassion for others. Will history remember us for the same thing? The answer has to begin with our values. Shall our relative prosperity be spent on our own well-being? Shall we, as altruists, share with others? Moreover, shall we, as true activists, stand up and fight against systems that oppress and exploit others? Shall we accept systemic sins as necessary evils or shall we determine to speak out against them?

Such a change of values hinges upon refocusing our eyes to the plight of people around us. Frankly, that action does not come easily in a world that is so segregated. The United States may have passed all kinds of laws against racial segregation, but the inclination to cluster with people most like us, along with the protection of property values and of cultural styles combined with the simple reality that most Americans buy or rent homes according to their income levels—all have enabled the haves to not even encounter the have-nots. People of privilege are afforded the luxury of blindness toward people of need. Transformation of the society has to begin by seeing the need that ought to be changed. Richard Foster suggests, "Our task is to envision and work to realize a society where it is easier to do good and harder to do evil; a society with institutions and laws and public policies that provide justice for all and enhanced life for all."[6]

Lest it not be obvious, such activism necessarily silences the claim that religion ought to be a private matter, a personal conviction. The Activist faith disrupts the equilibrium that a status quo fights to preserve.

At the same time, the Activist Christian will rise to a level that the secular activist will not. She or he will pray for God's intervention. Recognizing systemic evils to be the faces of principalities and powers, the Activist will wear the spiritual armor provided by God—i.e., truth, righteousness, the gospel of peace, faith, salvation, the word of God—in order to overcome the spiritual battle against the world (Eph. 6:10–17). Such prayers will focus on leaders of politics, industry, church, and public institutions. The prayers will be for peace in places of conflict and for justice where injustice and poverty arise. The prayers will be for insight for oneself and others to see the many forms of injustice that fly under the radar of most persons' consciousness.

Those Aggravating Activists

To be sure, like the believer who holds to a Confessionalist GodView, the Activist often disrupts others. For one thing, the Activist gains energy out of energizing others. A rabble-rouser at heart, the Activist needs to be changing things, stirring others to change things. In the church, the Activist brings an enormous energy for creativity, because she or he often carries an almost acidic burning that needs to destroy the works of evil. Auburn Seminary president Barbara Wheeler, a self-identified activist, upholds a high view of the church and its unity, but she also acknowledges the discomfort caused by pressing for the church's acceptance of homosexuality on the same terms as heterosexuality:

> Will vigorous conversation about these matters unsettle the church and upset some of its members? Probably it will, but that is no reason to hold back. The peace of Christ is not a sentimental blanket in which we hide and smother our differences. It is genuine reconciliation, obtained for us at a very high price, and we must expect to sacrifice some of our tranquillity to discover it among ourselves. A confessing church is a struggling church.[7]

One of the pressing struggles of Activists cuts to the core of biblical revelation. At a time when sociologists, anthropologists, and linguists have sensitized us to the destructive power of language—a tool often used to diminish and even oppress the powerless—many biblical passages fail the language sensitivity test. While some have offered more culturally sensitive, dynamically equivalent ways to express the essential thoughts of such passages, others have simply rejected such passages as the work of ignorant, thoughtless bigots. Needless to say, such radical rejection of some biblical passages stirs the ire of Confessionalists—and many others in the church.

Activists often swing the ax and let the chips fall where they may. That is, precision in research often gives way to a passion for action. One fundamentalist activist was criticized for being too reckless in his criticisms of others. His retort basically said, "I was like a person running through the halls of a hotel shouting that the fourteenth floor was on fire. So maybe it was the thirteenth floor. The hotel was still on fire and they needed to wake up and get out while they could!" Inaccuracies in details do not discount the real concerns raised by Activists, any more than their acidic style discounts the truth that they may convey.

Ultimately, the church needs its activists. They help clarify the church's mission in the world. As Foster says, "Christian social witness continuously holds before us the relevance of the impossible ideal. It points us to the new heaven and the new earth. It reminds us that 'God can make a way where there is no way.' It keeps alive the prophetic imagination. It never lets us forget the redemptive power of the active, self-sacrificial love that is imaged in the cross."[8]

When we lay hold of that ideal, when we determine to join with the Activist Christ, the one who came to turn things upside down, when we agree to loose the bonds of injustice, to undo the thongs of the yoke, to let the oppressed go free, to break every yoke, to share our bread with the hungry, to bring homeless poor into our house, to cover the naked, and to be present to and helpful to our own kin, then we shall see the promise fulfilled (see Isa. 58:6–8).

> Then your light shall break forth like the dawn,
> 　and your healing shall spring up quickly;
> your vindicator shall go before you,
> 　the glory of the LORD shall be your rear guard.
> Then you shall call, and the LORD will answer;
> 　you shall cry for help, and he will say, Here I am.
>
> If you remove the yoke from among you,
> 　the pointing of the finger, the speaking of evil,
> if you offer your food to the hungry
> 　and satisfy the needs of the afflicted,
> then your light shall rise in the darkness
> 　and your gloom be like the noonday.
> 　　　　　　　　　　　　　　　(Isa. 58:8–10)

Chapter 10

Pitfalls Await!

*D*id your heart soar with excitement as you read about each God-View? Was it not self-evident that you ought to be giving your all to fulfilling each of those missions that so obviously lay at the heart of the church's calling? I would like to think that each of the past five chapters thrilled you and stirred you. I would like to think that, halfway through each chapter, you threw down the book, picked up the phone, and joined a mission program specially suited to accomplishing the very vision being presented.

Not likely, I realize.

In fact, chances are that only one or two of those chapters caught your imagination. "He's got it," you thought to yourself. "This is what God is up to." Probably you did not need to throw the book down to enroll. Instead you heard positively an affirmation that the efforts in which you are already engaged are just what you ought to be doing.

Then again, as you read chapters less compelling to you, hopefully you still recognized the basic value of those GodViews. Hopefully you could readily recognize that each GodView does grow out of part of the message proclaimed by Jesus and extended through the church's unfolding story. Some GodViews—the one or two with which you most identify—seem worth dying for, whereas the others are not.

A Quick Summary

What is worth dying for?

The truth is worth dying for. Many people have died for truth's sake. It is, as Jesus said, the very thing that sets people free. People who are driven by a Confessionalist GodView are convinced that the truth has provided the dividing line between a life wasted and a life well spent. Truth has guided many a wise decision and redeemed many a wrong decision. And given that the highest truth is found in the identity of the Godhead and the gospel of salvation by grace through faith, the Confessionalist aims to proclaim, practice, and preserve the truth.

The Presbyterian Church (U.S.A.) certainly supports that conviction. On the opening page of the *Book of Order*, the six Great Ends of the Church begin with "the proclamation of the gospel for the salvation of humankind," and add, "the preservation of the truth." Immediately following the listing of the Great Ends, the *Book of Order* articulates the Historic Principles of Church Order. The fourth principle says,

> That truth is in order to goodness; and the great touchstone of truth, its tendency to promote holiness, according to our Savior's rule, "By their fruits ye shall know them." And that no opinion can be either more pernicious or more absurd than that which brings truth and falsehood upon a level, and represents it as of no consequence what a [person]'s opinions are. On the contrary, we are persuaded that there is an inseparable connection between faith and practice, truth and duty. Otherwise, it would be of no consequence either to discover truth or to embrace it. (G-1.0304)

The Confessionalist GodView is worth dying for.

Then again, other people have given their lives to hold on to and promote the experience of God. Devotionalists have fled to desert monasteries to deepen their religious life. They have pled with ecclesiastical leaders to abandon their shallow values, to cease accumulating wealth and goods, and to resist their secularizing tendencies in order to feed a hunger for God. They have good reason for doing so. The third listed Great End of the Church is the "maintenance of divine worship," which obviously implies more than "maintaining" the holy hour on Sundays. Divine worship is a comprehensive expression that calls for a thoroughgoing discipline of personal prayer as well as corporate praise, quiet meditation, and celebrative glorification of God. Such a lifestyle was pressed by the Westminster divines, whose two catechisms begin with the question, "What is the chief end of man?" The widely memorized and quoted response, from the Shorter Catechism, answers, "The chief end of man is to glorify God and to enjoy him forever." The Larger Catechism expands with just one word but it intensifies the point: "The chief end of man is to glorify God and *fully* to enjoy him forever" (emphasis added).

The Devotionalist GodView is worth dying for.

Perhaps not as many folks have given their lives—that is, actually died—for the church, per se, but a vast majority of Christians have invested countless hours, efforts, and capital for building up the church. Jesus did say that he was building the church, and apart from the church there is no real realm of salvation. While others go out on the town, the Ecclesiast GodView drives so many to stay up late Saturday evenings preparing sermons and Sunday school lessons, sweeping sanctuary floors and practicing organ anthems. Further, the ecumenical movement of the twentieth century has fueled efforts to repair breaches in the larger church, and for good reason. The second Great End of the Church is that of "the shelter, nurture and fellowship of the children of God." Moreover, the *Book of Order* reflects Jesus' words, "By this everyone will know that you are my disciples, if you have love for one another" (John 13:35), by stating glibly, "The Church is the provisional demonstration of what God intends for all humanity" (G-3.0200).

The Ecclesiast GodView is worth dying for.

Still again, many heroes of the faith, from Father Damien to Albert Schweitzer and from Corrie TenBoom to Mother Teresa, have given over their lives in service of the needy. People who follow an Altruist God-View would remind their sisters and brothers that the church must engage the world to present to them the promises and claims of the reign of God. In fact, of the points of light expressed so glowingly by recent national leaders, the vast majority of the organizations serving the needy were formed by faithful lovers of God who felt compelled to extend God's love to others, and for good reason. The final Great End of the Church is "the exhibition of the Kingdom of God to the world." That kingdom, or reign, is shown not in structures or buildings—as would be earthly king-doms—but in the loving, relating, and caring support of persons all around. The Confession of 1967 puts this calling in clear terms:

> The reconciliation of [humanity] through Jesus Christ makes it plain that enslaving poverty in a world of abundance is an intolerable viola-tion of God's good creation. Because Jesus identified himself with the needy and exploited, the cause of the world's poor is the cause of his disciples. The church cannot condone poverty, whether it is the prod-uct of unjust social structures, exploitation of the defenseless, lack of national resources, absence of technological understanding, or rapid expansion of populations. . . . A church that is indifferent to poverty, or evades responsibility in economic affairs, or is open to one social class only, or expects gratitude for its beneficence makes a mockery of rec-onciliation and offers no acceptable worship to God. (*Book of Confes-sions,* 9.46)

The Altruist GodView is worth dying for.

Still again, many people have given life and limb to take bold initiatives, to imagine and work for a radically different world, where captives are released, where the bonds of injustice are loosed, where discrimination and segregation are exorcised, and where inclusiveness, mutual respect, equality, and justice rain down on all. The Activist GodView prods people to challenge the status quo; to expose the indifference of those wielding power in society and culture; and to stand resolutely against injustice, the diminishment of persons, and the destruction of the environment, and for good reason. The remaining Great End of the Church is "the promotion of social righteousness." The Brief Statement of Faith reminds us:

> In a broken and fearful world the Spirit gives us courage to pray without ceasing, to witness among all peoples to Christ as Lord and Saviour, to unmask idolatries in Church and culture, to hear voices of peoples long silenced, and to work with others for justice, freedom, and peace. (*Book of Confessions* 10.4)

The Confession of 1967 adds:

> In each time and place, there are particular problems and crises through which God calls the church to act. The church, guided by the Spirit, humbled by its own complicity and instructed by all attainable knowledge, seeks to discern the will of God and learn how to obey in these concrete situations. . . . God has created the peoples of the earth to be one universal family. In his reconciling love, he overcomes the barriers between brothers [and sisters] and breaks down every form of discrimination based on racial or ethnic difference, real or imaginary. . . . [T]he church labors for the abolition of all racial discrimination and ministers to those injured by it. Congregations, individuals, or groups of Christians who exclude, dominate, or patronize their fellow men [and women], however subtly, resist the Spirit of God and bring contempt on the faith which they profess. (*Book of Confessions* 9.43–44)

The Activist GodView is worth dying for.

Simply put, each and every GodView motivates many godly people to seek to discern God's will and to exercise themselves energetically and faithfully to accomplish it.

Pitfalls Await

The GodViews do not bring unremitting good. Many godly people aiming to exercise themselves for good have become unwitting perpetrators of evil.

For one thing, the GodViews tend to isolate and subdivide the church. Ecumenist Clifton Kirkpatrick has said, "The greatest ecumenical challenge we are now facing is for us to find a way to get along not with other denominations but with one another within our own denominations."[1] One major impediment to getting along is the fact that within denominations, and even within many congregations, believers tend to gravitate together into enclaves of agreement. Humans, like the birds of a feather, naturally gravitate toward those who share common convictions about good and evil, truth and godliness, high goals and deep beliefs. God-Views, being the underlying value systems and missional convictions that drive believers, often provide the magnet that draw some believers together and push others away.

GodViews drive individuals to do good things. They also isolate like-minded groups from others, and set them at odds with those whose God-Views differ from their own.

Moreover, each particular GodView carries a self-destruct button, an inherent tendency to damage the very effort it is aiming to accomplish.

Confessionalist or Judgmentalist?

Love for the truth and preservation of the truth often lead to battling for the truth and seeking the destruction of people who challenge the truth as it is presently understood.

Given the Great End of preserving the truth, the very nature of "preserving" requires one to resist all germs that could infect. History is littered with movements that have infected the truth of the gospel. In fact, through twenty centuries the church found its gospel under assault by some force, either within or outside the church. The church has picked many a fight with people and institutions that have opposed its current message.

The word *current* is used intentionally. In every era, some of the message being proclaimed has been faithful to the revealed will of God. At the same time, in every era some of the message has required amendment. But all organisms instinctively protect themselves from anything that would disrupt their equilibrium, so the church has repelled new ideas—correctives or aberrations—like a world-class soccer goalie defending the net.

In the process, the labels "narrow-minded," "closed-minded," "judgmental," "Pharisaical," and worse have been attached to many a Confessionalist. Sometimes the church has allowed its zeal for the truth to lead it to violence. Ever heard of the Inquisition? Roman Catholic scholar

Hans Kung indicts his church for its history of inquisitions and its attendant violence against heretics.

> Few things [have] harmed the Church and its unity so much as the violent treatment of heretics, the evidence of a lack of love which made countless people doubt the truth and drove them out of the Church. The road to "pure doctrine" cannot be driven over corpses. Zealous faith must not be perverted into doctrinaire intolerance. . . . A Church deserts the Gospel at the point where it tries to liquidate all opposition by physical or spiritual murder, and makes a communion of love into a religion of executioners. . . .[2]

Lest Protestants take solace in that criticism of their Roman Catholic neighbors, Reinhold Neibuhr makes a similar indictment of his fellow Presbyterians.

> In the long history of religious controversy in England from the reign of Elizabeth to that of Cromwell, Presbyterianism pursued a policy very similar to that of Catholicism. It pled for liberty of conscience when it was itself in danger of persecution; and threatened all other denominations with suppression when it had the authority to do so.[3]

As Richard Hutcheson and Peggy Shriver expound, one of the "anomalies" of religious practice is that "certainty of conviction often breeds unintentional arrogance."[4]

Such arrogance is especially obvious when studying the recent history of conservative Christianity. In a remarkable study on the subject, Jon R. Stone suggests that conservative-evangelical Christians have obsessed over the dual questions, "Who's in?" and "Who's out?" In *On the Boundaries of American Evangelicalism*, Stone shows how evangelicals have struggled intensely since World War II to differentiate themselves from the other major streams of Protestantism. "This is especially noticeable in the writings of postwar evangelicals whose flood of books and articles documents a sustained effort at defining the limits of evangelicalism by affirming and reaffirming its boundary differences with both fundamentalism and liberalism."[5] The drawing of boundaries certainly helps any organization or movement to clarify its self-understanding. But such a boundary-drawing process easily reaches the level of obsession. Imagine two farmers each owning a huge tract of land who spend all their time fighting in court over a disputed meter-wide boundary between their farms. As their savings are wasted on legal fees, their massive farms lie fallow. So, too, the church obsessing over its boundaries probably is neglecting other duties to which it has been commissioned.

Accordingly, Confessionalist Christians have tended to exercise their efforts to define clearly the boundary between orthodoxy and heterodoxy, and, in the process, have often become exceedingly judgmental and contentious. Or as Miroslav Volf says, "Rightful moral outrage has mutated into self-deceiving moral smugness."[6]

What's more, a small but outspoken block of Confessionalist believers have seemed to enjoy the contest. Like students who join a debate club, or athletes who love to box or wrestle, they have adopted the notion that a church at war is the norm, not the exception. Such pugilistic Christians ride an adrenaline wave as they critique the lectures offered in seminary classes, as they sit in judgment of conferences designed to explore new ideas, and as they rake over the choice of words in every article written by ecclesiastical leaders. *Presbyterian Outlook* editor Robert Bullock did well to coin the label "ecclesiastical stalking" to summarize such practices (which by the way, are practiced by some Activist Christians as well). While motivated by a genuine desire to proclaim and preserve the truth, these champions of orthodoxy may have allowed their passion to become supercharged by the competitive spirit of sport.

What about the truth? Certainly, that's what sets people free. The truth must be learned and proclaimed by the church. But how? Does anybody really know that truth? Pilate asked Jesus, and Jesus did not answer very directly. But Jesus did say, "You will know the truth . . ." (John 8:33). At least enough of it can be known for it to do its liberating work. Perhaps Jerry Andrews gets close to the mark when he summarizes, "Every Christian has the right to claim to have knowledge of the absolute, but no Christian has the right to claim absolute knowledge."[7] Some ideas and concepts are clearly proclaimed in scripture, and some ideas and concepts are clearly repudiated. Other ideas are hinted at in the text, and they beg for further exploration—perhaps to be discovered in scientific study or artistic expression. And as the later chapter on biblical interpretation will show, some of the seemingly clear biblical passages still carry some ambiguity.

Reality: the Confessionalist GodView and those people who promote it can easily fall into narrow-mindedness, judgmentalism, and contentiousness. Perhaps others can help Confessionalists resist their worst inclinations.

Devotionalist or Superspiritualist?

Devotionalist Christians can happily exempt themselves from many of the pitfalls into which Confessionalists fall. Devotionalists typically are much less judgmental, much more open-minded, and more pleasant to be around! The great contemplative and pietistic traditions seldom have become embroiled in ecclesiastical wars, except when friends from more hard-line movements have recruited them into short-term partnerships. Devotionalists are not given toward conflict. It takes them away from their more important task of prayer.

As you may remember, Devotionalist Christians pour their energy into spiritual things, the contemplative life, and personal piety. However, when it really comes down to the exercise of extending Christ's work into the world, they often content themselves to stay on the sidelines. Devotionalists tend to be quietists.

As a specific movement, quietism spread rapidly in the seventeenth century due to the leadership of three key advocates: Fenelon, Molinos, and Madame Guyon. It spread in the subsequent centuries among Protestants in the efforts of the holiness movement, Pentecostalism, and the Keswick movement. More recently the reconnection with Roman Catholic mysticism of the medieval church has added new dimensions to it. In practice, quietism pursues an inner serenity, with its ultimate goal being a passive contemplation of the divine. The will and the intellect are perceived not as tools for spiritual service but as impediments to the quest for a boundlessness of the soul. In other words, quietism strategically promotes and organizes the experience of God as superior to service of God, thereby stifling Christian service.

While many Devotionalists do not specifically identify with the more formalized programs of quietistic spirituality, most have been influenced by the movements and the writings these programs have generated. In fact, many of today's popular texts of "classic devotion," including Oswald Chambers's perennial best-selling daily devotional, *My Utmost for His Highest*, were written by frequent speakers at the annual Keswick Convention, which has been held annually since 1875.

What's so wrong with all this? As the cliché goes, "They're so heavenly minded that they're no earthly good." The pursuit of the spiritual life naturally demands extended periods of undivided attention, and it often draws the participant away from many of the other endeavors necessary to live the complete Christian life.

Devotionalism commonly disengages the mind. The Reformed tradition, with its emphasis upon grasping an intelligent, reasonable faith based upon revealed truth, presses the believer to think through the faith that is being believed and experienced. Howard Rice explains, "Any spirituality that does not make full use of the intellect in the pursuit of truth is less than grateful to God for the gift of the mind."[8] Such spirituality degenerates into mere sentimentality, he adds, which is "excessive emotionalism [that] prefers feelings to careful thought." In the simple language of popular preaching, "You need the twelve-inch conversion. You need to move Christ from your head to your heart." Such imagery communicates effectively, but its message is dangerous. The empty-headed mystic becomes an easy target for "every wind of doctrine" that blows about (Eph. 4:14).

Devotionalism also disengages the will. The call to service, to actively love the neighbor, easily degenerates into sappy, vacuous sentimentality. "Sentimentality takes a particularly modern form as a kind of self-indulgent narcissism whenever people wallow in pity for the less fortunate without doing anything to change the situation that makes them suffer."[9]

Devotionalism often fuels an individualistic experience of God to the neglect of the larger community of faith. God has called the people of God into a personal relationship, insofar as one does know God as a person, and not merely as a force or principle. However, that relationship ought to be termed, more accurately, an interpersonal relationship, engaging God and Christian community altogether. The relationship carries over into one's individual times of prayer and contemplation, but it is constituted within the corporate experience of God as a shared experience with others.

While the pitfalls inherent in the Devotionalist GodView may not create the pitched conflict that the Confessionalist may unleash, nevertheless sloppiness of theology and passivity in service too often stifle its great potential. Perhaps others can help the Devotionalists to resist their worst inclinations.

Ecclesiast or Isolationist?

Ecclesiast Christians would not participate in the Confessionalists' inquisitions. Ecclesiasts are too intent on preserving the unity of the church to provoke such conflicts. They might attend a Devotionalist-sponsored retreat, but they would not linger in quiet monasteries. They have too much work to do. Sunday school class curricula need to be studied. Shut-ins need to be visited. Committees need to be organized. Covered dish meals need to be cooked. Presbytery meetings and ecumenical conferences need active participation. The Ecclesiast GodView keeps the church going.

Ecclesiasts can destroy churches, though. They kill the church slowly, by their resistance to change, by blindly protecting obsolete and unjust systems, by closing their eyes to the mission outside their doors, and by dodging issues they ought to be discussing. You might say that Ecclesiasts tend to circle the wagons.

Most Ecclesiasts circle around the status quo. Creative ideas have burst upon the church scene in the past few decades. Whereas church managerial books used to be published at a rate of just one or two a year, that genre mushroomed in the 1970s. The Alban Institute, Lyle Schaller, church growth researchers, megachurch pastors, contemporary worship advocates, liturgical renewalists—to name a few—have promoted their methods of church reinvigoration. Many of the ideas are truly innovative. Many are faithful to the Christian tradition and the scriptures. But adoption of new methods demands openness to change. Many Ecclesiasts would rather keep the worship style just the way it has been for decades. Many would rather keep the church small enough to know everybody. Many are willing to spend most of their God-service energy simply keeping things as they are.

Not that all innovations advance the cause of the gospel. In fact, some Ecclesiasts have burned the wagons in order to re-create the church in the image of their newest idea. For every good new idea several ought to have been vetoed. Some leaders are so enamored with new ideas that their "what's happening now" churches no longer reflect the gospel they have been entrusted to communicate. They spend most of their God-service energy trying innovations, running roughshod over church traditions and church people, all for the purpose of growing the church or making the church a unique identity—which in some cases means feeding the ego of the leader.

Whether they be the majority traditionalists or minority antitraditionalists, most Ecclesiasts circle the wagons around a managerial mind-set. Terms that a generation ago would never be used in the church, such as "marketing the church" and "total quality management," have become commonplace in church leadership circles. Much has been gained. But something is lost when pastors are called more according to their managerial skills than their preaching ability and theological acuity. A pastor-shepherd is one thing; a CEO is something different. Churches that see their mission as a set of programs to be managed, organized, controlled, and assessed eventually will find a lot of form and not a lot of content.

Ecclesiasts circle the wagons around safe conversation topics. When a church becomes too focused on itself, its programs, and its needs, it also loses the ability to take risks. Controversial theological topics are carefully avoided in pulpit and classroom—which clearly is in evidence in most rapid-growing megachurches. Exceptions exist, of course, but usually they amount to little more than rallying against a common and unanimously hated enemy—for example, "those liberals," "those abortionists," "those misogynists," etc. Potshot preaching at outside opponents may sound prophetic, but it still is playing safe. A church which opens a conversation about issues that can cause loud disputing ventures into a danger zone. Ecclesiasts' penchant for peace often leads to a dread fear of disagreements; but as any Confessionalist would say, some uncomfortable truths must be studied, and as any Activist would say, some daring initiatives ought to be taken—lest the church become little more than a safe haven.

Ecclesiasts circle the wagon around themselves. More than anything, Ecclesiasts tend to focus their ministry around their own congregations. One can feel very generous by tithing to one's church, by serving many hours in classes and committees, by singing in choir and serving in governing bodies; but at the end of the day, the only ones receiving all that generosity are one's friends, one's own fellowship. Such generosity camouflages what ought better to be called collective selfishness.

Denominational Ecclesiasts also tend to circle the wagons, especially in these embattled years. In the denominational arena, an enormous level of energy is spent solving disputes. The arm's-length distance between local bodies and national governing bodies affords local leaders the luxury of tossing controversy grenades into the larger church life. Even localist Ecclesiasts can sound like passionate Confessionalists or Activists in the national church. Some flip-flop between those roles as easily as Clark Kent putting on tights. As passionate Activists provoke conflict by challenging the status quo and as passionate Confessionalists decry the church's theological prostitution, the denominational Ecclesiasts are left to make peace. To the provocateurs, the Ecclesiasts can sound so compromising, so utilitarian, so unprincipled. Frankly, the criticism fits, when they say, "Let's not take a stand on this. Nobody is complaining, so let sleeping dogs lie." Sometimes the safe decision is wrong.

The ecumenical Ecclesiasts find themselves at an important crossroads. You remember the nursery rhyme, "Mary had a little lamb whose fleece was white as snow, and everywhere that Mary went the lamb was sure to go." Well, the conciliar ecumenical movement has journeyed on the path of a corporate understanding of the church which has assumed that if leaders could come together, the local churches would follow like lambs following Mary. But Mary's sheep have decided that they like pure democracy more than representative democracy, so they have eschewed the corporate model of the church in favor of "doing what is right in their own eyes." On the positive side, that approach has led to the formation of many expressions of ecumenical dialogue and cooperation in local communities, in chaplaincy ministries and in global missions. On the negative side, many of the particular initiatives of institutionally minded ecumenical Ecclesiasts have been shrugged off by localists. Fortunately, some recent initiatives of ecumenists, in particular the model of ecumenical relationships pioneered by the *Lutheran-Reformed Formula of Agreement*, offer enormous hope and help to people growing weary of the conflicts that divide us.

Yes, the Ecclesiasts do build churches. They pursue the unity for which Jesus prayed, they provide enormous service in the local church, and they nurture the growing discipleship of the church family where that family lives: in and around the local congregation. They help resolve the disputes created by Confessionalists and Activists. They pull Devotionalists out of their prayer closets to become involved in church life. Nevertheless, Ecclesiasts' tendency to insulate the church from troubles and especially from the outside world too often keeps the church playing safe. Perhaps others can help Ecclesiasts resist their worst inclinations.

Altruist or Secularist?

The readiness to see Jesus in the faces of the needy, the hungry, and the poor, and the effort to reach out to them with the love of Christ often live up to their hope. The care-receivers are really helped. But too often the needy, the hungry, and the poor return to the state from which they came. Their lives do not change because, while the Altruist shows forth the compassion of Christ, the good news of Christ is often left unsaid.

The greatest fear reported among Americans, even exceeding the fear of cancer and of heart attack, is that of speaking in public. Countless Christians have surrendered to this fear by choosing to "show" the love of Christ while leaving to others the task of telling the good news. In the process, their willingness to give themselves to altruistic ministries to the neglect of proclamation ministries has denied a listening audience the opportunity to hear the good news Christ would have the church proclaim.

For much of the twentieth century, the two loudest voices in the church were the fundamentalists' and the modernists'. While the modernists followed Rauschenbusch's lead on social justice, the fundamentalists countered by pressing the case for evangelistic missions. Theologians and ecclesiastical leaders sparred between social activism and evangelism. Sadly this dispute filtered down to the local churches, where the yen for privacy and the aversion toward hard-sell evangelists found its alternative in altruist ministry. "I show the love of Jesus. Others can tell the message," so it was said. "My faith is a private matter, but I'm happy to volunteer in the soup kitchen to feed the homeless," another would add.

This division of the mission endeavor has been reinforced by funding realities. Godly Altruist Christians have organized thousands of wonderful outreach programs. From food banks to after-school tutoring programs, from prison ministries to homeless shelters, from drug rehabilitation programs to AIDS care teams, the church has launched many high-impact ministries. But whence cometh the funding? As hoped, many of these ministries have taken on a life of their own, needing more and more funding to sustain the ministry in the light of such enormous needs. So they have applied for grants, only to discover that many granting organizations refuse to fund missions that propagate religious beliefs. So the grant receivers muzzle the voice of the gospel, and what began as a faith-based organization becomes just another secular organization with a religious sounding name—that is, if the name itself does not get changed, too!

The Altruist, given such secularizing tendencies, too easily addresses problems purely in socioeconomic terms.

The evangelical mantra, "I'm out to change the world one soul at a time," deserves a hearing in this context. While the individualistic thrust of evangelistic ministry is diminished by its inherent flaws, one strength it offers is the expectation that ministry should change a person's soul as well as body. Given our confession that all are sinners, it is not necessarily patronizing to recognize care-receivers as persons whose problems might have resulted from poor decisions, bad habits, or carryover from past woundedness—all of which are addressed by the biblical faith. The church ought not to shrink away from declaring that the sinner can be forgiven of one's sins, that the victim can be healed from one's injuries, that the ignorant can gain helpful information, that the addicted can regain control of one's life, and that, simply put, the lost can be found.

Jesus' public ministry provides the central paradigm for Altruistic ministry, as especially illustrated by the story of his healing of the paralytic. Seeing the man handed down through the roof due to the crush of the crowd, Jesus looked at him and said, "Son, your sins are forgiven." After some confusion among the crowds, Jesus then said, "Take up your mat and walk," and the man did so (Mark 2:1ff.). What did Jesus do? He healed the man of his immediate, physical need and he spoke to the man's ultimate, spiritual need. Jesus' ministry incorporated both kinds of ministry without drawing a line of demarcation between them. Repeatedly Jesus addressed people's immediate needs while simultaneously pointing beyond to their spiritual needs.

Jack Rogers puts these two ministry thrusts in perspective.

> Evangelism is the first priority of the church. If we do not keep evan-
> gelizing there will be no church. The unified witness of the creeds and
> confessions from the first to the twentieth century that the church is an
> ark of salvation is valid. . . . The church is unified by common beliefs.
> The center of that belief system is that there is one body and one Spirit,
> one Lord Jesus Christ, and one God and Father of us all. . . .
>   Justice is the second priority of the church. If we do not act for the
> good of all we will cease to behave as a church. The church is a
> covenant community created by God that has a responsibility to work
> for the renewal of the whole human community. The insight of twenti-
> eth-century confessions is valid that the church is to be in mission in
> the world, transforming it into a more just society as an implication of
> the sovereign claim of Christ over, and his love for, all creation.[10]

Yes, the Altruist GodView helps godly people provide help to the needy.
The unconditional, positive regard that they extend to the needy makes
them much more warm and welcoming than many of the Confessionalists. Their outreaching caregiving counters the Ecclesiasts' isolationist
tendencies. Their care of tangible needs balances the Devotionalists' tendency to be lost in esoteric orbits. But too many Altruists have become
"so earthly minded that they're no heavenly good." They call us all to ask
ourselves, "What would Jesus do?" but forget to ask, "What would Jesus
say?" In general, contrary to the children's school activity, they would
"show" but not "tell." Jesus would do both. Perhaps others can help
Altruists resist their worst inclinations.

Activist or Elitist?

The Activist GodView provides the church many a wake-up call, urging the people of God to count for something, to put their faith into action
out on the front lines of real human tragedy. In recent years, the Activists
have especially stood up against the tide of exclusion, xenophobia, and
exploitation—assaulting the traditions of the familiar.

In the process, Activists have commonly recast the gospel of forgiveness as a gospel of liberation. The exodus model of salvation, Israel's
emancipation from the money-grubbing, life-diminishing exploitation of
the Pharoah's slavery-supported economic system, has taken hold as the
true evil from which to be redeemed. Activists have stirred the church to
take on such evils in our time but often to the neglect of the searching of
one's own heart and the confession of one's own sins. Victim-centered

liberation does not replace sinner-centered salvation. Jesus died on the cross primarily to effect reconciliation for guilty sinners before God.

As modern sensibilities keep highlighting heretofore overlooked victims' plights, the church's liberating agenda seems to be taking its cues from the world around rather than from the scriptures already given. For some the Bible has ceased to be the director for mission. Indeed, during the past two centuries, critical studies of the texts have led guilds of biblical scholars to a hermeneutic of suspicion, a general assumption that the Bible's writers were writing with ulterior motives and a casual disregard of the truth. Their claim is that the scriptures, in effect, present manipulated propaganda for the sake of promoting the self-interests of the respective writers and editors. The passionate ideologies of Activists often have gone a step further into scorning some biblical writers and blandly disregarding others. In the process, the scriptures have become little more than a theological sourcebook, allowing readers to pick and choose from its many ideas only those that fit their interests. In fact, seminaries have codified such biblical interpretation in the language of "reader-response" exegesis—that is, claiming that the ultimate meaning of any text resides in the reader, who is free to respond to and quote from the text as she or he deems appropriate. Unabashedly, believers simply quote biblical passages that suit them and reinforce their convictions, and they feel free to dismiss biblical passages that challenge their convictions.

Sadly, the movement toward gender equality has reinforced this pattern of reader-response exegesis. In particular, while challenging the misogyny resident in church and society, many Activists dismiss biblical writings as products of women-haters. The apostle Paul especially has been scorned.

Was Paul a misogynist? Or was Paul, under inspiration of the Holy Spirit, speaking to specific situations sometimes reflecting the common wisdom of the day and at other times rising up against such common wisdom, even to the point of qualifying as a radical feminist? A strong case can be made for the latter position. The same writer who commanded all believers, "Be subject to one another out of reverence for Christ. Wives, be subject to your husbands as you are to the Lord," followed by commanding the husbands to love their wives as Christ loves the church—a requirement that finds no equivalent in an ancient culture, where women universally were treated just slightly better than slaves (Eph. 5:21–27). The apostle himself accorded husbands and wives coequal authority in matters of sexual intimacy (1 Cor. 7:1ff), a parity inconceivable in that era. Releasing wives' marital obligations due to husbands' abandonment (1 Cor. 7:15) was radical. Greeting women as fellow workers (Rom.

16:1–15) and even as an apostle (Rom. 16:7) models equality twenty centuries ahead of his time.

The failure of subsequent generations to hear this side of Paul's witness does not justify the common practice of writing off this source of scripture.

Lest this discussion focus too much on the example and too little on the issue at hand, the greater problem commonly exhibited in the Activist GodView is the tendency to redefine God's identity in ways almost unrecognizable to Bible students. In particular the feminist movement has correctly challenged us to set aside a male-image God in favor of one in whose image all of us have been created. However, the search for better language has led some to visualize the Christian God through the lens of other religions—even utilizing the language of goddesses and polytheistic pantheons of gods.

No doubt, the appeal for more female imagery is appropriate. Jesus spoke of himself as a hen who gathers her chicks under wing (Matt. 23:37). The prophet Isaiah spoke of the love of God as being akin to that of a mother who hardly could abandon her nursing child (49:15; 66:11–13). For too long those images have been underplayed by male-dominated leadership in the church. Nevertheless, to abandon and even discredit the images of God given in scripture has alienated such feminists from the larger church.

Another Activist problem has arisen as the penchant toward revisionism has converged with a genuine desire to help the Church relate magnanimously among interfaith relationships. How ought Christians to relate to their neighbors who profess other religious beliefs? If Jesus is the only way to God, then must Muslims, Jews, and Buddhists be damned to hell? How can a loving God condemn such devout persons to eternal punishment? The questions compel consideration. Sincere believers in every pew are asking them. Unfortunately two answers most often are posited. Some declare glibly, "That's just the way it is: Jesus is the only way," while others accommodate, "All roads lead to heaven." The former alternative forgets that God takes pleasure not in condemning people but in saving them. The latter alternative runs roughshod not only over the teachings of Jesus and the apostles, but also over the uniqueness of the Christ-event, i.e., the incarnation, the atoning crucifixion, the life-giving resurrection, the enthroning ascension, and the Spirit-outpouring.

The annual Presbyterian Peacemaking Conference in summer 2000 brought such struggles to the surface as Presbyterian minister, Dirk Ficca, the director of the World Congress on Religions, suggested that one way to better embrace adherents of other religions could be pursued simply by setting aside the instrumental role of Jesus' ministry in favor his revelational role. In other words, he suggests that Jesus should be viewed as one of many great persons who reveal aspects of divinity, but not as the one per se who is the instrument of salvation. Positively speaking, this view opens a door to fellowship without exclusion. However, as Ficca acknowledges, it does not mix well with the Great Commission to make disciples of all nations. He equates the commission to the ages-old confusion between Christendom and the kingdom of God, and thereby seems to dismiss it out of hand. What Ficca does not acknowledge is that the whole Christ-event—the incarnation, the crucifixion, and the resurrection—are stripped of any salvific value, being relegated to the simple function of showing the love and power of God.

The creedal faith is thrown out by the activist desire to include all religious strangers.

One other perplexity posed by the Activist GodView is its own inherent hesitation to find the way to be inclusive of those with whom it disagrees. Confessionalists frequently query, "If you all are so inclusive, then why do you work so hard to exclude us from roles of church leadership and decision-making power?" The inclusiveness of inclusive Activists seems to be selective, i.e., they are inclusive toward all those who share their ideology of inclusion and exclusive of all the rest. Here activists tamper not only with the historic, creedal faith; they also threaten the unity of the church. To press the church to rethink some of its beliefs certainly is needed, even to the point of redirecting the church's mission in more positive, loving ways. But to turn that effort to ultimately exclude others of differing ideologies, to try to win one's point by purely political, power-wielding means—as has been in evidence in many church legislative and judicial efforts by both Confessionalists and Activists—and in the process to run roughshod over the peace and unity of the church is problematic, to say the least.

Let there be no doubt that God has used the Activist GodView to change many errors in the church's community life and witness to the world around. Many forms of exclusion have been righted by those pressing the church to change its ways. They have stirred Altruist Christians to address not only individuals' needs but also to overturn systemic evils causing such needs. They have wakened many a sleeping Ecclesiast, rallying them to positive action. They have pressed Devotionalists not only to pray for just causes but also to take a stand. And they have forced Confessionalists to rethink long-held prejudices and power-holds, leading to a better discernment of God's will in the world. But too many times the truly life-giving grace of God has been sacrificed on the altars of noble causes. A kind of *reductionism* has set in as the central message of the gospel has been supplanted by more immediate, short-term causes that in some cases have been wrongheaded. A kind of *syncretism* has set in as the gospel has been mixed with foreign religious beliefs, some of them opposing the classical Christian faith. And a kind of *revisionism* has emerged, as intellectual arrogance has sacrificed the historic faith on an altar of personal enlightenment. Perhaps others can help Activists resist their worst inclinations.

Pitfalls?

As stated earlier in this chapter, the greatest pitfall resident in all of the GodViews is the fragmentation and balkanization they are visiting upon the church. To be more blunt, proponents of any one GodView tend to retreat into enclaves of agreement where one's allies can reinforce smug, elitist claims of superiority. Such enclaves often serve as foxholes from which ideologues toss grenades at one another. As Blaise Pascal has said, "Men never do evil so completely and cheerfully as when they do it from religious conviction."[11]

The church becomes increasingly impoverished by the silencing of voices who could offer so many correctives, so many valuable insights, so many lessons, leading ultimately to so much more wisdom. Ironically, in an era that daily is multiplying mechanisms of communication, we seem to be hiding more and more in safe circles where the conversation is painfully predictable. Is there any hope for us to come together?

Chapter 11

We Really Do Need Each Other

We are like a family living in one house trying to kick the other members out of the same house, but we can't. We have to share the living room, bath, and kitchen, but we hate each others' guts. We don't want to share the bedroom, so we hire divorce lawyers to try to force the other parties out of the house. But no one wants to leave. So we just threaten, 'If you won't leave, I will oppress you and make your life as miserable as possible.'" These words come not from an unhappily married spouse but from Salim Munayer, explaining the plight facing Jews and Arabs in Israel-Palestine.

As director of Musalaha (moo-SAH-la-hah), the Arabic word for reconciliation, Dr. Munayer arranges gatherings of Christians, Muslims, and Jews in order to help them share hopes, solve common problems, and seek mutual understanding. But the challenges are huge. He explains, "We are living on the same parcel of land. We have to live together. One people cannot eliminate the other people. If one rules the other, then it has a destructive effect on both. One is oppressed and impoverished. The other becomes a police force, a powermonger; it glorifies violence and power over other values."[1]

Consider those same words paraphrased for a conflicted church: "We are serving God in the same denomination. We have to live together. One GodView group cannot eliminate the other GodView groups. If one group acquires dominance, then all will be damaged. Some groups will feel oppressed and stifled. The dominant group or groups will become mere power brokers, trading the gospel for the thrill of legislative victory, judicial enforcement, and successful ecclesiastical politics."

What a sad state that would be. What a sad state that has been. Sadly, we are never far away from that state. The twentieth century saw American denominations living out conflicts of power and control in some of the ugliest ways, even when hidden under a genteel, sanctimonious veneer.

Now that we understand better the GodViews that are driving such conflicts, perhaps we should simply redefine the denominational landscape. Perhaps all the Confessionalist Methodists, Presbyterians, Lutherans, and Episcopalians could form the Confessionalist Church, another multidenominational group could form an Altruist Church, and so forth. The whole idea sounds really appealing!

Of course, a reshuffling of the denominational deck would spell disaster. Put all Confessionalists together and soon they will reengage old divisive debates, such as free will versus predestination, or believer's baptism versus infant baptism. Similar scenarios would unfold in other GodView camps. One division would beget more divisions. Moreover, each group would be impoverished by censoring the unpleasant voices that contrary GodViews bring to the ecclesiastical table.

Is there a way to stay together? Is there a will to find the way to learn and grow together? Do we really need to try?

Calvin Says: Stick Together

While questioning the value and viability of maintaining unity amid such diversity, we discover that our questions are merely added to questions asked throughout the history of Christianity. Unlike our Hebrew forerunners, our lack of common blood, common heritage, or close proximity have long tested our ability to function as one people. From the days of the apostles, we have struggled against our own innate tribal instincts, which have only been compounded by our tendency to lock into the convictions to which our varying GodViews have led us.

Those struggles reached breaking point during the persecutions that assaulted the Christians between the time of the apostles and that of Emperor Constantine. While the persecutions were not constant, they did arise with a ferocious intensity during various emperors' reigns, Domition and Nero being two who took special pleasure in the humiliation and suffering of believers. But even such evildoers did not kill every believer they encountered. In most cases they gave their would-be prey the option to recant their faith. Those believers faced enormous pressure to do as offered, especially in the light of the fact that their premature death might well spell doom for spouses and children who depended upon their livelihood to provide the daily bread. "What am I to do?" would ask one husband-father of his cell mate. "How can I abandon my children and wife? Either they will starve, or she will end up selling her body for other men's pleasure." Women of the day were afforded very few honorable forms of gainful employment. Some believers would make the painful decision to retain their religious conviction, maintaining their loyalty to their Lord and praying for the family as they were lit up at the stake. Others made the equally painful decision to retain their family conviction, choosing to return to their spouses and children and praying for the Lord to be merciful to them for recanting their faith under such pressure.

The warm embrace that welcomed the freed convicts back home inevitably was followed by them telling their account of their release. Soon the townspeople were abuzz with discussions. In the back of their minds they could hear those words of Jesus, "Everyone therefore who acknowledges me before others, I also will acknowledge before my Father in heaven; but whoever denies me before others, I also will deny before my Father in heaven" (Matt. 10:32–33). Those words of the Savior had motivated some of their own fellowship to choose the way of suffering over the way of ease. How could they now welcome back this coward? Was his faintheartedness any more to be commended than Peter's denial of Jesus at the time of the crucifixion?

As the congregations struggled to walk the road between these two terrible options, the bulk of the churches determined to allow the recanting individual to return to full-member status after a trial period. After an extended period of service, instruction, and examination, typically one to two years in duration, the traitor would be restored to full-believer status, sometimes even allowed in time to take a leadership role. However, some believers found such an option to be too indulging. "If Jesus said, 'I also will deny [them] before my Father in heaven' (Matt. 10:33), who are we to presume that they can be restored?" The cowardly recanting of Christ equated to the unthinkable, unpardonable sin, and could not be restored, they reasoned. For years the church argued between these two alternatives. Finally, one group severed ties with the rest. Led by Montanus from the city of Phrygia—who also was intent upon reviving the exercise of spiritual gifts, especially spontaneous prophesyings—this group claimed to be the truly faithful people of God. They might serve as just a footnote in church history were it not for the fact that Tertullian, the leading and most prolific writer/theologian of the early third century, became a Montanist.

While the Montanist movement died out after a few centuries, it did articulate an understanding of the church that has persisted in many a movement since. As far as the Montanists were concerned, the broad church was far too compromised with the secular culture and far too indulging of sinfulness. For the Montanist, to put their standards in contemporary terms, "You can join the church only when I am 100 percent sure that you are 100 percent pure." Through the centuries this requirement has been revived again and again. Most notably, during the days of the Reformation, conflicts arose between the Lutheran-Reformed leaders and those who became known as the Anabaptists. The Anabaptists were so named because of their practice of being baptized not just once but in some cases as often as a person would need to repent for committing any sin, even daily. Although the movement's label reflected their revisionist approach to the sacrament, the essential theological conviction among them echoed that of the Montanists, "You can join the church only when I am 100 percent sure that you are 100 percent pure." In the Anabaptists' case, you could join and rejoin the church again and again, but your participation always would hinge upon your being 100 percent pure.

To this day, Baptists continue to baptize only those who have personally professed their repentance and faith, believing that admission to the body of Christ depends upon one's having fully confirmed one's commitment to Christ. In this tradition, to be a child of believers makes one no more a part of the family of God than being a child of registered Democrats gives one the right to vote. In contrast, the Reformed tradition recognizes baptism to be in continuity with the Abrahamic practice of circumcision, by which a newborn is welcomed into the believing community and numbered as "one of us." Obviously, the ultimate aim and expectation is that the child should grow in the faith, taking it as the child's own, but the infant is treated as a part of the church body from the time of the baptism. In the meantime, the Reformed body into which the child has been included openly acknowledges that its membership is far short of pure.

As over against the Montanist church, the Reformed church is unabashedly brackish: somewhat sinner, somewhat saint. According to John Calvin, "some fault may creep into the administration of either doctrine or sacraments, but this ought not to estrange us from communion with the church. For not all the articles of true doctrine are of the same sort. Some are so necessary to know that they should be certain and unquestioned by all men as the proper principles of religion. Such are: God is one; Christ is God and the Son of God; our salvation rests in God's mercy; and the like." Beyond that, he opens the door wide: "But since all men are somewhat beclouded with ignorance, either we must leave no church remaining, or we must condone delusion in those matters which can go unknown without harm to the sum or religion and without loss of salvation."[2]

How could Calvin admit such brackishness? Because he, like Luther before him and the Westminster divines to follow, believed that the true "invisible church" is only imperfectly and incompletely represented by the visible church. The invisible church is comprised of the truly elect, "those who are children of God by grace of adoption and true members of Christ by sanctification of the Holy Spirit," that is, both the "saints presently living on earth" and "all the elect from the beginning of the world." The visible church includes not only those true members of Christ but also all those spread over the earth "who profess to worship one God and Christ" . . . in which "are mingled many hypocrites who have nothing of Christ but the name and outward appearance. There are many ambitious, greedy, envious persons, evil speakers, and some of quite unclean life. Such are tolerated for a time either because they cannot be convicted by a competent tribunal or because a vigorous discipline does not always flourish as it ought." Shall we disassociate ourselves from such an imperfect body of sinners? No. Calvin concludes, "Just as we must believe, therefore, that the former church, invisible to us, is visible to the eyes of God alone, so we are commanded to revere and keep communion with the latter, which is called 'church' with respect to men."[3]

In other words, we all are faced with two basic alternatives. We could adopt a purist, Montanist ecclesiology, which necessitates the establishment of a fully developed list of particular beliefs and practices that must be fully subscribed by anybody wishing to be a part of the fellowship. In the process we will have established a church in whose membership none of us could be welcomed. Our other alternative is to throw the doors wide open—as Peter did on the first Christian Pentecost—and allow the Lord to add "to [our] number daily those who [are] being saved" (Acts 2:47). Calvin promoted that kind of church—yes, a church that is and always will be brackish, a little bit sinner and a little bit saint, and thus is ever in need of reformation. In the process, that church simply matches up to the real world; sinners are welcomed into their fellowship of Christ—solely on the merits of his holiness—and are miraculously declared saints, yet know that their lives fall short of that regal title.

Parenthetically speaking one might ask, "But different folks have different denominations, each with its own emphases. Why can't we just accept those differences and go our separate ways?" In other words, shy of becoming Montanist purists, why not make a more pragmatic decision to affiliate with people who share more common ground and disaffiliate with those who do not? This argument hinges upon one simple assumption of the church, namely, that it exists as a voluntary association of like-minded persons. The proliferation of denominations and parachurch organizations in the modern era could easily be interpreted as proof positive that churches are nothing more or less than such voluntary associations. The ongoing debate over the separation of church and state also lends itself to a "voluntary association" definition.

However, such a definition of the church flies in the face of biblical and Reformed understandings of the church. Jesus said he would build his church, a single institution owned not by a board of trustees but by Christ himself. Scripture does not hint in the least of multiple-choice options for choosing churches in any locality. Even with the proliferation of denominations occurring during the Reformation, Calvin and others assailed anybody who would divide or separate from the existing church. As Presbyterian evangelical theologian Mark Achtemeier says it, "To break fellowship with other persons who show any signs at all of being in Christ is to deny our own oneness with Christ and our own hope of salvation."[4] Achtemeier then quotes church father John Chrysostom, "Nothing angers God so much as the division of the church; even if we have done ten thousand good deeds, those of us who cut up the fullness of the church will be punished no less than those who cut his body."[5]

So what does it mean for us to work not only for the peace and unity, but also the purity of the church? Well, certainly such a calling demands that we all study the scriptures so that our proclamation of the word of God be more and more faithful to the intended meaning of the text. We ought to administer the sacraments responsibly and faithfully. We need to exercise loving, careful discipline. But in order to do so, we need to be together. We need to challenge each other. We need to instruct each other as we understand God's word spoken to us, and we need to learn from each other as we express what that word means to us.

The purity of the church does not come about by piously evicting those who challenge her traditions, who question her assumptions, who provoke controversial conversations, not even those who defy her polity. Both political correctness ideologues and theological correctness ideologues commonly misguide the church's mission. Quite the contrary, it is not the censoring of such provocations but the mutual pursuit of God's will from a variety of starting points and a diversity of passionate mindsets—and the very, very difficult task of working together across our lines of division—that ultimately build up the body of Christ. That variety of passionate believers, that variety of GodViews, is part of the design built in to the Lord's body.

Paul Says: Work Together

Returning to First Corinthians, the core theological insight provided by the apostle Paul is the body-of-Christ analogy. This analogy is significant enough in the apostle's thinking to have been utilized not only in the Corinthian correspondence but also in his theological tome, the letter to the Romans. It also plays a prominent role in the letter to the Ephesians. But focusing on the First Corinthian letter, the twelfth chapter opens by introducing the very question on the minds of the Montanists, the Anabaptists, and the many frustrated, conflicted believers of our day: "Do not some of those sinners stand outside the true body of Christ?" What are we to make of those who are cowards, hypocrites, and deceivers? The apostle says that some of them clearly stand outside the realm of God's grace, and others clearly stand within the community of grace. What kinds of errors set one outside that body? What sinful practices constitute apostasy?

Only one dividing line is offered. "I want you to understand that no one speaking by the Spirit of God ever says 'Let Jesus be cursed!' and no one can say 'Jesus is Lord' except by the Holy Spirit" (1 Cor. 12:3). In other words, no one declaring their confession that "Jesus Christ is Lord" could be doing so except by the electing call, the indwelling presence, and divine inspiration of the Holy Spirit. That person must be a part of the body of Christ. In contrast, the electing, indwelling, and inspiring presence of the Holy Spirit could not bear the declaration, "Let Jesus be cursed!" Therefore anybody saying so clearly stands outside the body of Christ. That one dividing line presses an uncomfortable point: Many folks who proclaim beliefs that sound un-Christian and many folks who practice behaviors that appear unethical nevertheless are Christian, if they profess Jesus Christ to be their Lord. One's assessment of others' beliefs and behaviors may be accurate, but the inference that such excludes them from Christ's church does not follow. Wrong as their belief and practices may be, they are a part of his body.

Certainly this word did not settle well for the sectarian Corinthians, so the apostle elaborated his point. "Now there are varieties of gifts, but the same Spirit; and there are varieties of services, but the same Lord; and there are varieties of activities, but it is the same God who activates all of them in everyone" (12:4–6). The operative term of the paragraph is "varieties." Commonly, the contemporary church focuses much of its mobilization of members around God's gifting of the church with a variety of gifts. But equally important are the varieties of services and activities. Many single-minded, unidirectional churches welcome a variety of gifts, all of which can be utilized to fulfill a common vision. However, a variety of services (Greek: *diaconia,* ways of serving) and a variety of activities (Greek: *energemata,* exertions of energy) can press a church in diverse directions at the same time. So it is with the variety of GodViews. Each one presses the church to direct its efforts in different kinds of service and in organizing different types of activities. Indeed, sometimes such a variety of service and activities sends parts of the body in seemingly opposite directions. Like the complex mix of human activities our bodies are capable of performing—such as chewing gum and walking—all at the same time (actually, you might add pumping blood, breathing, dreaming, digesting, washing, singing, etc.), the body of Christ does perform many complex and contrary tasks under the guidance of the one head of the body, Christ himself.

A sample list of the variety of endeavors, activities, and gifts then is enumerated, and then two very specific applications are outlined. First, let nobody devalue your contribution to the body; and second, don't you devalue anybody else's contribution to the body. The point of application to church leadership is crucial for the contemporary church. No matter what gift you bring, what service to which you feel called, what activity you wish to lead, or underneath all those, which GodView drives you, you must neither devalue your contribution nor devalue anybody else's contribution to the church's ministry. No matter how mundane your call may appear, and no matter how misguided others' dreams may seem, if you and they proclaim the lordship of Jesus Christ, the body of Christ will be malnourished if either of you is stifled in pursuing your various perceptions of call in that body. And lest there be any doubt about your mutual value, the apostle directs "that there may be no dissension within the body, but the members may have the same care for one another" (12:25). To be blunt, the Activist cannot diminish the value of the Confessionalist and vice versa. The Devotionalist must not tear down the Altruist and vice versa. The Ecclesiast must not dismiss the Activist or the Confessionalist or anybody else.

We really do need each other, if only because the apostle says so. Then again, we need each other also because we really have a lot to learn from one another.

Affirming Admonishers Say: Learn Together

If the twentieth century is to be remembered in part for its great ecumenical initiatives, perhaps one of the most far-reaching successes will prove to have been one that involved just four denominations. The Lutheran-Reformed Formula of Agreement, approved by the Evangelical Lutheran Church in America, the Reformed Church in America, the United Church of Christ, and the Presbyterian Church (U.S.A.), was adopted by each denominational body by overwhelming margins. In the process these four denominations entered into full communion. That is, they now recognize each other as churches in which the gospel is rightly preached and the sacraments rightly administered; they have withdrawn any historic condemnation against one another; they recognize each others' sacraments; they recognize each others' ordained offices and allow for the exchange of clergy; they have established consultative and decision-making channels; they have committed to continuing ongoing theological dialogue; and they have pledged to live together via the principle of mutual affirmation and mutual admonition toward the building of trust, respect, and love.

How did these four churches form such a comprehensive agreement? Could the success of this peacemaking, reconciling effort between the churches help each respective church rebuild within its own denomination esprit de corps, mutual trust, shared service, and a cooperative learning experience? The answer to those questions boils down to the key operative expression of the Formula of Agreement, namely, *mutual affirmation and mutual admonition.* "This breakthrough concept, a complementarity of mutual affirmation and mutual admonition, points toward new ways of relating traditions of Reformation churches that heretofore have not been able to reconcile their diverse witnesses to the saving grace of God that is bestowed in Jesus Christ, the Lord of the Church."[6] Quoting from the doctrinal consensus articulated in *A Common Calling: The Witness of Our Reformation Churches in North America Today,*[7] the Formula asserts, "The theological diversity within our common confession provides both the complementarity needed for a full and adequate witness to the gospel (mutual affirmation) and the corrective reminder that every theological approach is a partial and incomplete witness to the Gospel (mutual admonition)." Simply put, this guideline invites each tradition to bring "its 'corrective witness' to the other while fostering continuing theological reflection and dialogue to further clarify the unity of faith they share and seek."[8]

The Formula of Agreement does not promote a "least common denominator," generic religion. Quite the contrary, it makes it "clear that in entering into full church communion these churches:

- do not consider their own traditional confessional and ecclesiological character to be compromised in the least;
- fully recognize the validity and necessity of the confessional and ecclesiological character of the partner churches;
- intend to allow significant differences to be honestly articulated within the relationship of full communion;
- allow for articulated differences to be opportunities for mutual growth of churchly fullness within each of the partner churches and within the relationship of full communion itself."[9]

It then articulates "a Fundamental Doctrinal Consensus," namely belief in justification by grace through faith, the practice of baptism to receive human beings into Christ's fellowship of salvation, and the presence of Christ in the Lord's Supper (though articulated in various ways).[10] It then unabashedly articulates known differences as ground for further discussion and learning. Finally, with its adoption, the Formula declares that "the churches acknowledge that they are undertaking an act of strong mutual commitment. They are making pledges and promises to each other. The churches recognize that full commitment to each other involves serious intention, awareness, and dedication. They are binding themselves to far more than merely a formal action; they are entering into a relationship with gifts and changes for all."[11]

Is there a model for interdependence that can be appropriated for the individual churches in times of conflict? Most assuredly so! Consider the two-pronged methodology of the Formula.

First, "mutual affirmation" declares that there exists common convictions that center the faith of the participating denominations. In that case, that center is relatively small, namely common belief in salvation by grace through faith and a partial common agreement regarding the administration of the sacraments. For those who serve together within any one denomination, the center is much larger; as the Sun compares to the Moon, the common beliefs and commitments are much larger and much brighter. At the center of Presbyterian faith and practice we find not only the Bible, but also the *Book of Confessions* and the *Book of Order*. In the opening chapters of that *Book of Order* we read of preliminary principles, such as the Great Ends of the Church and Historic Principles of Church Order; we hear the core values articulated as the Confessions are summarized; we see the church's mission unfolded; and we are reminded of the Christ-centered basis of the church's unity. Later on, requirements of its leaders are enumerated, as are questions of commitment to be asked and confessed by every ordinand. In responding to such questions, the candidate declares one's trust in Jesus Christ as Savior and Lord, one's acceptance of the scriptures, one's reception of the Reformed confessions, one's commitment to obey Jesus Christ, etc. In a very pointed section, the *Book* also addresses all ordained leaders who may at any time depart from the faith once subscribed:

> It is necessary to the integrity and health of the church that the persons who serve in it as officers shall adhere to the essentials of the Reformed faith and polity as expressed in The Book of Confessions and the Form of Government. . . . His or her conscience is captive to

the Word of God as interpreted in the standards of the church so long as he or she continues to seek or hold office in that body. The decision as to whether a person has departed from essentials of Reformed faith and polity is made initially by the individual concerned but ultimately becomes the responsibility of the governing body in which he or she serves. (G-6.0108a–b)

When you add up the convictions held and the commitments made by all clergy, elders, and deacons in the Presbyterian Church (U.S.A.), the common core of faith is formidable—far greater than that held among the four participating churches in the Formula of Agreement, which themselves outline a far greater, more comprehensive litmus test than the one offered by the apostle Paul (declaring "Jesus Christ is Lord" vs. "Let Jesus be cursed"). Is it not obvious that for all of our differences, we cannot help but affirm a whole body of beliefs and practices that are non-negotiable core values? Can we not engage in *mutual affirmation* as brothers and sisters in Christ?

Not so fast, you might say. Do not our differences on sexual ethics constitute radically different understandings of sin and scripture? Do not our differences on biblical interpretation lead to real differences on the identity and mission of Jesus himself? Are we going to paper over our very real differences?

Certainly the differences are genuine, significant, and sometimes disturbing. That is where *mutual admonition* fits into this picture. To minimize our differences would be pointless. To dismiss them would be dishonest. But the ecumenical model of *mutual affirmation, mutual admonition* presumes a common table around which each participant is expected to admonish those who are believed to be in error. None of us enjoys being corrected, whether by a disciplining parent, school principal, police officer, or colleague in ministry. However, everyone who accepts the call to lead in the church by implication is submitting oneself to the council (both affirming and admonishing) and the guidance (both affirming and admonishing) and the discipline (both affirming and admonishing) of the scriptures, the Confessions, the *Book of Order,* the courts, the governing bodies, and the fellowship of one's colleagues in ministry. At the same time, all church officers when being ordained and installed are accepting the responsibility to lead, that is, to give counsel, guidance, and discipline to others growing in their discipleship, whether they be colleagues in leadership or church members growing in their personal discipleship. Effective leaders and church officers will affirm and admonish those entrusted into their circle of service.

Obviously, we tread here on bumpy terrain. The sectarian map claims that a smooth superhighway lies ahead for those who quit the church or divide the church into separated enclaves of agreement. On paper that alternative relieves us of the need to confront groups or people with whom we differ. Of course, as has been said earlier, that superhighway offers the most dangerous route of all—as the earlier analogy suggested, the shrapnel effect brings too much collateral damage—but the appearance of a high-speed, easy journey looks appealing because it allows us to live in ecclesiastical denial. It affords us the luxury of avoiding issues we think an unnecessary, aggravating waste of time. To meet at the table with folks whose GodViews conflict with ours seems a terrible waste of effort, a foolish, bumpy route that ought to be bypassed via other routes.

To be sure, few actions seem to aggravate believers more than being forced to discuss issues we think irrelevant. Often when holding such discussions one person or group casts the issues in a way that shames others into silence. Often one person uses terms that sound to others to be beyond the pale, totally outside Christian faith and common sense. So often, it seems that when all is said and done, much more has been said than done.

Nevertheless, conflict avoidance does not solve conflicts. Ecclesiastical denial allows issues to fester, encourages the status quo to prevail over better alternatives, and does not serve the proclamation of the truth. At the very minimum, truth must be open to testing, reformulating, and correcting. *Mutual affirmation, mutual admonition* paves a bumpy road, but it sure beats the other available routes.

Such a road reminds one of the road taken by some heads of state a few decades back. It was called détente.

Ecclesiastical Détente

Though the context and stakes are obviously different, the call to engage the differing GodViews does equate to the decision of the administration of Richard Nixon to adopt a policy of détente in its dealings with the then–Soviet Union. Sadly, that chapter of history largely has been crowded out of our memory banks by the scandal of Watergate and by communism's ultimate collapse. However, the tearing down of the Berlin Wall never may have happened were it not for Nixon's determined vision. "Probably the most abiding tribute to Nixon's legacy is that most of the relationships and strategies launched during his presidency have sustained the foreign policy of all of his successors to this writing," says Henry Kissinger in the third volume of his memoirs.[12] Kissinger acknowledges that this conservative leader was criticized intensely by other conservatives as being "overeager for accommodation with the Soviet Union in the name of détente, which, in their view, compounded bad policy with French terminology."[13]

In reality, the distrust his colleagues felt toward the Soviets was fully subscribed by Nixon. He considered the Soviet Union to be "ideologically hostile and militarily threatening."[14] However, he faced several perceptions and possibilities. On one hand, the threat of Soviet expansionism, along with its massive nuclear buildup, meant that any military encounter could bring about mutual destruction. On another hand, "the American public was drained by twenty years of Cold War exertions and the increasing frustrations with Vietnam."[15] Americans increasingly were seeking to claim a moral high ground, pursuing peace above all else. A subtle underpinning to all these conflicting trends was an American attachment to generations-old Wilsonianism.

Woodrow Wilson, one of the most thoughtful leaders to serve in the Oval Office, was, you will recall, the president who brought us "the war to end all wars." In so doing, he articulated an approach to peacemaking that is built not on a balance of power but upon the formation of a singular moral consensus. Wilsonianism "sees foreign policy as a struggle between good and evil, in each phase of which it is America's mission to help defeat the evil foes challenging a peaceful order."[16] Such an approach holds forth the hope and expectation that total victory and vindication is always just one breakthrough away. "Such a foreign policy tends to be segmented into a series of episodes and not perceived as a continuum requiring constant attention and adjustment, a quest for absolutes rather than as the shaping of reality by means of nuances."[17] Accordingly, throughout the Vietnam conflict, as divided as the country was between doves and hawks, most Americans, both Democrats and Republicans, kept searching for one decisive breakthrough, whether that would entail a full frontal attack on the communist North Vietnamese or a unilateral withdrawal from the conflict altogether.

In contrast, both for the Vietnam War and for the subsequent attempts to warm the Cold War, Kissinger recalls,

> nothing in Nixon's personal experience led him to share the conviction that great ideas could be realized in one grand ideological assault. Both Nixon and I enlisted our firm anti-Communist convictions in the services of a complex strategy designed to achieve our objective in stages, each of which by definition was bound to fall short of the ultimate ideal and could therefore be castigated as amoral. We viewed foreign policy as a continuing process with no terminal point, unlike the dominant

view among liberals and conservatives, who were seeking a series of climaxes, each of which would culminate its particular phase and obviate the need for a continuing exertion.[18]

In the process, Nixon and Kissinger "strove for a strategy which calibrated the benefits of restraint and the penalties to recklessness to keep Soviet leaders from mounting a challenge during our period of national turmoil."[19]

So how did they implement a policy that sought peace with a dangerous enemy? One thing they did not do was become naïve. "We explicitly rejected the proposition that Communist leaders 'have already given up their beliefs or are just about to do so. . . .'"[20] What they did do was see the Soviet Union as a nation that in a time of peace could be more vulnerable to cultural influences for change than it was in times of conflict. That is, the Soviet people would not accept for long their poverty and isolation if there were no war to convince them that they ought to make such sacrifices.

> We did not view the Soviet Union as a monolith but as an amalgam of ideological, nationalist, and imperialistic tendencies. It had been placed on the defensive by the combination of Khrushchev's revelations of Stalin's crimes and Soviet repression of upheavals in Eastern Europe. In light of its vulnerable economy and geopolitical isolation, we intended to nudge the Soviet colossus into transforming itself from a cause into a state capable of being influenced by traditional calculations of reward and punishment, thereby at first easing the Cold War and ultimately transcending it.

In that light, Nixon chose to meet his Soviet opponents face to face. He had no intention of compromising the ideals for which America stands, and he had no interest in watching the others parade before him the glories of their communist system. But in a desire to avoid all the collateral damage that armed conflict would produce and in the expectation that a tense peace could allow the Russian people to foment change from within, he met his counterparts at the table to talk. Those encounters were not easy. The two parties did not share anywhere near the amount of common ground that ordained church leaders do, but they did share two common goals: the desire to avoid armed conflict and, toward those ends, the need to slow the pace of the nuclear arms buildup. Their motives were different: Nixon was being pressured by the American people to slow the arms race, whereas the pressure being felt by the Soviets was economic. Nevertheless, the very act of meeting together, of wrestling hard-fought negotiations together, and of opening mechanisms for communication pushed the seemingly inevitable third world war off to the edge of the horizon.

In the meantime, and through the following decades, the payoff finally came. Two decades later, with the addition of Ronald Reagan's instinctive ability to rally American idealism (Nixon never had been effective at rallying people's enthusiasm!), the policy of détente bought final victory, symbolized in the tearing down of the Berlin Wall.

The ecclesiastical implications of the Nixonian policy of détente should be self-evident. First, the expectation that the church's present conflicts ought to be brought to a decisive conclusion in short order does not match with the lessons of history. Wilson was a great statesman but a Wilsonian vision for decisive, complete victory is an unreachable dream. A more realistic expectation calls for the church to live in a state of ongoing tension, as passionate believers of varying GodViews continue to vie for the right to shape the church's mission in the world.

Second, patience in times of peace will generally bring about more substantive change than will a frontal attack. In times of direct conflict, such as churchwide votes on controversial amendments, fixed, hardened, and polarized positions inevitably result as advocates do all they can to castigate their respective opponents in absolute, radical, conspiratorial terms. When put on the defensive, we all harden our positions and paint ourselves into ideological corners that we would have happily avoided if the circumstances had not pushed us there. Prior to Nixon's presidency, the Soviet system had continued in force for two generations, and the people made enormous sacrifices to support it, as long as a perceived threat—the czars, then the Nazis, and then the evil American empire—was pressing them to make such sacrifices. But when the dangers were minimized, even that highly controlled nation discovered things like Western TV and radio broadcasts, rock and roll music, and blue jeans. Soon the Soviet system changed from within. So, too, when church leaders come to the table to talk—and resolve not to misrepresent one another but, instead, seek to affirm and admonish one another—the church can pull back from extremist, polarized positions, it can back away from fundamentalist takeovers and apostate backsliding and find a semblance of peace, albeit a tense peace.

Third, while resisting the tendency to paper over real differences between those holding different GodViews, we need also to avoid the opposite tendency to presume the worst of those with whom we disagree. We ought to listen carefully for the nuances in each others' thinking, for the ambiguities that necessarily come with any genuine effort to live at once in the two realms—of God's rule and of secular society. If church history teaches us anything, it tells us that conflicts, debates, and disagreements have been with us always and that the polarization of those debates has brought upon the cause of Christ foolish and unnecessary shipwrecks. We need to listen to and to beg for a change in rhetoric, away from that which accuses and defends to one that explains and seeks to understand.

Fourth, leaders will lead either the assault or the reconciliation. While the scriptures do utilize militaristic language to speak of God's mission in the world, the prevailing language of the New Testament is that of reconciliation. "So if anyone is in Christ, there is a new creation: everything old has passed away; see, everything has become new! All this is from God, who reconciled us to himself through Christ, and has given us the ministry of reconciliation . . ." (2 Cor. 5:17ff).

In William Westom's analysis of the pluralism that prevails within Presbyterianism, he poses the notion that a healthy competition results when such voices come to the table.[21] Georg Simmel's research points out that within the tension of "competitive pluralism . . . competitors are induced to give their best efforts in order to achieve their own ends, while society as a whole benefits from the sum of these best efforts."[22] That is particularly true when among the GodViews, the Confessionalists and Activists so often play off one another. The tradition-challenging Activist GodView and the tradition-preserving Confessionalist GodView tend to be the most outspoken in denominational battles, and indeed they do tend to play off one another's ideas with counter-ideas.

That competition is not limited to the realm of the Activists and Confessionalists. The Devotionalists and Altruists play off one another, too. The interplay of these mind-sets is powerfully manifest in Luke's telling of Jesus' conversation with a lawyer.

> "Teacher," he said, "what must I do to inherit eternal life?" He said to him, "What is written in the law? What do you read there?" He answered, "You shall love the Lord your God with all your heart, and with all your soul, and with all your strength, and with all your mind; and your neighbor as yourself." And he said to him, "You have given the right answer; do this, and you will live." (Luke 10:25–28)

But then he pressed the question, "And who is my neighbor?" (Luke 10:29). Jesus proceeds to tell the story of the Good Samaritan, which brings the clear message that one must love neighbor as self, even if that delays the fulfillment of one's religious duties. The Good Samaritan story shouts forth the Altruist calling. But then Luke immediately tells the story of Jesus' visit in the home of Mary and Martha, where the one doing service is scolded in favor of the one who "has chosen the better part," namely, to listen adoringly to Jesus (Luke 10:41). The story of Mary and Martha shouts forth the Devotionalist calling. Which message should prevail in the church's life and ministry, the love of neighbor or the love of God? In the Great Commandment, love of God and of neighbor come together to be a two-pronged call for all of us, even if one comes more naturally than the other.

When church leaders gather around a table to press for the priority on their GodViews, they effectively press for part of the message presented in the gospels themselves. Ought not all the voices be at the table together? Can we not gain from the interchange that comes when we—who may not instinctively trust one another and who will want to press our own points—talk and listen to one another around a common table?

Some certainly may suspect that their theological sparring partners are wolves in sheeps' clothing, but as Calvin and others are quick to remind us,

> let them hear the parable from Christ's lips that compares the church to a net in which all kinds of fish are gathered and are not sorted until laid out on the shore [Matt. 13:47–58]. Let them hear that it is like a field sown with good seed which is through the enemy's deceit scattered with tares and is not purged of them until the harvest is brought into the threshing floor [Matt. 13:24–30]. Let them hear finally that it is like a threshing floor on which grain is so collected that it lies hidden under the chaff until, winnowed by fan and sieve, it is at last stored in the granary [Matt. 3:12]. But if the Lord declares that the church is to labor under this evil—to be weighed down with the mixture of the wicked—until the Day of Judgment, they are vainly seeking a church besmirched with no blemish. (*Institutes* IV, I, 13).

Two Models

To change from the ancient farming and fishing images to a more contemporary one, imagine a giant, enclosed stadium like the Astrodome wherein all the risers have been removed. Instead, the whole area is but one giant floor on which are found round café tables, about fifteen inches in diameter, around each of which are five chairs. Imagine that at each of those tables are seated five visionary, impassioned believers, each of which is driven by a gut-level conviction regarding God's work in the world. Each of the GodViews is represented at each table. Imagine all five at every table being so close that their knees keep bumping in to each other. Imagine all five praying together expressions of thanks for their oneness in Christ and the gospel. Imagine then the five engaging a discussion on any one of a number of controversial subjects. Needless to say, this vision is not a quiet vision. The discussion would be boisterous, argumentative, and conflicted. At the end of the day they all would be exhausted for having had the exchange. But just before the end of the day, they set aside their differences, they relax their shoulders, they slow their breathing, and they pass a loaf of bread and a cup of wine around each table. They share the Lord's Supper with some folks they now know without doubt to be sisters and brothers in Christ.

As the gathering is dismissed they take with them a few surprise insights. For one, they now realize that some substantial points of agreement exist between them and their discussion partners. For another they realize that some of the things they were sure the others believe—well, they don't. For yet another, they are struck with an insight or two that they gained into their own faith. Most of all, they feel that, without doubt, they had been heard, their calling has been affirmed, and their faith has been strengthened.

Too idealistic? Well, such a vision would not solve all the conflicts of the church. A Nixonian realism tempers the Wilsonian dream. But a few such events strung together over time could help the church adjust the volume of its arguments. It might moderate the polarization of its debaters. It might help find ways to solve this generation's pressing theological and moral issues that could prove more effective than did past generations of the church.

Coming together to talk has value, if that conversation is structured carefully and thoughtfully.

Imagine another vision for conversation. This one comes by way of Salim Munayer's reconciliation ministry in Israel-Palestine. I put the question to him bluntly, "How can you possibly get Christians, Muslims, and Jews to talk together?"

"That's easy," he said. "I take a few dozen of them out on a five-day wilderness journey in the Sinai peninsula. I pair them up with a stranger and put them on the back of a camel for the trek. They both are so scared of the camel that they forget to hate each other."[23]

Munayer elaborates that the unchosen alliance formed against the camel opens the door for real conversations around evening campfires. A few weeks after the trek, they reunite, this time to visit together a site or two where one's people committed an atrocity against the other's. In the midst of the exchanges, they discover ways to talk about their common hunger for peace and their diversely different dreams for how it might be realized. It's working for some Palestinians and Israelis. Perhaps it could work with some Protestants, too.

We do need each other. That need finds its greatest hope and challenge in one book. We need to take a look at the book to see if it its pages can help plot our course through the wilderness.

Chapter 12

Rethinking Our Believing

So what do you want to talk about?" It always makes me nervous when a group leader opens the discussion that way. Sounds like he or she has not prepared anything, and I wonder if my time would be more productively spent taking a nap. Worse, such an open question sets the stage for all the participants simply to share what's on their minds, what agendas they bring, and what opinions they have formed. In early 1998, as presbyteries launched into voting on the Fidelity-Chastity Amendment, the first and last "Common Ground" meeting for Presbyterians brought competing leaders to the table to redirect their conversations away from controversies to their common fellowship in Christ. The conveners asked the participants to share the story of their spiritual journey. For two days, one story after another was shared—heartwarming stories, dramatic stories, deep-felt stories. A spirit of mutuality seemed to fill the room. Then as time was nearing the end, one of the guests spoke up, "Folks, we've got an elephant in the living room. Are we going to deal with it, or are we just here to share stories?" Suddenly the sense of koinonia was broken, debate erupted, and the leaders left in a huff. Some were offended that their time had been stolen by folks wanting to relive a high-school campfire experience. Others were angered that one person had the gall to overturn their attempt to build bridges where only walls had existed.

Other attempts at dialogue have followed that one, and usually with better results. Usually they have acknowledged the elephant— the heated controversies that divide—and increasingly they have met around an open book.

For Christians to fellowship together with integrity, a common source of information is needed. Just as the past chapter outlined the common core of beliefs and practices required of church officers—the essential starting point for meaningful dialogue—the follow-through on that dialogue, the ability to converse about the hot-button issues, hinges upon our ability to read together from that book, the holy Bible. There can be no other starting point. Sure, we say that Jesus, the living Word, has priority over the written word; we worship the Savior, not the book written about him. But just as philosophy invariably begins with epistemology—how we come to know what we know—so, too, faith begins with the revelation of God, the vehicle by which God has become known to us.

The opening paragraph of the Westminster Confession states the point clearly:

> Although the light of nature, and the works of creation and providence, do so far manifest the goodness, wisdom, and power of God, as to leave men inexcusable; yet are they not sufficient to give that knowledge of God, and of his will, which is necessary unto salvation; therefore it pleased the Lord, at sundry times, and in divers manners, to reveal himself, and to declare that will unto his Church; and afterwards for the better preserving and propagating of the truth, and for the more sure establishment and comfort of the Church against the corruption of the flesh, and the malice of Satan and of the world, to commit the same wholly unto writing; which maketh the Holy Scripture to be most necessary; those former ways of God's revealing his will unto his people being now ceased. (6.001)

As stated in the second chapter, the priority of mission over theology ("theology divides, mission unites") has tended to push the Bible off the table and onto the shelf. That tendency has been compounded by the bewilderment that overwhelms Bible students who have encountered fields of scholarly biblical studies. Given that no other book in the history of the world has been scrutinized even one tenth as much as the Bible, the sheer glut of critical studies has caused many to throw up their hands in despair at the first thought of doing Bible study in the midst of real controversies. "You can make the Bible say whatever you want it to say," says one of the dismissive conclusions. "Everyone has their own interpretations," says another. "I don't know Greek or Hebrew; what right do I have to claim that I know what it says?" queries still another. So the Bible collects dust.

Yet for good reason the Reformed tradition in particular and the universal Christian church as a whole draw their identity, their self-understanding, their mission, their doctrine, their ethics, and their morals all from this one book. Apart from our own subjective experiences, which are individually perceived without any objective standard of measurement, the only reliable source for all our believing is the collection of writings called the Bible. If the church has any hope of addressing its present-day issues as well as future ones, it must read the Bible together.

In spite of the popular books and movements pointing in a contrary direction, there never has been a better time to read scripture. After two hundred years of scholarly suspicion hovering like a dark cloud over scripture study, several breakthroughs in recent years have refounded scholarly interest in the Bible. For one thing, great biblical scholars of the liberal tradition have changed their approach from one of arguing against the scientific and historical accuracy of scripture to one that favors listening to its originally intended meanings. Over the past two hundred years, the academic world has been enamored with empirical studies: whatever the scientists could observe, could discover, and could manipulate through experimentation—that would be believed. In that light, biblical stories like a seven-day creation, like a man spending three days in the belly of a fish, like a talking donkey, like a child being born to a virgin—all brought guffaws from science departments of leading universities. Add the fact that several historical accounts in scripture contradict other accounts of the same event, and historians have just rolled their eyes when enthusiastic students tried to convince them to "Believe the Bible!"

However, a curious thing has happened of late in the universities: confidence in the empirical task has waned. Modernistic empiricism has given way to postmodern pluralism, and the need to substantiate these ancient writings by modern scientific-historiographic standards has given way to a genuine desire to hear the manuscripts on their own terms. "What were they trying to say?" has become the dominant question in the study of scripture. Oh, the Jesus Seminar and a few other iconoclastic scholars still retain their affection for empirical study of the manuscripts in a 1950s approach to scholarly study; and many excellent scholars caution anybody who claims to get inside the head of any ancient author, but the vast majority of biblical scholars has followed the lead of Brevard Childs, Walter Brueggemann, and others who are reviving the traditional aim of biblical interpretation. They are asking, simply, "What does the text say?"

Getting to the Point of the Text

The reformers spoke often of the need to grasp the plain meaning of the text of scripture, and for good reason. The Roman Catholic Church had maintained an exclusive hold on biblical interpretation, telling the masses that only the priests could adequately interpret its meaning. Indeed the translation of the text into the language of the people was forbidden for centuries. But at the initiative of John Hus, John Wycliffe, and their followers, the scriptures were translated for the people. As the reformers began unfolding the text for the people, it became increasingly clear to them that God had spoken in these texts not just for scholars or clerics to understand, but for all the people both to read and to grasp its meaning. They came to lift up before the people the simple need to read the scriptures for the plain meaning of the text, working with the assumption that the writers were writing what they intended to mean and meaning what they wrote. The biblical authors were communicating God's word to the recipients to be understood by them, and now centuries later those listening in on those ancient conversations ought to listen accordingly. Westminster elaborates:

> All things in Scripture are not alike plain in themselves, nor alike clear unto all; yet those things which are necessary to be known, believed, and observed, for salvation, are so clearly propounded and opened in some place of Scripture or other, that not only the learned, but the unlearned, in a due use of the ordinary means, may attain unto a sufficient understanding of them. (6.007)

Of course, some interpretive challenges arise when one is reading somebody else's mail, or in this specific situation, when reading scriptures written thousands of years ago and thousands of miles away. But utilizing an informed common sense, we need to do our best to hear the texts on their own terms.

In order to do an adequate job of listening faithfully to the scriptures, especially when facing tough controversies, one must set one's sight upon the original writer's intention when writing. What was Paul trying to convey to the Galatians? What was John's point in writing his first letter? How did the writer of Acts expect his recipients to apply what he was writing? What was David trying to convey when writing the twenty-third Psalm? What was Koheleth trying to say in writing Ecclesiastes? Several related questions must be asked to arrive at least at a preliminary answer.

First, what writing style did the writer or writers utilize to convey the message? If the style was a direct communication like a letter or a sermon, then its message will be direct. If the style is recounting history, then its moral, if there is one, probably will be more subtle. If the style is poetic, then its meaning will be more evocative and suggestive. If the style is proverbial, then it mostly will provide wise insights into how life generally—but not always—works. This already may sound unnecessarily complicated, but these differences are pretty obvious to anybody who reads the daily newspaper. We all know the difference between front-page headlines, comic strips, editorials, classified ads, and weather reports. We instinctively interpret each one within the context of its own style.

Second, each verse of scripture falls within the context of a conversation that shapes its meaning. That context entails both the historical situation that occasioned the writing and the flow of ideas that move through the communication itself. In order to understand that particular verse, the whole communication needs to be read in its entirety, keeping a particular eye to hints regarding the situation being addressed—the historical context—and paying particular attention to the movements of ideas that carry through the communication—the literary context. A simple example: Philippians 4:19 reads, "And my God will fully satisfy every need of yours according to his riches in glory in Christ Jesus." At face value that sounds like a blanket guarantee that no person will ever lack any need at any time in life. However, even a quick review of the letter reveals that one of the central reasons for this epistle was that the apostle wanted to express thanks and commendation to the Philippians for taking up a generous offering to support his ministry needs. In large part, this is a thank-you letter. In the context of the thanksgiving, he closes his letter by applying to these ministry partners the principle expressed by Jesus, "Give, and it will be given to you . . ." (Luke 6:38). Does this constitute a promise for all people at all times? Not really. But it certainly is a reminder of God's blessing that awaits those who give generously to the service of the Lord.

Context helps spell out the meaning of any text.

Third, the plain meaning of any text is weighed and applied best when compared with other scriptures relating to it. Westminster helps here: "The infallible rule of interpretation of scripture, is the Scripture itself; and therefore, when there is a question about the true and full sense of any scripture (which is not manifold, but one), it may be searched and known by other places that speak more clearly" (6.009). This principle of the analogy of scripture is necessitated by the varying modes of communication used by God in providing the scriptures for the church's use. Not all scriptures speak with the same voice on a topic. For example, fidelity in marriage between a man and a woman is clearly taught at points in scripture, but at other points leaders such as Abraham, Moses, and David take more than one wife, with no apparent condemnation for those acts. Should the church indulge infidelity in that light? Surely not. But the church's call to fidelity for married couples emerges only when comparing all texts and teachings on the subject and weighing the particular teachings within their contexts wherever they appear in the scriptures.

Other teachings become less dogmatically held—such as the competing views on baptism, predestination, and freewill; the nature of Christ's presence in the Lord's Supper; and the fulfillment of future prophecies—when we allow all texts on relevant topics to be weighed together. Frankly, the church does well when it exhibits sufficient humility to admit where the word of God is intentionally ambiguous.

These first three principles, namely the need to read the texts within their literary style, within their context, and in comparison to other related texts, is well summarized in the words of the Second Helvetic Confession:

> THE TRUE INTERPRETATION OF SCRIPTURE. The apostle Peter has said that the Holy Scriptures are not of private interpretation (II Peter 1:20), and thus we do not allow all possible interpretations. . . . But we hold that interpretation of the Scripture to be orthodox and genuine which is gleaned from the Scriptures themselves (from the nature of the language in which they were written, likewise according to the circumstances in which they were set down, and expounded in the light of like and unlike passages and of many and clearer passages) and which agree with the rule of faith and love, and contributes much to the glory of God and man's salvation. (5.010)

Consistent Ambiguity or Inconsistent Clarity?

While following the particular commonsense approach to interpreting scripture outlined above, well-meaning Christians still too often find themselves at odds with one another over the meaning of particular scriptures. The need to draw overarching conclusions, that is, to do theology, presses us to deal with those challenges. From the point of this observer, it appears that many in the church have gravitated to one answer or its alternative. Generally speaking, the Confessionalists have opted to focus on what is clearly spoken in scripture and to proclaim that message unambiguously, even if that word does not apply equally in all circumstances. For example, most Confessionalists believe and teach that sexual relations should be shared only within the confines of a marriage, a life-long covenant. They will proclaim "fidelity in marriage and chastity in singleness" as a moral absolute and will bemoan the loss of such moral absolutes in society. However, the vast majority of the population does not wait until the wedding night to share their first intimate act. When an engaged couple, already living together, asks a Confessionalist minister to perform their wedding, in all likelihood that minister will perform the wedding, perhaps asking the couple to refrain from any additional intimacy until the wedding, perhaps saying nothing at all. Does that couple meet the moral standards the minister proclaims? Absolutely not. Does the minister change the standards to indulge the behavior? No. But does the minister go ahead and perform the wedding anyway? In most cases, yes. How absolute is the absolute? The standards continue to be taught with clarity, even if they are not applied consistently. Approximations and exceptions may be allowed, but they are not discussed.

Other leaders cry foul. Activist clergy insist that the Confessionalist is playing loose with the truth. "If you really believe in moral absolutes, then you ought to apply them absolutely," they say. In order to have what they consider to be a more honest and consistent set of standards, they will generalize those standards to fit all situations. Terms like "committed relationship" are offered as a substitute for covenanted marriage. Nobody should be having sexual intimacy outside a committed relationship, they may say, and if and when that relationship has progressed to the point of making a lifelong commitment (moving from "exclusive for now" to "exclusive for life"), the marriage will be performed. This model of fidelity then embraces exceptions and approximations as equally valid to the covenanted marriage, and, while ambiguous in its proclamation, still is applied consistently.

Which is better, inconsistent clarity or consistent ambiguity? An argument can be made for either approach. That very question begs for conversation by those seated around the café tables, upholding the various GodViews. In the meantime, the basic, commonsense principles of interpretation still beg for more principles to guide such discussions.

The Decisive Christ

When it comes to interpreting and applying biblical teachings on such things as marriage, fidelity, divorce, and many other issues, we need more help than the commonsense, plain-meaning counsel offered above. We need to be given some criteria with which we can judge which biblical texts should overrule others when we find ourselves truly caught between contradicting options.

The central criterion for Christian biblical interpretation is the person and work of Jesus Christ. The life, ministry, death, and resurrection of Jesus mark the decisive act that has changed everything for the Christian. Yes, the revelation of God made throughout the Hebrew scriptures still remains in force, but the most significant teachings of the Old Testament are reinforced and clarified by Jesus. Some are disregarded by Jesus. Others are completely recast by Jesus. What's more, the followers of Jesus, the authors of the other New Testament books, also reshaped the meaning of numerous Old Testament teachings in the light of the decisive impact of Jesus in human history. Getting specific . . .

Given that the Bible is Jesus' story, a Christ-centered interpretation of scripture will always ask first, "How does Jesus' incarnation, teaching, ministry, crucifixion, resurrection, enthronement, and sending of the Holy Spirit recast this particular scripture?" Some scriptures, such as the servant texts in Isaiah, surge to front-page status while Levitical requirements for blood sacrifice find their fulfillment (and in the case of animal sacrifices, their cessation) in the Christ event.

Second, given Jesus' mission to reach the lost and needy, a Christ-centered interpretation of scripture will ask, "How does this text align with and/or reflect Christ's mission in the world?" As the late mission scholar David J. Bosch has said, "Contemporary New Testament scholars are thus affirming what the systematic theologian Martin Kahler said eight decades ago: Mission is 'the mother of theology.'" He continues:

> The New Testament writers were not scholars who had the leisure to research the evidence before they put pen to paper. Rather, they wrote in the context of an "emergency situation," of a church which, because of its missionary encounter with the world, was forced to theologize. The gospels, in particular, are to be viewed not as writings produced by an historical impulse but as expressions of an ardent faith, written with the purpose of commending Jesus Christ to the Mediterranean world.[1]

In that vein, the GodViews all seek to understand and fill out the mission to which they have been called largely by appropriating the example and instruction of Jesus. Whereas the Judaism into which he was born fostered an isolationist outlook and a survival mentality, Jesus was born to do mission. He commissioned the disciples to do mission. Driven by the love of God, scripture was provided to give direction to our mission. That mission calls us to consider the Christ-mission whenever we seek to understand and interpret any biblical text.

Third, Christ-centered biblical interpretation recognizes that Christ is our clarifier. Given his mission focus, Jesus reshaped our understanding of many texts in that light. In the Sermon on the Mount he reminds his followers of the teachings of the Hebrew scriptures, "You have heard it said." But he then rejoins, "But I say to you. . . ." He sets his teaching above and beyond that which preceded him. One key example comes when wrestling with sabbath laws. He recasts all ceremonial laws, and perhaps all laws altogether, with his summary statement, "Sabbath is made for humankind, not humankind for the sabbath" (Mark 2:27). To him, the Law was given to help accomplish God's mission to love people, not simply to preserve divine sanctity. Accordingly, our interpretation of scripture must follow his pattern of putting higher priorities on the teachings in which he placed higher priority, and on the teachings his disciples emphasized.

Along these lines it might be helpful to revisit the fundamentalist-modernist debate and ask a century after the fact, "Are there nonnegotiable fundamentals, essential tenets that can be articulated in simple terms to finally establish boundaries between truth and error?" Confessionalist Christians often will say that, in order to find the center, one must define the boundaries. "If there are no boundaries there can be no center," so they say. However, as Vernon Broyles suggests, "That makes great sense until you consider the solar system."[2] There exists no known boundary, but there certainly exists a core, and that core defines not only the location of all that revolves around it; it determines the heat or lack thereof on every object following an orbit around it. Those whose orbit is closest at hand bask in the heat the sun emits. Those far away suffer paralyzing cold. So, too, with the faith. Those beliefs and believers who hover near the core enjoy the power of the truth inherent in those essential tenets. Beliefs and believers who deviate far away from the core suffer the chill that distance creates. While the actual articulation of a particular list of essential doctrines continues to elude anyone's grasp—for many good reasons—the existence of core convictions provide the power, light, and heat that illumine and warm the faith of the believers. And what is that core? It is Jesus Christ—incarnate Son of God, teacher, healer, suffering savior, resurrected lord, ascended sovereign. Jesus Christ is the core. While a bounded-set theology would make life a little simpler, a centered-set theology makes life more exciting and energizing.

With Christ at the center, two other key interpretive principles remain. First, one ought always to interpret the Bible today in the light of how it has been interpreted through the ages. Faithful interpretation of scripture will "be guided by the doctrinal consensus of the church, which is the 'rule of faith.'"[3] Deviations from traditional beliefs—necessary as they are at times—ought to be embraced and promoted only after thorough reflection, study, and counsel.

Finally, all interpretation of scripture requires the active role of the Holy Spirit, whom Jesus promised would "remind you of all that I have said" (John 14:26) and would "guide you into all the truth" (John 16:13). More shall be said on this in chapter 15, but suffice it to say that it is the third member of the trinity whose presence and gifts of knowledge, discernment, and wisdom are the only ultimate hope for sainted, sinful students of scripture to fall into accurate understandings of God's word. We need the Holy Spirit to lead, teach, and interpret.

Can our hope for meaningful dialogue come to fruition? Can we anticipate a mutual experience of learning to result, as we gather around café tables, in "speaking the truth in love" as we understand that truth and love? If we follow these basic methods of biblical interpretation—ones shared with a broad consensus of reformed beliefs—then we can expect to learn together with God's word to be our rule of faith and practice.

In *The Divided Church*, Hutcheson and Shriver offer an encouraging word along these lines.

> Yet if it is our view of Scripture that most basically divides us, it is also our common commitment to the Bible that offers our greatest hope. We Protestant Christians are inescapably a people of the Word. We may regard the Bible as the Word of God, as the heart of 'the tradition' or as a witness to humankind's struggle to understand the nature and purpose of God. But to the extent that it is authoritative for us, Scripture itself points inexorably to the need—indeed the absolute necessity—for reconciliation among quarreling people who consider themselves disciples of Jesus Christ. 'Is Christ divided?' Paul asked the squabbling Corinthians. This remains the question that a polarized church must ask itself when seeking to live out a gospel of love.[4]

Yes, there is hope in the revelation of God given in scripture. But how do we talk about it? How can we discuss our beliefs, our convictions, our GodViews and find some points of connection as well as ways of learning from each other? If it is true that one should never talk in social situations about such things as religion—given the volatility that can erupt—is there any way we who have invested so much of ourselves into our faith can actually talk about it in a mannerly way? We surely need help here.

Chapter 13

Redignifying Our Disputing

*I*t's been over ten years since the big event, but the favorite family story Barbie, David, Kelly, and I love to retell is of the famous Haberer family food fight. Barbie had undergone minor surgery a few days before, and after three days of eating the canned and boxed soups I knew to prepare, she was ready for a real meal. She even felt energetic enough to get out of bed and prepare the family's favorite, "Skull Valley Special"—named not for its ingredients but for the town in California where it was created. The kitchen table was filled with serving dishes, each containing one of the ingredients that were to be piled one on top of the other on our individual plates: white rice, cooked chopped beef, grated cheddar cheese, chopped lettuce, chopped tomatoes, homemade salad dressing, and crushed Fritos.

After saying grace, each plate was piled high, and we dug into our feast. The conversation was lively, given the ages of our chattering kids, David being ten and Kelly eight. However, as we emptied our plates, Barbie's remained full. Staring down at her food, and poking at it with her fork, she said, "I thought I had an appetite, but the sight of the food turns me off." Feeling devious, I perched a grain of rice on my fork, turned it upside down, and cocked it as if ready to fling it at Barbie. The kids looked at me and then at her, the expressions of expectant glee coming over their faces. Barbie looked over at me and realized she was about to become a target. "Don't you dare," she said, "or you'll be sorry."

Never one to turn down a dare, I let fly that single grain of rice. But Barbie is quite the competitive type, a natural athlete. As one who has embarrassed many a self-assured male in the game of ping-pong, she was not about to let me fire the last shot. Quickly surveying the plates, she realized that she had more food remaining than the rest of us combined. In the blink of an eye, she picked up her plate and machine-gunned her food a full 270 degrees, splattering all three of us. Immediately we picked up whatever we had left on our plates and threw it back at her. Soon every serving dish was emptied; then eight hands scrambled to scoop whatever food had landed on the table and hurl it at any available target. In about a minute's time, no food remained on the table. The floor, walls, and sliding glass door were plastered with our leftovers.

"I'm not feeling well," Barbie said nonchalantly. "I'm going back to bed." She disappeared.

"I need to take care of Mom," I stated. "It's kids' night to clean the kitchen." I disappeared too.

"Lady! Brandy!" yelled the kids to the two family dogs. "We've got homework to do." Lickety-split, we all vanished.

An hour later, I checked out the mess. Sure enough, the dogs did an admirable cleaning job. The kitchen looked quite clean, all except for the small starch spots remaining on the sliding glass door.

To this day, when the kids visit home for holidays and reminisce about favorite memories, this story is the first one told: a family food fight to beat all family food fights . . . and the happiest of memories to tell.

Fighting the Bad Fight

Unfortunately, not many fights leave happy memories in the minds of all the participants. Some fights do produce satisfied victors, especially in the world of boxing, wrestling, and other contact sports. But each of those victors leaves behind a defeated foe. Many fights produce many more losers than winners, as in the NCAA Basketball tournament, which begins with sixty-four teams, of which sixty-three end their season with a loss; only the champion ends with a win.

As we have seen, when churches fight, the whole church suffers, if only because the shrapnel effect scatters collateral damage in every direction. However, as we also have seen, only a Polyanna is naïve enough to think that we can avoid conflict simply by deciding to get along. We cannot paper over our differences, many of which are driven by passionate GodViews, which can be instructed but must not be suppressed. The church needs to be informed and guided by the variety of ideas, dreams, visions, and fears that such GodViews bring to the laboratory of church inquiry.

Can we learn to get along even when we don't get along? Can we at least learn to fight fairly?

Our culture has grown accustomed to dirty fighting. Such has become the stock-in-trade of many television and radio interview programs, where guests willingly endure humiliation in order to experience their fifteen minutes of fame. Dirty fighting has cut a path to victory for some politicians, who make false, scandalous accusations of their opponents, and then, when counteraccused, claim that their opponent is playing dirty. And then there are the movies: what's more popular than Mafia movies, or *Dirty Harry* movies, or countless movies that herald the sly, underhanded maneuvering of the unscrupulous hero?

We are accustomed to fighting. In fact, the very language used in everyday conversation is replete with expressions befitting war colleges. Athletes *battle* for gold. Senators *fight* to get votes. The government *declares war* on poverty. A mother waiting for a tardy teenager mutters, "I'm going to *kill* him when he gets home."

In the book, *The Argument Culture*, sociolinguist Deborah Tannen warns of the damage such warfare metaphors have on all our lives: "Our spirits are corroded by living in an atmosphere of unrelenting contention—an argument culture. The argument culture urges us to approach the world—and the people in it—in an adversarial frame of mind. It rests on the assumption that opposition is the best way to get anything done: The best way to discuss an idea is to set up a debate . . . the best way to begin an essay is to attack someone; and the best way to show you're really thinking is to criticize."[1]

One would hope that the church could be exempt from such thinking, but the culture of criticism and personal attack is thriving in the church. Passionate believers scrutinize the activities of other passionate-but-contrary-minded believers; they draw inferences from what they observe, and soon vituperative denunciations fill religious news reports. Internet chat rooms flood their participants with breaking news and comments (with little, if any, attempt made to differentiate news from comments). Interest groups rally protests and prosecutions. And those caught on the critics' radar screens take on a siege mentality, defending not only the good they were doing but promoting even the aspects that they'd just as soon disavow—were it not for the vilification being published by their critics. Soon every issue, whether a new idea or an old tradition, finds proponents and opponents arguing for votes for or against. Charges are filed to reverse errors. And the two-party theory reemerges as the pat summary of all conflicts.

Just as the two-party theory misrepresents the much more complicated convictions of those so categorized, so, too, a debate that polarizes into two opposite positions robs the church of intelligent inquiry. So many issues beg for options that lie somewhere between the two extremes of totally "A" or totally "Z." How about "G" or "R"? Polarized debates disallow such options even to be considered. So many issues, such as that of human sexual orientation, are replete with so many ambiguities. Will anybody out there please acknowledge that human sexual desire is more complex than that which can be boiled down to a singular genetic chromosome? The two options offered by a two-option debate that insists on winning "all the way" defy intelligent reflection.

To Debate or To Dialogue?

The present climate in the church, one that divides into two opposite options between which the masses must make an all-or-nothing choice, requires all passionate believers to engage in debate. As good debaters, they press the point for their positions while the opponents press the point for their opposite positions. As Tannen points out, this approach has become the method of choice for most investigative reporting and much academic research, but it often blocks the way to significant insight:

> Our determination to pursue truth by setting up a fight between two sides leads us to believe that every issues has two sides—no more, no less: If both sides are given a forum to confront each other, all the relevant information will emerge, and the best case will be made for each side. But opposition does not lead to truth when an issue is not composed of two opposing sides but is a crystal of many sides. Often the truth is in the complex middle, not the oversimplified extremes. . . . If you begin with the assumption that there must be an "other side," you may end up scouring the margins of science or the fringes of lunacy to find it.[2]

Not only that, but the very process of framing issues into only two options between which thinking persons must argue ends up muzzling key thinkers. People who like to argue do argue; people who don't, don't.

Nowhere is the dropout rate more obvious than in the churches, where most Devotionalists and Ecclesiasts shy away from debating the hot-button issues facing denominational governing bodies. In fact, many clergy, who will speak out passionately on the national scene regarding those controversial issues, know better than to do so when preaching to everyday Christians in the pews. In most congregations the hometown folks are more concerned about the experience of worship and the effectiveness of the church's youth ministry than they ever will be on the denomination's policies on ecumenical relationships or capital punishment. Sadly, though, the hot-button issues do flame up at those national assemblies, and the most convinced, dogmatic voices are amplified while the more negotiable voices are muzzled.

It need not be this way. While debates will rage, unavoidably so, the church can also set the table for dialogues.

A world of difference stands between a debate and a dialogue. For one thing, a debate aims for victory, while a dialogue aims for insight. When engaged in a debate the whole purpose is to win. The key to winning is that of stating your points as clearly and compellingly as possible and dismantling the other's points as decisively and irredeemably as possible. Consequently, "you're usually not trying to understand what the other person is saying, or what in their experience leads them to say it. Instead, you're readying your response: listening for weaknesses in logic to leap on, points you can distort to make the other person look bad and yourself look good."[3] On the other hand, dialogue seeks to learn together, as in a group research project to which one might be assigned in high school or college.

That's not to say that dialogue exists as an end in itself. Neither, as some charge, is a call to dialogue simply a device created by antitraditionalists to bend the minds of traditionalists. Dialogue as an educational method invites participants both to offer understandings that they bring to a subject and to hear the understandings others bring. In such a process, one person may prove to be the true expert and all other participants totally ignorant, but not very often. In most cases, different participants bring to a dialogue a mix of good information and bad, a mix of truth and prejudice, a set of experiences that color one's perception but can add color to the perceptions of the others sharing together. Do all dialogues produce greater wisdom? Of course not, but their noncombative structure lends itself much better than the debate format to the ultimate possibility of reaching insight, both on the receiving end and the giving end.

Second, a debate criticizes others' ideas, whereas dialogue reports one's perceptions. Experts in human relations always insist that in conflicted situations, one of the first rules is the need to report feelings rather than to accuse or blame the other person. In *Caring Enough to Confront*, David Augsburger advises, "When angry, I want to give clear, simple 'I messages.' 'You messages' are most often attacks, criticisms, devaluations of the other person, labels, or ways of fixing blame. 'I messages' are honest, clear, confessional. 'I messages' own my anger, my responsibility, my demands without placing blame."[4] This is no less true when discussing issues of theological, ethical, or ecclesiastical significance. Without doubt, many a theological controversy could have been avoided if only the critics would have checked out their information before drawing conclusions. So often—though not always—the real problem has been more one of miscommunication than of misbelief or misbehavior.

What a difference when folks check out their perceptions before jumping to conclusions! It usually does not take a lot of effort to do so: for example, "I hear that your conference speaker belittled the crucifixion as a picture of God being an abusive father; can you correct or clarify that report?"—or "I'm troubled to hear others quoting you as opposing the church's policy on inclusive language; please fill me in." Such inquiries can go a long way to encourage insight-seeking dialogues and to avert polarizing debates. Simply put, debates accuse, but dialogues inquire.

Third, a debate impugns others' motives, whereas a dialogue trusts others' sincerity. As a Yankee transplant to Texas, I've been slow to adopt most of the traditions of this "Old West" region of the country. One thing I did learn up north—watching old Westerns—is that the "bad guys" wear black cowboy hats and the "good guys" wear white cowboy hats. Over these years, I have concluded that, in the church, *all cowhands wear white hats.* That's because, by the very nature of the fact that persons of faith are aiming to be faithful to God's will, they see themselves as ones on the Lord's side. As theologian Miroslav Volf says, "in a world so manifestly drenched with evil everybody is innocent in their own eyes."[5] Sadly, though, as the church engages in debates, one of the first things reported is that the other side is plotting a takeover. Conspiracy theories abound when you don't know the conspirators. On the other hand, when sitting down together to discuss a whole range of issues and a variety of options regarding those issues, one can gradually come to recognize the genuine sincerity of the others' convictions. Why should it be otherwise? You hold your beliefs sincerely! So do others! We need to see the others as we would have them see us—a slight twist on the Golden Rule. To put it simply, debates demonize our opponents whereas dialogues humanize them.

Fourth, a debate tells the truth selectively where a dialogue engages the truth openly. Let's face it. Some of the ideas others raise contrary to yours sure do make some sense. But when engaging in a debate, you dare not admit that. You have to cover the flaws in your argument. Better to disregard such points and switch to your strongest arguing points. In fact, anybody coached in preparation for a radio or TV interview has been told, "If the interviewer asks a question you don't want to respond to, just change the subject to what you want to say." That is textbook advice for engaging a potentially confrontational, debating format. Far better to avoid that very style of engagement by choosing dialogue over debate. In a conversational format, all ideas can be given fair hearing, white lies can be acknowledged for what they are, half-truths can be completed to become full truths, ambiguities can be embraced, and inconclusive endings can be allowed.

Fifth, whereas a debate radicalizes ideas, a dialogue moderates them. Gregory Bateson has coined the term "symmetrical schismogenesis" to summarize the tendency for debate opponents to do "more and more of the same thing in reaction to the other."[6] Deborah Tannen illustrates:

> An illustration in a book by communication theorists shows two people in a small sailboat, holding on to opposite ends of a rope attached to the mast, leaning in opposite directions. As one pulls toward one side of the boat, the other has to lean toward the other side to prevent the boat from capsizing. This prompts the first to lean farther out, and so on, until they are hanging dangerously over opposite edges of the boat. How much better, the authors suggest, for one to let up slightly. To keep the boat balanced, the other person will have to let up, too, until both are sitting comfortably in the boat instead of hanging over its sides.[7]

The tendency to react in the extreme is especially magnified where the issues involve ultimate claims to truth, eternal salvation, and life's purpose. Debates radicalize those positions. But as the illustration suggests, dialogue invites disagreeing parties to separate misunderstandings from real differences; it encourages them to focus on major issues and deemphasize minor ones; it invites change by refraining from using intimidation as the method of choice; and it cools tempers. To put it succinctly, a debate drives weak arguments to the point of foolishness, whereas a dialogue invites participants to learn together.

The Five Most Amazing Bible
Words Regarding Human Relationships

Dialogue really works better than debate as a means both to discover truth and to encourage unity and reconciliation in relationships. Those two goals were clearly in mind when the apostolic writer addressed the Ephesians:

> We must no longer be children, tossed to and fro and blown about by every wind of doctrine, by people's trickery, by their craftiness in deceitful scheming. But speaking the truth in love, we must grow up in every way into him who is the head, into Christ, from whom the whole body, joined and knit together by every ligament with which it is equipped, as each part is working properly, promotes the body's growth in building itself up in love. (4:14–16)

What would the writer have us avoid? Immaturity, indecisiveness, gullibility, and temptation. What are we to seek? To be mature in Christ, equipped for ministry, and promoting growth in the body of Christ. How are the pitfalls to be avoided and goals to be accomplished? By "speaking the truth in love." These five words offer the most amazing, comprehensive, and instructive words on human relationships you will ever find.

What does it take to "speak the truth in love"? A love for the truth is where it begins. Commitment to the truth as revealed in scripture is central. A hunger for truth that can be discovered through scientific experimentation, logical deduction, and poetic imagination is also essential. And the attitude of an inquisitive student, recognizing that one cannot possibly have all the truth, is critical. As Oliver Cromwell put it, "I beseech you in the bowels of Christ, think it possible you may be mistaken."[8]

In a determination to love others, this five-word phrase frames one's commitment to the truth. Measured by the standard of the Great Commandment, to love neighbor as self, loving another in this context means communicating truth in the way we would wish it to be conveyed to us. Doing so requires one to avoid embarrassing the other; no one enjoys being humiliated. Doing so requires one to treat the other as a peer not as a child; no one likes to be patronized. Doing so requires one to acknowledge incomplete understanding; isn't it easier when others admit up front that they may be wrong? Doing so requires one to avoid lecturing; it is always preferable to be engaged in conversation over being scolded. Simply put, speaking the truth in love requires us to utilize the good manners our parents' generation tried to teach us. Though many of us learned them as children, sadly it seems that as adults we somehow think we now are exempt from such social requirements.

The other key element in this phrase is the action intended: speaking. Modeling the truth in love is not sufficient. That does not suffice for giving witness in a court of law, and it does not suffice for giving witness within the church. Certainly skirting the issues and avoiding the person is easier, but love says you must speak, if only for their sake—all the more for the sake of your relationship to the other.

Jesus himself articulated a couple of rules for the exercise of speaking the truth in love:

> "If another member of the church sins against you, go and point out the fault when the two of you are alone. If the member listens to you, you have regained that one. But if you are not listened to, take one or two others along with you, so that every word may be confirmed by the evidence of two or three witnesses. If the member refuses to listen to them, tell it to the church; and if the offender refuses to listen even to the church, let such a one be to you as a Gentile and a tax collector." (Matt. 18:15–17)

On only two occasions do the gospel writers quote Jesus speaking of the church. In the one instance he promises to build that church upon the rock. In this other instance he unfolds the essential rules for communication ethics, teaching dialogue as the primary means of communication in times of conflict, and only when dialogue proves unsuccessful should one use more imposing means. What are we to do if in conflict with another? We are to confront them alone and in private, providing "the maximum amount of information" with "the minimum amount of threat."[9] The goal in mind? To have the other member listen to you and for you to regain that one—that is, to persuade the other to redress the wrong and to restore the relationship. If successful, then the private conversation can remain that way, and the restored relationship will have been strengthened. If unsuccessful, then one ought to meet again, this time with two or three witnesses, who might be able to persuade or interpret the process to you and the other party, and testify after the fact as to what transpired. If, and only if, that second conversation fails should the offense become a public matter; then, and only then, should the charge be published to the court of the church and addressed under the church's disciplinary procedures.

In other words, apart from giving the church a glimpse of Christ's essential construction plans, his only other specific directives for the church—according to the gospel writers—were specific methods on how to speak the truth in love to one another within the church. Can anybody claiming to follow Jesus do otherwise than he has commanded?

A Revival of Manners

When Christians of varying GodView persuasions plead with God to revive the church, one may well hope to see it revived in its truth-telling, another its spiritual passions, and yet another in its community-building, its caregiving, or its justice-advocacy. But one revival that is desperately needed by all is a revival of manners, the manners our mothers taught us.

I well remember the manners my mother taught me. She taught me to treat people the way I would like to be treated. She taught me to listen before speaking. She taught me to check the facts before drawing conclusions. She taught me to try to trust others' intentions, no matter how ill-advised their actions might be. She taught me to express my words as graciously as possible. She taught me to be nice. She also taught me that God wanted me to use manners like these, and in fact, that Jesus taught us to do so.

If any one of us hopes to follow Jesus, we cannot follow him only when he leads us to pursue the fulfillment of our favorite GodViews. We also must follow him when he teaches us to use good manners. John Calvin did so. The premier reformed theologian, in writing his unequaled exposition of theology, the *Institutes of the Christian Religion*, apparently considered good manners to be an essential component of the theological enterprise, especially when facing conflicts within the church:

> In bearing with imperfections of life we ought to be far more considerate. For here the descent is very slippery and Satan ambushes us with no ordinary devices. For there have always been those who, imbued with a false conviction of their own perfect sanctity, as if they had already become a sort of airy spirits, spurned association with all men in whom they discern any remnant of human nature. . . . There are others who sin more out of ill-advised zeal for righteousness than out of that insane pride. . . . But on their part those of whom we have spoken sin in that they do not know how to restrain their disfavor. For where the Lord requires kindness, they neglect it and give themselves over completely to immoderate severity. Indeed, because they think no church exists where there are not perfect purity and integrity of life, they depart out of hatred of wickedness from the lawful church, while they fancy themselves turning aside from the faction of the wicked. . . . [T]hey are vainly seeking a church besmirched with no blemish." (IV, I, 13)

We need to move from debate to dialogue. We need to allow the five most amazing Bible words for human relationships, "speaking the truth in love," to guide our interactions, especially whenever we encounter those driven by different GodViews. But will we ever encounter one another? Given the ease with which we retreat into our enclaves of agreement, is there a chance of us gathering around the café tables of fellowship, conversation, and dialogue? Will somebody throw a party for us all to get together?

Chapter 14

Rerouting Our Networking

*Y*es, we need to get together. Some great party host must organize the gathering. Then again, we have to find a way to create contact between the parties. Just how might that happen?

Few trends in recent decades have had even a fraction of the impact on everyday life as has the massive expansion of communication technology. Between the multiplication of telephones, television broadcast stations, and e-mail communications, it's never been easier to "reach out and touch someone." Yet the church has never been more factionalized than it is today. How can that be? One unfortunate by-product of the information-communication explosion is its proliferation of enclaves of agreement. Of course the tendency to draw toward "people of our own kind" is nothing new, but the modern creations of specialized publications and Internet correspondence groups have lifted the single-minded interests to a level inconceivable even a decade ago. Today if you wish to engage in a conversation over the subject of "the ethical implications of subatomic research on the Dead Sea scrolls' excerpts of the Book of Isaiah" (or any other obscure subject), all you need do is create a Web site and invite inquirers into a conversation. Soon you will have a whole circle of similarly interested friends conversing electronically. The conversation may become so engaging that you end up organizing weekly conference calls, monthly regional retreats, and semiannual, international conferences. An enclave of common interest has been born!

Given the energy most Christians invest in causes and efforts corresponding to their particular GodViews, like-minded allies would only naturally band together into organizations or affinity groups. A particular cause draws us together, and the by-products of friendship, appreciation, significance, and recognition keep us together. Soon we are traveling in an orbit with people who are continually reinforcing our convictions, our passions, and our senses of call. Natural social habits and psychological needs build such affinity groups. Unfortunately, we end up missing out on the chance to learn from others who gravitate into other groups, and they miss out on what we could bring to them. The net result is that we splinter into hundreds or even thousands of disconnected affinity groups.

Governing Bodies: The Incapable Answer

When observing such splintering of the church, denominational leaders shake their heads in dismay. "This isn't what John Calvin had in mind," their troubled voices say. "We are a connectional church, united through its governing bodies." Some Ecclesiasts join in the leaders' chorus. But most believers laugh a cynical laugh and ask, "Huh? Governing bodies are supposed to connect us?"

Governing bodies, the official expression of connectionalism in the Reformed churches, certainly were created to help leaders work better together. The Confession of 1967 confirms that intention when it states that "A presbyterian polity recognizes the responsibility of all members for ministry and maintains the organic relation of all congregations in the church. . . ."[1] That organic relation finds its highest expression in the parity between laity and clergy that is central to Presbyterian polity. The governing bodies above the Session bring together the clergy and elders in a region (presbytery, synod, or national synod/assembly) to enact legislation. When necessary, they function as a court (or delegate that task to a judicial commission made up of a sampling of its members) to hear judicial cases and exercise discipline. In those meetings the ministers and elders also worship together and may share together other expressions of fellowship and mutual edification. But in many places and for many members, the connectionalism ends with adjournment until the rapping of the gavel calls the next meeting to order. For most, the connecting between meetings goes on via affinity groups.

The lack of genuine, lasting fellowship within regional governing bodies ought not surprise us. The governing bodies are, well, just that: governing bodies. They are structured to order and govern the church's service to God, congregation, and world. In the opening pages of the Presbyterian Church's *Book of Order*, the historic principles all emphasize governance. Even the chapter titled "The Church and Its Unity" says little about such values as mutual respect, friendship, and support. Rather, a sampling of phrases unveil the chapter's real emphasis: "shall be governed," "the right of review and control," "ecclesiastical jurisdiction is a shared power," "administrative authority."[2] It is all about governance.

In our day, most people who yearn for genuine friendships with colleagues resist the whole notion of church government. Sure they may welcome it when congregational conflicts require the presbytery's intervention to bring reconciliation. But for the most part, the whole notion of hierarchical power structures is anathema. Ever since the Watergate crisis, all authority figures have been just one John Dean away from being accused of corruption and power abuse. Even corporate America has flattened its pyramids and substituted "work teams," thereby bringing their workers together on equal footing with equal status and power. Relationships of trust and partnership build better among peers than among "superiors" and "subordinates."

Further still, interest in regional governing bodies has waned due to the lack of "the need to know." In past generations, clergy and active elders attending presbytery meetings would expect to hear from the leaders breaking news coming out of denominational headquarters and ecumenical councils, not to mention the latest gossip about colleagues in other parts of the presbytery and country. Regional denominational executives provided the pipeline of information. But who needs such a pipeline when news reports from denominational headquarters arrive daily in your e-mail—and when friends keep e-mailing friends their friends' news?

Frankly, affinity groups organized around common causes and interests, and facilitated by modern technologies, are replacing governing bodies as the primary point of connection between clergy and lay leaders. But we do need to join together across the lines of our affinity groups. How can we come together for mutual ministry, mutual learning, and mutual support across the lines of our GodViews? Who is going to throw a party that we all will want to attend?

A Parallel Universe

Most Protestants do not know that the Roman Catholic Church, with its history numbered in thousands of years rather than hundreds, crossed this bridge over a millennium before the beginning of the Protestant Reformation. Ask Protestants how the Roman Catholic Church is structured and they will say, "The pope rules the cardinals, the cardinals rule the bishops, the bishops rule the priests, and the priests rule their congregations." Though stated in the simplest terms, that summary is essentially correct, but only for part of the church. In the early Christian centuries, some church leaders yearned to serve God in ways that broke from typical parish duties. Some wished to enter into a more concerted, contemplative life, as in the desert fathers heading to monasteries; others wanted to become specialists in such fields as education, mission work, or church administration. So they clustered together in what today are called religious institutes, such as orders, monastic congregations, or clerical communities. Such institutes were (and continue to be) organized around an essential charter known as the "rule," as in the Rule of St. Francis or the Rule of St. Benedict. Given their popularity as vehicles through which those called to consecrated religious service can serve God in a very focused manner, these institutes have multiplied in number, with some of them—such as the largest group, the Jesuits—numbering thousands of ordained leaders serving on every continent.

The spread of these institutes posed a problem: To which local bishop should they be subject? There was no obvious answer until, in A.D. 710, the Cluny monastic center in southwest France was organized by a wealthy man who, wanting the bishop to leave him alone, submitted the whole order directly to the pope. The investiture of the order's abbot was granted directly by the pope and thereafter has continued for that order and all other orders and institutes. In other words, given the broad regional—and in some cases, international—reach of the institutes, they were brought into a direct affiliation with the pope and into parallel status with all the other institutes and orders. In effect, they were formed into a parallel universe, that is, a structure for the religious institutes that is separate from the hierarchical pyramid overseeing the noninstitute parish ministries. Within the churchwide Roman Curia (or courts), ten departments—called congregations—were later organized, including the Sacred Congregation for the Affairs of Religious. To this day all of the institutes give account directly to the pope through this Vatican City office. Whenever needed, the pope calls the leaders of the institutes to a gathering of the sacred congregation in order to discuss issues regarding the religious life, enabling them to compare, contrast, and integrate their various mission and ministry efforts and to formulate norms for all to follow.

This Roman Catholic structure cannot match up to, or meet all the needs of, mainline Protestant bodies, but it offers some lessons that might help. For one thing, the larger church needs to capitalize on the energy such groups can offer. The mainline churches typically have discouraged the organization of pan-regional affinity groups, given that they often have launched controversies and criticisms of the official policies, practices, and leaders in the churches. In the 1980s the newly reunited Presbyterian Church (U.S.A.) inherited from the northern branch a process for regulating these groups and incorporated such a structure into the ninth chapter of the Form of Government. These Chapter Nine Organizations met so much resistance that, in ten years' time, those paragraphs were excised from the *Book of Order* and the organizations were liberated from any official relationship to the denomination. The organizations continued to multiply, although this time lacking denominational recognition or oversight. What has remained is a spirit of suspicion. Indeed, galvanizing issues continue to proliferate; pan-regional communications become more efficient and broadly spread; racial-ethnic minorities seek a fair hearing; new mission strategists press their visions; and the multiplication of such diversities promises to further balkanize an already fragmented church. The time has come to stop opposing such affinity groups and, instead, to encourage their formation. Let the energy and vision be lauded, encouraged, and welcomed as hothouses for ministry and mission growth!

A second lesson to be drawn from the Roman Catholic experience is their ability to come to terms with the overlay of these two structures. Local churches are governed by bishops as they oversee their respective dioceses. At the same time, any order or monastery situated within any particular diocese draws its mission vision from the headquarters of its respective institute's rule, but also exercises that mission in concert with the authority of the bishop for the local diocese. Similarly, affinity groups have drawn and ought to draw their particular mission vision from their own mission statement that sets the direction for the organization, whether it be Presbyterians for Restoring Creation, The Witherspoon Society, Presbyterian Elders in Prayer, Presbyterian Association of Musicians, Presbyterian Writers Guild, and so on. At the same time, the respective members need to continue to serve in their local contexts under the authority of the local presbytery.

A third parallel to be drawn relates to the gathering of leaders together. Where the Roman Catholic institutes' leaders may be called to the Vatican once in a while to discuss and reformulate their norms of ministry, Protestant affinity group leaders could gather together as well—but a whole lot more frequently. The historic practice of governing the orders under the clear, uncompromising authority of the Roman pope makes frequent gatherings unnecessary. On the other hand, affinity groups among the Protestants have cropped up mostly during the latter decades of the twentieth century, lacking any consistent pattern of organization or authority structure, except as required by state laws governing nonprofit organizations. Also, the one Presbyterian attempt to manage these organizations flopped. Consequently, leaders of these groups ought to gather frequently—at least annually—to share together, to compare ministry visions together, to dream together, and to dialogue together. In the meantime, the technologies ought to be fully engaged in order to network such groups together for ongoing fellowship, consultation, and détente-minded dialogue over tough issues.

The one key exception to the Roman Catholic structure regards authority. For this structure to function effectively within Protestantism, at least within Presbyterianism, it needs to stay out of the governance business. The fellowship and interdependence need to be cultivated, and the experience of learning together through mutual affirmation and admonition requires the differing GodView leaders to be free to share candidly without fear of reprisal. The legislative and judicial oversight of the church certainly would continue to be exercised in the official governing bodies of the church, lest traditions seem constantly to be in play and disorder overwhelm the church's peace; and yes, those legislative, judicial actions still would generate controversies as the governing bodies seek to resolve them. But a network of affinity groups could function in a nongovernmental, relationship-building way, one that produces win-win learning and win-win mission partnership results.

Several decades ago, missiologist Ralph Winter proposed a similar structure for the mobilization of world missions ministries. "How can a pluralistic church do mission in a pluralistic world if it insists on doing so from a central office?" Winter asks. While this book has already suggested that church splits generally occur when conservatives grow impatient with the adventurous innovations of revisionists, Winter also points out that the ultimate point of argument always has been the doing of mission "my way." In fact, the harbinger of most denominational divisions has almost always been the formation of an alternative mission board to send the right *kinds* of missionaries to do the right *kinds* of mission. In 1961, he published an article calling upon the Presbyterians to follow the Roman Catholic model by encouraging the formation of orders of mission. Each one would be regulated by church standards but would be administered by its own leaders and funded by its own supporters. As he wrote, "If the Catholics have found the key to being a diverse, pluralistic church that nevertheless is one, why can't we learn from them?"[3]

Getting to the Party

This chapter opened by asking, Who's going to throw the party? And who is going to come? Well, the time is now. The time has come for denominational leaders to throw the party and to invite leaders of every conceivable affinity group to gather around those café tables for peacemaking through animated conversations.

In order to throw such a party, the actual groups must be identified. The most visible groups include those that have played active lobbying roles in national ecclesiastical policy-making. They need to be there. But many less visible groups ought to be there, too. Pastors' support and accountability groups ought to be there. Lectionary study groups ought to be there. So ought to be prayer groups, global mission support groups, inner-city mission groups, racial-ethnic minority groups, addiction recovery groups, family life groups, gender justice groups, and most certainly all groups who feel themselves unrepresented and undervalued, including self-avowed, antitraditionalist iconoclasts.

Would such a "party" produce anything helpful for the church? That remains to be seen. The annual gathering of Presbyterian leaders to the General Assembly produces hot controversies and an ever-enlarging body of church laws within a three-ring-circus atmosphere. Yet few attending those Assemblies really connect, or share mutual affirmation and admonition, with sisters and brothers in the faith who happen to feel passionate about differing GodViews. As Fuller Theological Seminary President Richard Mouw says, "Deep does not call to deep in legislative bodies."[4] Perhaps by gathering together for a party in a large auditorium, where believers of differing GodViews sit around café tables with their knees bumping into each others', and where difficult topics are discerned within an overall commitment to engage one another within an ecclestical détente . . . well, maybe it could produce some good.

Something good is needed. Something good is especially needed from churches of the Reformed and Presbyterian family, because quite frankly, they are the ones most capable of bringing forth a positive result. And the whole body of Christ—Protestant, Catholic and Orthodox, Western and Eastern, Anglo and African, Asian and Arab—has come to depend upon that particular family of Christians to lead the way.

Chapter 15

So Who Cares?

Who cares? Who really cares if the Presbyterian Church (U.S.A.) stays together? If they go out of business, the whole kingdom of God will go on without them. Who really cares?" Those questions slapped me like a tornado, especially since they were coming from one of the leading ethics scholars in American Christianity, Max Stackhouse. "Of course," he added with a wry smile, "I'm a member of the UCC, so I have the luxury of saying this." Nevertheless, his questions did startle me. With just 2.5 million members, the PC(USA) comprises less than one-fourth of 1 percent of the world Christian population. And given our rate of shrinkage in the midst of a worldwide church that is expanding rapidly, our piece of the pie keeps getting smaller.

Who does care about the fights going on in this tiny sector of the church? Would a lot be lost in God's larger economy if our church, and the relatively few other shrinking churches that are wrestling with similar controversies, were to go out of business? Why not shut down the institutional and cultural machinery that fosters such contentions? Why not send our members to other churches that are not struggling with controversies? Why not liquidate all our assets and give them to other mission agencies? Why not spend our time doing the mission rather than "dialoguing" about the theology behind that mission? Is it worth all the energy we are investing to seek unity while applauding our diversity?

In a long-developed pedagogical style, Dr. Stackhouse was baiting my thinking, pressing me to ask myself, *What is it that my church denomination brings to the larger world church that would be tragic if squandered?* He hinted at the answer, "Consider the motto you Presbyterians always quote."

"*Reformata semper reformanda,*" I said.

"That's right," he said with a nod. "*Reformata semper reformanda.* 'Reformed, always reforming.'"

"Always being reformed," I qualified, "by the word of God and the work of the Spirit."

"That's exactly right," he said. "That's why the Presbyterian Church has to find a way through all its controversies."

My visit with Dr. Stackhouse at Princeton Seminary was immediately followed by a visit to my sister's home, just an hour away in northern New Jersey. A strange thing has happened to Tobi. She's just been ordained an elder in her church. I say "strange" thing, because she attends a non-denominational, conservative, charismatic church that never even has considered ordaining a woman before. As conservative Christians, they read the scriptures in a more matter-of-fact way, and their read of the texts—consistent with so many other nontraditional, conservative, independent congregations—has seemed self-evidently opposed to "elevating" women to such leadership roles. But something has happened in her church. They've become Presbyterianized. Now don't tell them I said that. They wouldn't know what to do with such a claim. But the facts are indisputable. We Presbyterians—and other mainline, Reformed church bodies—wrestled for decades over the role of women, and having embraced a Spirit-inspired, truly biblical commitment to gender justice, we have set the stage for others to follow.

We never would have arrived where we are if it were not for the Activist Presbyterians provoking us, troubling the waters of the status quo. Usually people with an Activist GodView have been the ones to provoke such change. Then again, those resistant Confessionalists dragged their feet, exegeting every text, wrestling all the theological implications, fighting through the legislative process, and ever-so-slowly articulating a precise theological defense for egalitarian marriage and women's ordination. Ecclesiasts fretted all along the way, worrying about the conflicts such debates were unleashing; then again, many of them were salivating over the practical gains the church would be able to appropriate with all those women serving as pastors. Altruists came on board, knowing that women long have led the way in providing significant mission service to the needy. And Devotionalists—who at first were slow to join in, their inclinations being not so politically-power-brokering-minded but focused on prayer—came on board as they realized that the whole spiritual tenor of leadership surely would be deepened substantially by women in such leadership roles.

Over several years and through many legislative debates, the Presbyterians not only changed the church's policies, they also wrote extremely articulate, broadly accepted policies that both directed our practices and provided a catalyst for other denominations to follow.

Reformata Semper Reformanda

The Presbyterian Church long has provided American Protestantism—indeed world Christianity—its think tank. As church historian and author of *Dynamics of Spiritual Life*, Richard Lovelace, summarizes, "The Presbyterian Church is and has always been an arena of theological recovery and discovery."[1] It is that arena of thought, analysis, study, conversation, and deliberation—all carried out in the midst of doing ministry and mission (we're not just an institution of higher learning)—that has caused the Presbyterian Church and its sister Reformed bodies to exercise an enormous influence upon the whole unfolding mission of Christ throughout the world.

Though none are quite like the Presbyterians, other ecclesiastical traditions bring many other contributions to the larger church. The Catholic Church has demonstrated an amazing ability to adjust to varying cultural contexts, all the while maintaining an essential unity. The Anglican and Lutheran communions have nurtured the liturgical experience of worship, all the while bridging relations between the Roman Church and Protestant bodies. The Methodist, Baptist, and Pentecostal churches have led the way in world evangelization and enthusiastic worship. And racial-ethnic churches have blended the best of the rest and added a whole lot more that each particular culture draws upon in its experience of the gospel. But the Reformed churches have consistently provided the "arena of theological recovery and discovery" that the larger church long has needed.

Reformata. This first word of the motto bespeaks the theological recovery that is critical for the church to be faithful to the gospel. No doubt the gospel proclamation prior to the Reformation had fallen away from the central proclamation presented in the Holy Scriptures. The groundbreaking leadership of Martin Luther and the theological brilliance of John Calvin provided the church a new beginning. They helped recover the theological center of the gospel—salvation by grace through faith—that has continued to provide the benchmark for the living faith ever since. That gospel always faces challenges, threats, and, given the human sinful condition, the tendency to compromise its clarity and to minimize its power. To be a church *reformata* is to be one that harkens back to that central benchmark again and again.

Semper Reformanda. These two active words bespeak the theological discovery that has been a central task of Reformed theological studies since the Reformation. It also sets the agenda for the church's interaction with other fields of study, so that the general revelation of God written in nature, logical reasoning, and creative expression may all speak into the church's continuing education in the things of God. Although he was a Baptist, the remarks of John Robinson in his send-off sermon to the Pilgrims on July 21, 1620, paraphrased in a hymn of George Rawson (1807–89), are pertinent to this Presbyterian mission:

"We limit not the truth of God to our poor reach of mind—by notions of our day and sect—crude, partial and confined. No, let a new and better hope within our heart be stirred, for God hath yet more light and truth to break forth from the Word."[2] This expression has been claimed by one advocacy group, "More Light Presbyterians," and opponents have resisted it accordingly, but it still reflects this role the Presbyterian Church does play as think tank for the larger church.

Into All Truth

Who would be so foolish as to think that there remains more truth to burst forth from the word of God? Jesus would. "On the night when he was betrayed . . ." (1 Cor. 11:23) he not only instituted the Lord's Supper, he also instructed the disciples how to discover and discern the truth in the days ahead. In a word, he told them of the coming *paraclete*.

The twelve were hoping beyond hope that Jesus' warnings of his coming departure would prove inaccurate. But as the ominous, immanent reality was setting in, their anxieties were growing. "What will we do without you? Where should we go? Will this movement end? What about all your teaching about the coming kingdom?" The questions could have filled a long scroll. We do not know whether those questions were voiced or if Jesus simply anticipated them and lectured, but we do know that John ultimately recounted Jesus' upper-room discourse—presented in this form over four chapters, even longer than the Sermon on the Mount. In that discourse John presents Jesus' plans for the twelve, shares Jesus' hopes for them, and promises his continuing support of them. Jesus assures them that all will be okay. And the reason for that, although they will no longer see him, is that he will send the paraclete to be with them. And the paraclete will "guide you into all the truth" (John 16:13).

Who is the paraclete? It is the third member of the Trinity, the Holy Spirit. When thinking of the Spirit, one commonly thinks of the biography of the Spirit presented in the book of Acts. There the Greek word *pneuma*, meaning "spirit," is used interchangeably with the word *dunamis*, meaning power, and for good reason: the Holy Spirit repeatedly brings about miraculous transformations of people's lives, not to mention healings, speaking in tongues, etc. But here in John's gospel, the Spirit is equated very little with power. Rather, the role of the Spirit highlighted in this gospel, and in particular in the upper room, is one dealing most in the realm of truth.

This word *paraclete,* from the Greek *parakaleo* ("to call in"), has been translated variously as counselor, comforter, or advocate. Given the present use of terms, the best translation might be "consultant"—that is, one who comes in and gives wise counsel, insight, and support—because it fits the whole message Jesus gives in this discourse:

> "I still have many things to say to you, but you cannot bear them now. When the Spirit of truth comes, he will guide you into all the truth; for he will not speak on his own, but will speak whatever he hears, and he will declare to you the things that are to come. He will glorify me, because he will take what is mine and declare it to you. All that the Father has is mine. For this reason I said that he will take what is mine and declare it to you." (John 16:12–15)

To promise that the Spirit will "guide you into all the truth" implies that they have not received all the truth as of yet. Three years of traveling with Jesus had not answered their every question, and it certainly had not helped them to anticipate every situation in which they would someday find themselves. They would need a source of truth for the days ahead. The spirit "will guide you into all the truth."

Two thousand years later, the church continues to find itself in need of the truth, but discerning that truth seems a bit too enigmatic and elusive for analytical folks like Presbyterians. Rightly so. The Holy Spirit has taken up residence in the life of all those in Christ, assuring one's place in the family of God. But the voice of the Spirit can never be discerned so purely and distinctly as to be exempt on the one hand from our own preferences and prejudices, and on the other hand from our own fears and shame. How were the disciples, and how are we, to discern the word of the Lord from the words of a counterfeit? In that same upper-room discourse, Jesus gave the disciples a filter through which they could clarify the voice of the Spirit:

> "I have said these things to you while I am still with you. But the Advocate, the Holy Spirit, whom the Father will send in my name, will teach you everything, and remind you of all that I have said to you." (14:25–26)

The first essential part of the filter is that the Spirit would remind them and will remind us of what Jesus has said. That benchmark was followed closely by the disciples throughout their ministries. It was followed so closely that, in the rare instances when Paul was addressing issues not previously addressed by Jesus, he was careful to point that out:

> To the rest I say—I and not the Lord—...
> Now concerning virgins, I have no command of the Lord, but I give my opinion as one who by the Lord's mercy is trustworthy. I think that ...
> (1 Cor. 7:12, 25–26a)

By inference the rest of what he wrote was apparently consonant with teachings of Jesus, with which he had authoritative, trustworthy familiarity, which is to say that when the consulting Holy Spirit leads us into the truth, that truth will be consonant with the teachings of Jesus, the apostles, and by implication the body of the Hebrew scriptures that Jesus and the apostles recognized to be their written authority for God's word. The Spirit leads into all truth, which certainly will be consistent with the truth revealed in scripture.

Second, the consulting Spirit will lead us into the Truth with a capital T. "When the Advocate comes, whom I will send to you from the Father, the Spirit of truth who comes from the Father, he will testify on my behalf" (John 15:26). The core belief of the faith is not simply the body of teachings Jesus presented us, but the person of Christ Jesus himself. Accordingly, says Jesus, the Spirit will continually point us back to Jesus; the Holy Spirit will testify on Jesus' behalf. That is why John 3:16 is universally recognized as the core message of scripture: "For God so loved the world that he gave his only Son, so that everyone who believes in him may not perish but may have eternal life." That message is elaborated in Paul's letter to the Romans: "But God proves his love for us in that while we still were sinners Christ died for us" (5:8). The Christ-act of dying for our sins is summarized in Second Corinthians: "For our sake he made him to be sin who knew no sin, so that in him we might become the righteousness of God" (5:21). And John himself reminds us of our essential response to this gift of God: "But to all who received him, who believed in his name, he gave power to become children of God" (1:12). The Holy Spirit, in order to lead us into the truth, will always be leading us to the living Truth, the living Word, Jesus himself.

On the night in which he was betrayed ... Jesus did teach those disciples about the one who would come to lead them into the truth. How would they recognize that truth? It would remind them of what Jesus had said and it would remind them of who Jesus is. Accordingly, on that same night he said, " ... Do this in remembrance of me" (1 Cor. 11:24), which at minimum meant, do this so you do not forget the most important part of what you need to know: Jesus.

The third benchmark of the Spirit's illumination is that the consulting Spirit will correct our errors.

> "Nevertheless I tell you the truth: it is to your advantage that I go away, for if I do not go away, the Advocate will not come to you; but if I go, I will send him to you. And when he comes, he will prove the world wrong about sin and righteousness and judgment: about sin, because they do not believe in me; about righteousness, because I am going to the Father and you will see me no longer; about judgment, because the ruler of this world has been condemned." (John 16:7–11)

Face it, as suggested above, the single greatest deterrent standing in the way of our hearing the Spirit's voice is ourselves: our prejudices, our special interests, our shame, our avoidance of discomfort. We are quick to put words into God's mouth. In fact, nothing thrills us more than hearing others proclaim confidently the same prejudices we hold. The next time you visit a demonstrative church—the kind that shouts "Amen" during the minister's sermon—take notice of when the congregants respond with their enthusiastic endorsements. Do they shout their affirmations when the minister is instructing them about things they have never heard before? No. Do they shout their affirmations when the minister discusses the ambiguities that attend life's struggles? Of course not. They shout "Amen" when the minister tells them what they already know and believe. They are excited to hear the minister articulating—eloquently, hopefully—beliefs they already hold dear. If you participate in a more sedate congregation, the phenomenon may not be as outward, but internally it is just the same. The beloved sermons are the ones that restate what the people already know and remind the people of what they already believe. That is a good thing insofar as the Spirit's primary task is to remind us of what Jesus said and to point us to who Jesus is. But given that the Spirit also comes to convict us of sin and judgment (that is, our sins and our judgmentalism toward others' sins), we should expect the consulting Spirit to call us to repentance.

Reminding us of the teachings of Jesus, pointing us to the person and work of Christ Jesus, and convicting us of our sin and judgment: those are the benchmarks by which we can discern how well we are hearing the consulting Holy Spirit as the Spirit leads us into truth.

It's Working

Ever since the days of the Reformation, the Presbyterian and Reformed churches have been living out the motto that attaches to the tradition. *Reformata, semper reformanda:* Reformed, always being reformed . . . by the word of God and the Holy Spirit. From time to time, we have found ourselves distracted from the central teachings of the Reformation. By the work of the Spirit being active in the official legislative and judicial processes, and being active in theological and dialogical discussions, the Spirit has repeatedly recovered the proclamation of the gospel within the church. Throughout the same centuries we have found ourselves struggling through the birth pangs of new ideas, disruptive proposals, and newfangled doctrines. And through those same legislative, judicial, theological, and dialogical processes, sometimes we have disposed of them as aberrations; other times we have embraced them as more light shed from God's word, illumined by the Spirit.

Some changes were risky. At a time when many threatened that we would be discredited around the world for equalizing the authority between women and men, we moved ahead, trusting God to lead us. To our happy surprise, our international partner churches did not disown us; many have followed suit. We also set the pace for change on other issues, such as relieving divorcees of the scarlet letter of shame, welcoming charismatic gifts within our typically staid churches, embracing (albeit slowly) new music into our worship, leading the way in peacemaking, committing energy to an applied theology of the environment, standing up for justice, leading in virtually every major ecumenical effort. And at the same time, we've given leadership to the recovery of biblical studies, the renewal of theology, the empowering of preaching, the equipping of educational ministry; all of these are just a glimpse of the work of the Spirit among us.

In short, a long list of successes exists in which every member in the Presbyterian-Reformed family, and especially in the Presbyterian Church (U.S.A.), may jump up and shout, "Amen!" That is to say, every member including the Confessionalists, the Devotionalists, the Ecclesiasts, the Altruists, and the Activists.

So Where Do We Go from Here?

While I was training church officers last spring, one of the deacons-elect asked me, "Do you know why I am proud to be a Presbyterian?"

"You tell me," I said to her.

"Because we Presbyterians fight in the open," she said. The others all laughed, but they also understood her point. Although I'd rather use non-militant lingo, the point is true: Presbyterians are not afraid to discuss issues that would embarrass others—no issue is too radical to be proposed to a General Assembly for study and/or action. Presbyterians then hold open dialogues; they publish widely their ideas—both the orthodox and unorthodox. They repudiate some dumb ideas and they promote some new, groundbreaking policies.

But these are perilous days. Many are the controversies. Varied are the passions. Diverse are the cultures. Deep is the pain. Overwhelming is the anxiety. Searing are the hot-button issues. How can the church be a faithful church through such times as these?

By recognizing the God-designed, God-given diversity of GodViews that fuels the comprehensive vision God has placed before the church . . .

By embracing the ambiguities that a brackish Reformed ecclesiology presents us . . .

By struggling through the discomfiting détente that can demilitarize our disagreements . . .

By determining to affirm one another as sisters and brothers in the Lordship of Jesus Christ . . .

By choosing to talk together in dialogue, in mutual affirmation and mutual admonition . . .

By opening our Bibles together to plumb the message and meaning of the scriptures as they address our contemporary issues . . .

By gathering in new ways, utilizing the network patterns of relationships and modern communications technologies, in order to have substantive dialogues . . .

By recognizing that God has blessed this church, and the tradition in which it plays the primary role, with the essential calling to be the think tank for world Christianity . . . *Reformata, semper reformanda* . . .

And, as in everything, by resolutely determining to stay together, to struggle together, to study together, to serve together, and to worship together—thereby being the church Jesus has built upon the rock, against which the gates of hell shall not prevail.

Notes

Notes to Chapter 2

1. Bradley Longfield, *The Presbyterian Controversy* (New York: Oxford University Press, 1991), 23.
2. Ibid., 212.
3. Ibid.
4. John Leith, *Crisis in the Church* (Louisville, Ky.: Westminster John Knox Press, 1997), 29.
5. John Calvin, *Institutes of the Christian Religion*, IV, I, 14–15, ed. John T. McNeill (Philadelphia: The Westminster Press, 1960).

Notes to Chapter 3

1. Douglas Jacobsen and William Vance Trollinger Jr., eds., *Re-Forming the Center* (Grand Rapids: William B. Eerdmans Publishing Company, 1998), 447.
2. Salim Munayer, conversation, July 2000.
3. Douglas Jacobsen and William Trollinger Jr., "Re-forming the Sloppy Center by and with Grace," *Interpretation,* 51, no. 2, (Apr. 1997), 162.
4. Richard Hutcheson Jr. and Peggy Shriver, *The Divided Church: Moving Liberals & Conservatives from Diatribe to Dialogue* (Downers Grove, Ill.: InterVarsity Press, 1999), 62.
5. Jacobsen and Trollinger, *Re-Forming the Center,* 91–108.
6. Avery Dulles, *Models of the Church* (New York: Image Books, 1987).
7. Richard Foster, *Streams of Living Water* (San Francisco: Harper SanFrancisco, 1998).
8. William Westom, *Presbyterian Pluralism* (Knoxville: The University of Tennessee Press, 1997).

Notes to Chapter 4

1. "Presbyterian Conflict: The Modern Ecclesiastical Context," in *The Nature of the Unity We Seek in Our Diversity: Discovering Our Fundamental Unity in Jesus Christ* (Louisville, Ky.: Office of the General Assembly, 1999).

2. Richard Hutcheson and Peggy Shriver, *The Divided Church* (Downers Grove, Ill.: InterVarsity Press, 1999), 43.
3. Miroslav Volf, *Exclusion and Embrace* (Nashville: Abingdon Press, 1996), 69–70.
4. Karen Horney, *Neuroses and Human Growth* (New York: W.W. Norton & Co., 1991), 377.

Notes to Chapter 5

1. Joe Donaho, *Good News Travels Faster!* (Decatur, Ga.: CTS Press, 1990).
2. John Leith, *Crisis in the Church* (Louisville, Ky.: Westminster John Knox Press, 1997), 22.
3. (G-1.0200).
4. Leith, *Crisis,* 42.

Notes to Chapter 6

1. J. Mary Luti, "Keeping the Great Commandment," *The Christian Century,* 22 March, 2000, 348.
2. "The Whole World Singing: A Journey to Iona and Taize," *The Christian Century,* 22 March 2000, 338.
3. Augustine, *The Confessions of Saint Augustine,* trans. Edward B. Pusey (New York: Random House, 1949), quoted in Howard L. Rice, *Reformed Spirituality* (Louisville, Ky.: Westminster John Knox Press, 1991), 22.
4. Ibid.
5. Donald Bloesch, *Crisis of Piety* (Colorado Springs: Helmers & Howard Publishers, Inc., 1988), 15.
6. Thomas C. Oden, *Requiem: A Lament in Three Movements* (Nashville: Abingdon Press, 1995), 109.
7. John Calvin, *Instruction in Faith* (Philadelphia: Westminster Press, 1959), 19, quoted in Bloesch, *Crisis of Piety,* 26.
8. Douglas Jacobsen, "Pietism and the Postmodern Context of Ecumenical Dialogue" (paper presented at Annual Meeting of NAAE, September 26, 1999), 2.

Notes to Chapter 7

1. Hans Kung, *The Church* (New York: Image Books, 1976), 158.
2. Loren B. Mead, *The Once and Future Church* (Washington, DC: The Alban Institute, 1991).
3. Stanley Hauerwas and William H. Willimon, *Resident Aliens* (Nashville: Abingdon Press, 1989).
4. Jack Rogers, *Claiming the Center: Churches and Conflicting Worldviews* (Louisville, Ky.: Westminster John Knox Press, 1995), 165.
5. Rick Warren, *The Purpose-Driven Church* (Grand Rapids: Zondervan Publishing House, 1995).

6. Augustine, *De Baptismo,* IV, 50.17.24.
7. Dietrich Bonhoeffer, *Life Together,* trans. John W. Doberstein (New York: Harper & Row, 1954), 30.

Notes to Chapter 8

1. Charles M. Sheldon, *In His Steps . . .* (New York: Permabooks, 1949).
2. Stanley Hauerwas and William H. Willimon, *Resident Aliens,* (Nashville: Abingdon Press, 1989), 55.
3. John M. Buchanan, *Being Church, Becoming Community* (Louisville, Ky.: Westminster John Knox Press, 1996), 38–39.
4. Walter Rauschenbush, *A Theology for the Social Gospel,* chap. 13, quoted in *American Christianity: An Historical Interpretation with Representative Documents,* eds. H. Shelton Smith, Robert T. Handy, Lefferts A. Loetscher (New York: Charles Scribner's Sons, 1963), 2: 404.
5. *General Assembly Minutes* (New York: PCUSA, 1937), 220.

Notes to Chapter 9

1. E. M. Howse, *Saints in Politics* (Toronto: University of Toronto Press, 1952), 32, quoted in Richard Lovelace, *Dynamics of Spiritual Life* (Downers Grove, Ill.: InterVarsity Press, 1979), 370.
2. Ibid., 370, n. 34.
3. Martin Luther King Jr., "Pilgrimage to Nonviolence," quoted in *American Christianity: An Historical Intrepretation with Representative Documents,* eds. H. Shelton Smith, Robert T. Handy, Lefferts A. Loetscher (New York: Charles. Scribner's Sons, 1963), 2: 557.
4. Jane Hanna, "Private Fulfillment or the Well-being of the Whole," *Witherspoon Society Newsletter*, October 2000.
5. Richard Foster, *Streams of Living Water* (San Francisco: HarperSanFrancisco, 1998), 171.
6. Ibid., 175.
7. Barbara Wheeler, "True Confession: A Presbyterian Dissenter Thinks About the Church," (Plenary for Covenant Network Conference, Atlanta, Ga., November 5, 1999), 6.
8. Foster, *Streams,* 178.

Notes to Chapter 10

1. Clifton Kirkpatrick, speech, n.d.
2. Hans Kung, *The Church* (New York: Image Books, 1976), 328–29.
3. Reinhold Niebuhr, *Nature and Destiny of Man,* vol. 2 (New York: Charles Scribner's Sons, 1943).
4. Richard Hutcheson and Peggy Shriver, *The Divided Church* (Downers Grove, Ill.: InterVarsity, 1999), 109.
5. Jon R. Stone, *On the Boundaries of American Evangelicalism* (New York: St. Martin's Press, 1997), 179.

6. Miroslav Volf, *Exclusion and Embrace* (Nashville: Abingdon Press, 1996), 58.
7. Jerry Andrews, (Lecture given at the Gathering of Presbyterians, sponsored by the Presbyterian Coalition, Dallas, Tex., October 1999).
8. Howard L. Rice, *Reformed Spirituality* (Louisville, Ky.: Westminster John Knox Press, 1991), 55.
9. Ibid.
10. Jack Rogers, *Claiming the Center: Churches and Conflicting Worldviews* (Louisville, Ky.: Westminster John Knox Press, 1995), 167.
11. Carroll E. Simcox, ed., *3000 Quotations on Christian Themes* (Grand Rapids: Baker Book House, 1988), 28.

Notes to Chapter 11

1. Salim Munayer, conversation, June 2000.
2. John Calvin, *Institutes of the Christian Religion,* ed. John T. McNeill (Philadelpha: The Westminster Press, 1960), IV, I, 12.
3. Ibid., IV, I, 7.
4. Mark Achtemeier, *The Church and Its Unity* (Louisville, Ky.: Office of Theology and Worship, 1999), 22.
5. Ibid.
6. *Formula of Agreement,* in *Book of Order*, 2000–1, C-3.
7. *A Common Calling: The Witness of Our Reformation Churches in North America Today* (Minneapolis, Minn.: Augsburg Fortress, 1988–92), 66.
8. *Formula of Agreement,* C-3.
9. Ibid.
10. Ibid., C-4.
11. Ibid., C-8.
12. Henry Kissinger, *Years of Renewal* (New York: Simon & Schuster, 1999), 92.
13. Ibid., 93.
14. Ibid., 99.
15. Ibid., 96.
16. Ibid., 97.
17. Ibid.
18. Ibid., 98.
19. Ibid., 99.
20. Ibid., 102, quoted in Richard Nixon, *Public Papers of the Presidents of the United States, Richard Nixon, 1970* (Washington, D.C.: U.S. Government Printing Office, 1971), 178.
21. George Simmel, "Conflict," in *Conflict and the Web of Group-Affiliation,* trans. Kurt Wolf and Reinhard Bendix (New York: Free Press, 1955) 58–60, cited in William Westom, *Presbyterian Pluralism,* (Knoxville: The University of Tennessee Press, 1997), 128.
22. Ibid.
23. Salim Munayer, public address, Clear Lake Presbyterian Church, Houston, Tex., October 2000.

Notes to Chapter 12

1. David J. Bosch, *Transforming Mission* (Maryknoll, NY: Orbis Book, 1977), 16.
2. Vernon Broyles, conversation, May 1999.
3. Jack Rogers, *Reading the Bible and the Confessions* (Louisville, Ky.: Geneva Press, 1999), 39.
4. Richard Hutcheson and Peggy Shriver, *The Divided Church* (Downers Grove, Ill.: InterVarsity Press, 1999), 66.

Notes to Chapter 13

1. Deborah Tannen, *The Argument Culture* (New York: Random House, 1998), 3–4.
2. Ibid., 10–11.
3. Ibid., 9.
4. David Augsburger, *Caring Enough to Confront* (Ventura, Ca.: Gospel Light Publications, 1981), 42.
5. Miroslav Volf, *Exclusion and Embrace* (Nashville: Abingdon Press, 1996), 79.
6. Tannen, *Argument Culture,* 165.
7. Ibid.
8. Jack Rogers, *Claiming the Center* (Louisville, Ky.: Westminster John Knox Press, 1995), 44.
9. Augsburger, *Caring Enough to Comfort,* 51.

Notes to Chapter 14

1. *Book of Confessions,* 40.
2. *Book of Order,* G-4.0300.
3. Ralph Winter, conversation, November 2000.
4. Richard Mouw, conversation, May 2000.

Notes to Chapter 15

1. Richard Lovelace, conversation, October 2000.
2. George Rawson, "We Limit Not the Truth of God," in the *Pilgrim Hymnal* (New York: The Pilgrim Press, 1931), no. 259.